THEATER
IN THE
AMERICAS

A Series from
Southern
Illinois
University
Press
ROBERT A.
SCHANKE
Series Editor

Documentary Trial Plays in Contemporary American Theater

JACQUELINE O'CONNOR

Southern Illinois University Press
Carbondale and Edwardsville

16 15 14 13   4 3 2 1

Library of Congress Cataloging-in-Publication Data
O'Connor, Jacqueline.
Documentary trial plays in contemporary American
theater / Jacqueline O'Connor.
pages cm — (Theater in the Americas)
ISBN-13: 978-0-8093-3236-6 (pbk.)
ISBN-10: 0-8093-3236-1 (pbk.)
ISBN-13: 978-0-8093-3237-3 (ebook)
ISBN-10: 0-8093-3237-X
1. Historical drama, American—History and criti-
cism. 2. Theater—Production and direction—United
States—History—20th century. 3. Literature and
history—United States—History—20th century.
4. Trials in literature. I. Title.
PS338.H56O25 2013
812'.051409—dc23   2012043920

To my husband, Derek Jeffery, with gratitude for his love, support, and companionship

Contents

Acknowledgments ix

Introduction: Legal Representation 1

1. Judicial Identification: *The Trial of the Catonsville Nine* and *The Chicago Conspiracy Trial* 22

2. National Investigation: *Inquest* and *Are You Now or Have You Ever Been* 63

3. Ideological Confrontation: *Execution of Justice* and *Greensboro (A Requiem)* 97

4. Individual Interrogation, Communal Resolution: *Unquestioned Integrity*: *The Hill/Thomas Hearings*, *Gross Indecency*: *The Three Trials of Oscar Wilde*, and *The Laramie Project* 126

Conclusion: Cultural Legislation 169

Notes 189
Select Bibliography 207
Index 215

Acknowledgments

Documentary theater calls attention to the multiple communities involved in the production of texts, so it is fitting and with enormous gratitude that I thank the members of the many communities of which I am a part and without whom I could not have written this book.

This project emerged from my membership in an academic writing group made up of colleagues from the Departments of English and Theatre at my home institution, Boise State University. I am very grateful to Marcy Newman for organizing this community of female scholars; without it, I would not have had the courage to begin or the confidence to continue. Three members of the group, Tara Penry, Michelle Payne, and Leslie Durham, have become the kind of professional colleagues and friends who transform a career, infusing work with joy and fulfillment. I am particularly grateful to Leslie Durham for sharing her professional expertise in contemporary theater throughout the book's long gestation period, and for acts of friendship too many and frequent to enumerate. I could not have completed this project without her advice and support.

Michelle Payne also supported this book in her position as English department chair; her successful leadership and effective management of resources has led to increased time for faculty research, and my project benefitted greatly from these efforts. Both she and our previous chair, Bruce Ballenger, contributed to my progress with scheduling allowances, letters of support, and much-needed encouragement. Thanks to all the scholars, writers, and teachers who make up our vibrant and diverse department; they contribute to an intellectual community to which I am proud to belong. I am very fortunate to be able to teach various courses in my area of expertise every semester, and I thank all the students in my undergraduate and MA drama courses for the engaged and enthusiastic class discussions that have helped me to develop my ideas. Several former students, now dear friends, continue to enrich my life and require individual mention: Echo Savage, Marc Dziak, and Christy Claymore Vance.

Boise State University has provided financial support at several key points along the way. A College of Arts and Sciences Faculty Research Grant supplied seed money for the project, and sabbatical funding allowed me valuable time for drafting several chapters.

During an early stage of manuscript revision, I received a National Endowment for the Humanities grant to participate in a 2009 Summer Institute, "The Rule of Law: Legal Studies and the Liberal Arts," at the University of New England in Biddeford, Maine. Institute leaders Matthew Anderson and Cathrine O. Frank conceived of and created a singular interdisciplinary experience and selected a wonderfully diverse group of university faculty to take part in five weeks of intensive study and discussion. My thanks go to the entire group of participants and distinguished faculty speakers who helped to make those five weeks one of the most exciting and intellectually rich periods of my life. The readings and discussions proved essential to me as I drafted and revised this manuscript.

I continue to rely on the advice and friendship of several members of a 1997 NEH Summer Seminar community of which I was a part: Jerry Dickey provided me guidance and advice on publication, and Bob Duxbury read an early version of the manuscript. Another member of that group, Deborah Martinson, was my companion at the first documentary theater play I attended, in New York City, and several more since then. Most significantly, however, she has been one of the most ardent supporters of all things I attempt, and she inspires me regularly with the example she sets as a scholar, teacher, and friend.

My thanks go to scholars and editors William W. Demastes and Iris Smith Fischer for including my essay "Facts on Trial: Documentary Theatre and Zoot Suit" in their collection *Interrogating America through Theatre and Performance*, and thus providing me an early opportunity to develop my ideas on this topic. I am also indebted to editors Austin Sarat, Matthew Anderson, and Cathrine O. Frank for including my essay "Performing the Law in Contemporary Documentary Theater" in their volume *Teaching Law and Literature*.

I am enormously grateful to everyone at Southern Illinois University Press. Series editor Robert A. Schanke generously put his expertise and his expert editorial eyes to work on multiple versions of this manuscript; whatever contribution the book may make to the field, I owe to him and to SIU Press editor Kristine Priddy, whose patience and advocacy were crucial to the completion of this project. Thanks go also to the editorial team, particularly project editor Wayne Larsen and copy editor Kathleen Kageff, for their excellent work on my manuscript, and to Suzanne Sherman Aboulfadl for her preparation of the index.

I am blessed by the love and support of my siblings, Rose O'Connor, John O'Connor, and Kathy O'Connor, and my sister in spirit, Susan Carroll. My husband, Derek Jeffery, to whom this book is dedicated, devotes himself to our wonderful life together with a loyalty that I do not deserve but am grateful for daily. I am indebted to him for enduring, with grace and good humor, the long period of research and writing that produced this book.

Finally, none of my work in American drama and theater studies would be possible without Ruby Cohn. She remains the singular influence on my academic life. The honor of knowing her, the benefit of her mentoring over the course of two decades, the quality of her friendship; all of it and more remain with me and continue to guide me in ways that I could never have anticipated but without which my career would be unimaginable.

DOCUMENTARY TRIAL PLAYS IN CONTEMPORARY AMERICAN THEATER

Introduction: Legal Representation

The most sensational United States trials of the late twentieth century offer an amazing array of dramatic spectacle, plot twists, and shocking finales. Courtroom antics by both Yippie defendants and Judge Julius Hoffman transformed the 1969 Chicago Conspiracy Trial into a farce. Charles Manson's determination to loose helter-skelter on Southern California by directing his followers to kill a group of wealthy Los Angelenos was followed by a trial with grisly murder details and an account of Manson's plan to stir the underclass, inspired, as he claimed, by Bible verses and Beatles songs. He and his accomplices came to embody the kind of violent drug-induced social revolt that mainstream America most feared. During Dan White's 1979 trial for the murders of San Francisco mayor George Moscone and city supervisor Harvey Milk, the "Twinkie defense" provided an unexpected variation on a classic narrative of crime and punishment. But criminal trials were not the only sources of newsworthy legal proceedings: the 1990s are bookended by congressional hearings that held a nation spellbound, as Supreme Court nominee Clarence Thomas and impeached president Bill Clinton faced testimony about the personal sexual proclivities that had allegedly led them to transgress legal boundaries on workplace harassment and perjury.

Furthermore, the public events that preceded or surrounded these trials are themselves part of the performance record of contemporary American history: theatricalized moments of political discord, violent outbreaks of urban violence, and incendiary debates about minority rights. The justice system, designed to serve as a neutral platform for the resolution of private and public discord, often fails to achieve or maintain proposed neutrality, fostering skepticism about whether courtroom procedures and decisions can produce both just and satisfactory denouements during times of major social conflicts. Politically explosive and emotionally charged issues that called for justice resisted the closure that legal decisions are expected to foster, the court proceedings and the attending press only increasing community polarization, fueling difference rather than resolving it. Such trials make visible that justice is rarely uncomplicated, and that our legal system ought not be the only recourse we have for settling disputes or for healing the individual and collective trauma that remains after a crime has been committed, a verdict has been rendered, and court is adjourned.

The cases mentioned joined the ranks of legal proceedings from earlier in the century, all of them at one time or another hyperbolically dubbed "trial of the century": the Sacco-Vanzetti trial, the Leopold and Loeb murder case, *State of Tennessee v. John T. Scopes.* While the phrase may be overused, it conveys something significant about a trial so categorized: that it is newsworthy and culturally polarizing, but perhaps more importantly, that it has a clear connection to its historical moment and conveys information about its era. Legal scholar Robert Ferguson defines such high profile trials as "a distinct phenomenon at the nexus of the legal system and public life," in part because they "surprise by attracting massive attention beyond the locality in which they take place and by influencing social thought generally."[1] While high profile trials, Ferguson argues, may "come in many different forms and situations," they "share qualities that aid the interpretation of history and culture," and as such, they lend themselves to representational reenactments.[2]

Although congressional hearings are not considered trials, they are legislative actions that proceed along similar lines and share many components of a criminal or civil courtroom case: questioning, evidence, the possibility of censure or punishment, the polarization of public opinion. They also have the capacity, as did the many "trials of the century," to underscore the fissures that are an intrinsic part of the structure and values of a pluralistic society. They thus provide a kind of detailed history, formed with equal parts court or hearing documentation and news coverage or other commentary, of the episodes and events that have reflected or affected social change in the contemporary era. They contain fundamental cultural narratives that are noteworthy in their inherent drama and in their persistent repetition.

Not surprisingly, then, the controversies that prompt or result from these proceedings, fired as they are with narrative tension and ambiguity, have not languished in historical archives but have been recounted in biographies, critical studies, and film, theater, and television documentaries or dramatizations. Whether on the page, stage, or screen, contentious legal cases lend themselves to afterlives in representational forms, their investigative and performative elements readily adaptable to a variety of narrative genres. Harvey Milk's political career and assassination has been the subject of documentary and bio-pic films, while the HUAC hearings have prompted dozens of retellings, both historical and allegorical. While such retellings may be produced primarily for entertainment, their origins in actual events expand their purpose as they disseminate information and shape perspectives on the most notorious legal transgressions and decisions of the recent past. They demonstrate the ongoing impetus and importance of examining historical narratives in order to reflect shared values, confirm the boundaries on acceptable public and private behavior, and promote dialogue on social change.

One representational genre deeply indebted to the judicial procedures of the twentieth century is the contemporary documentary theater; indeed, the development of this dramatic form emerged directly from and has been shaped by the many trials and tribunals that punctuate the traumatic events of the twentieth century. Originating in Germany, documentary theater was developed by Erwin Piscator; one year after Piscator staged *In Spite of Everything* (1925), which examined World War I in Germany using documentary film footage to accompany stage action, Bertolt Brecht first used the term "documentary theater" to describe this performance style. Although "documentary theater" remains the most common designation for this fact-based theatrical genre, it has been called, alternatively, "documentary drama," "theater of testimony," "theater of fact," and "verbatim theater" by practitioners and critics.[3] These generic tags all reflect the idea that existing documents, many of them factual, have determined the genesis and development of this form; however, the proliferation of descriptors also implies a certain instability or ongoing development of the form, as well as indicating the skepticism that has surrounded the development of a theatrical form that veers so closely to history while maintaining its identity as an artistic form.

The term "documentary drama" and its shortened version, "docudrama," have also been used to describe other kinds of fact-based representations. Derek Paget points to this problem of naming in his study *True Stories:*

Documentary Drama on Radio, Screen and Stage, when he notes on the first page of his book that he will not use "documentary theater" and "documentary drama" interchangeably, but rather will distinguish between acted performance designed for a theater *building* or *space*—"theatre," and that very much wider range of practice that includes all media using acted performance—"drama."[4] Later in the book, he reiterates this distinction, reminding his readers that his use of the term "documentary drama" describes "the full range of dramatic practices in which the True Story invokes the special power of the document."[5] For the purpose of my study, I will further develop this distinction by noting that "documentary theater" often relies significantly, even completely, on texts from the public record but gives voice to those words with actors. Documentary film, in contrast, regularly features the actual participants of a narrative telling their own versions of events and rarely depends on reenactments to tell a story. Television docudramas, on the other hand, often begin with a factual frame but then depart from it significantly by adding fictionalized dialogue and situations. So while all three genres share commonalities, such as the dependence on a collection of different source materials and the use of editing to create a narrative of viewable length and thematic coherence, the documentary theater represents a unique marriage of fact and fabrication: the text is usually completely factual, but the performance is a unique artistic creation.

As a genre that contributes to the century's preoccupation with fact-based narratives, the contemporary documentary theater has not limited itself entirely to texts composed of legal reenactments, but a major strain of these plays has been centered around a notorious court case or a divisive government hearing. The intertwining of legal tropes and themes with theatrical practice that has produced what I call the "documentary trial play" comes about through the blending of verbatim excerpts from legal transcripts, media coverage of the events, and first-person interviews, the last compiled either at the time of the trial or, in some cases, months or years later. In the documentary trial play, the court or hearing room, already evocative of and theorized as a space of performance, takes center stage quite literally as legal space is transformed into theatrical space. The dramatic elements of a trial are heightened as the playwright and production team edit, arrange, and reproduce the court narrative, transforming it into a performance of the events. The audience is explicitly informed, by way of production notes or some other kind of written or spoken message, that the play has been constructed, often in its entirety, from other documents.

Eric Bentley provides an example of what has become a tradition for the documentary theater playwright, prefacing the published version of the dramatic text he created with transcripts from the HUAC hearings as follows: "The dialogue of *Are You Now or Have You Ever Been* is taken from hearings before the Un-American Activities Committee. Hence no resemblance between the witness and the actual person is coincidental. These characters wrote their own lines into the pages of history. Though I did abridge and tidy up the record, I did not write in additional dialogue."[6] Note the tension between the read and the constructed in the language of Bentley's disclaimer, the distinction made between "witness" and "actual person," no longer the same person, as the former has become one of the "characters" who have written their own "lines" into the pages of "history." This style of playwriting, here described as abridging and tidying up the record, is in fact a much more complicated reimagining of historical documents. While these scripts often rely completely on transcriptions and other oral or written sources, we shall see that it is not only in the inclusions but in the omissions, not to mention diverse elements of staging, that the play and the performance are created.

Bentley's note also makes clear that documentary trial plays are, simultaneously, theater texts and cultural documents; they situate themselves on a shifting border between imagination and law; they enact not just dramatic events but legal crises as well. The trials that are being staged are not just any trials, for they are, almost without exception, legal procedures that display the diversity of the nation, define the national imagination, and delineate the cultural parameters of the American rule of law. As Carol Martin argues, "How events are remembered, written, archived, staged, and performed helps determine the history they become." Moreover, she says, documentary theater has "the capacity to stage historiography. At its best, it offers us a way to think about disturbing contexts and complicated subject matter while revealing the virtues and flaws of its sources."[7] The documentary trial play specifically does all this and more with legal history, which is in turn an integral part of the nation's social and political histories. By recreating a courtroom in the theater and restaging significant sections of the judicial proceedings, the trial play not only records the virtues and flaws of the way that legal history is remembered, it reconfigures that history. The word-for-word testimony from the most contentious courtroom proceedings of the twentieth century is transformed into dramatic dialogue and theatrical spectacle.

These performances present a very particular kind of dramatic enactment of the law, for as each play incorporates existing trial rhetoric or other kind of legal language (that of the deposition, the criminal interrogation, the statute) into its theatrical event, it participates not only in ongoing dialogues within the legal community, but in a larger cultural examination of the judicial institution in all its complexities. These plays remind us that the work of defining and endorsing a rule of law is taken up in a variety of public and private venues: in law schools and in other academic enclaves; in courts, lower to Supreme; on the streets, as citizens negotiate a complex social system; in living rooms, as those same citizens witness enactments of law in entertainment and educational formats. The documentary trial plays under discussion here offer to theatergoers and readers narratives constructed of procedurals, interrogation transcripts, trial testimony and cross-examination. Objection and confirmation are positions built into this fact-based genre that synthesizes law and theater. Certainly, conceptions of contemporary theater and its development, particularly its use of existing documents to create the play script, inform any discussion of documentary theater; however, if this fact framing is done within the limits of certain key legal procedures, the performance pieces may also develop a new vision of a trial's purpose or outcome, help to explore law's complexity and contradictions, and challenge the tradition of proclamations and the seemingly unshakeable foundations of a judicial system as well as its citizens' understanding of it. As such, then, the documentary theater may illuminate ongoing conflicts within the law itself; not only the dissensions that become visible in specific judicial decisions, but the ongoing arguments about what law can do and should do.

As such discussions about issues of justice, morality, and the reasonable use of force are represented in these dramas, the dualism of artistic purpose and political purpose employs history, journalism, dramatic arts, and film (whether through video incorporated into the performance or a video version of the performance).[8] The focus on law and the examination of the rule of law in the documentary trial play brings legal structures as well as legal theory to bear on this theatrical aesthetic. The existence and proliferation of the documentary trial play demonstrate the significance of the legal system to our culture and our national identity, while also demonstrating that law's tropes are a foundational structure and enduring format for this style of artistic representation. As trial proceedings are adapted for the theater, as they are moved out of the courtroom and into other public venues, the cases themselves are not reopened, but the cross-examinations are cross-examined and the decisions that emerged from them are scrutinized. With their narrative elements honed and polished, made sharper and clearer under the playwright and director's creative choices, these cases convert history into a cultural experience. However, as Bentley's preface reminds us, history and representation are not the same, no matter how closely they may resemble or reflect each other.

Although a new narrative is created from the existing one and staged as a theatrical event, not a legal event, the stage trial reanimates the original proceeding and confirms the significance of law and law's structures to contemporary life. The chronology and the contents of the legal events are rearranged and edited, as thousands of pages of trial transcript recorded over weeks of testimony are reduced to less than a hundred pages of text or several hours of performance. The condensation of material need not mean that the judicial conflict becomes less significant than it was in its original form; indeed, its importance, not to mention its impact, is expanded by the dramaturgical changes that have been imposed on the historical material. Editorial distillation may actually make visible issues that are buried within the bureaucratic language and the length of official transcripts, as the documentary playwright draws out linguistic and thematic patterns in order to underscore ideas or insights that may have been obscured in previous versions of the narrative in question. The trial transcript might become the foundation from which to launch a love story; the government hearing may demonstrate the oppositional pull between personal and professional loyalty; the criminal investigation of an individual may conclude with the indictment of a community. The interconnections and the tensions between law and family or law and society may be laid open in the performance, as the emotional and even traumatic impact of enacting the rule of law are manifested in a form that requires us to experience, in the live theater, the bodies of those who practice law or those who reside in the courtroom: judge, defendant, witness, spectator.

The structure of the judicial proceeding allows for a particular type of theatrical realization, and this realization, in turn, puts pressure back on what happens and what has happened in court—also on what will happen, for as documentary theater confronts history, it exposes the limitations that come with relying on the documentation of events to tell the stories of the past. The personal narrative may be inconsistent with the judicial narrative, and both may conflict with the journalistic narratives of the events. Official stories produce a monolith of information against which the plays' protagonists are forced to defend themselves; in some cases, both legal and dramatic, the media champion the public's right to knowledge and its right to participate in public forums. Words that were originally spoken in the courtroom or hearing room and then reduced to a written record, often available to the public but rarely accessed, become once again part of the speech acts performed repeatedly during the run of the performance. Audiences have the opportunity to experience and to witness the reenactment of a legal proceeding that they may have only read about, as the documentary trial play provides the opportunity for citizens who only rarely find themselves in a real courtroom to attend the documentary trial play and serve as spectators to justice or injustice reenacted.

An often-employed convention of the documentary trial play presses the audience into service as jurors, explicitly calling for participation and judgment from the theater patrons; as these patrons witness the trial recreated in a theatrical venue, they serve as the "symbol of representative democracy and official listener until the moment of decision."[9] This sharing of documents across judicial and artistic lines exerts influence on both the legal and the theatrical spheres. It underscores the significance of legal narratives, for with their selection they are identified as central texts through which we determine and decide society's major conflicts. It calls attention to the cultural significance of the performance text, as we recognize the value of such narratives in achieving and maintaining consensus about the need for a rule of law and for its effective processes. For as Martin reminds us, evidence and testimony are used in documentary theater "in ways not unlike a court of law. . . . In both the theatre and the courtroom, the evidence serves as a pretext for the testimony of actors, of witnesses and lawyers." And, as she goes on to argue, "In court, as in documentary theatre, the forensic evidence stored in the archive is as much constructed as it is found."[10] This notion of constructed legal narrative, as we shall see, may extend beyond the level of evidence as the documentary trial play calls attention to the extent that legal principles themselves emerge from an ongoing historical narrative. As conceptions of the rule of law, as well as our understanding of it will, no doubt, continue to evolve, the documentary trial play contributes to other ongoing examinations of law and its close engagement with issues that determine our lives, from economic to psychological.

The trials that attract the interest of documentary theater practitioners are judicial proceedings that have originated in or resulted in traumatic events; exposure of the archival records to the light of day demonstrates that certain documents of legal history continue to reverberate with the aftershock of the events that engendered them. The dramatizations, created from the historical records compiled at the time of the trial, thus serve to release the pain otherwise stored in history but may not do so until months, years, even decades after the original incident has passed into memory. The playwrights and companies whose texts are discussed here thus do the difficult but necessary work of providing new audiences an opportunity to consider some of the most challenging historical moments of law, to ponder their significance, and to engage in new dialogues about them.

Through a variety of narrative and performative strategies, documentary theater explicitly calls attention to its factual content and to its creation from existing documents, challenging the division between reality and representation; however, textual similarities and connections extend further, as we recognize with the help of Robert Ferguson's description of what he calls the "continuum of publication at trial." In explaining the "misplaced communal agitation" endemic to a high-profile trial, a result of the "publication" and "publicity" that attends it, he notes that courtrooms are "compulsive generators of texts." So much is written during a high-profile trial that "actual reading becomes a selective process fraught with conscious and unconscious choices." He suggests that the "the presentations around a high profile trial form a *continuum of publication*, and the synergy between texts is an ignored resource in understanding what happened" (emphasis in the original).[11] Through its process of selection, the documentary trial play not only makes such selections for its audiences, it calls attention to the complexities and possible contradictions in this "*continuum of publication*" that Ferguson describes.

As these documentary plays reflect and project cultural trauma, they transcend or complicate their artistic purpose by illuminating legal principles or challenging assumptions about law's power and law's effectiveness. Not until the twentieth century have the documents of law been so exactingly and expertly taken over for dialogue, as what had been first produced for or included in a legal proceeding was now reproduced on a stage set, the rhetorical skill originally woven into a transcript cross-stitched into the fabric of public performance. Ferguson notes the ease with which it is possible to adapt legal transcripts for other kinds of narratives: "The cannibalism of a legal transcript for other uses is made easier by the fact that nonlegal narratives are invariably embedded in it. Trials, particularly high profile trials, unfold through narratives that strain for heightened effect. . . . The winning story in a controversial trial almost always has an extralegal dimension familiar to a community, and the greater the familiarity, the more its form attracts nonlegal narrators into the continuum of publication in search of new variations on its success."[12] By participating in a unique and extensive kind of narrative cannibalism, these trial or tribunal performance texts replay key national crises that test the resiliency of a democratic government or that expose social disharmony; whether the history is past or present has mattered less than the play's capacity for revelation of or insight on the complexities of twentieth-century cultural politics.

In the search for authenticity in representation, documentary theater must balance the demands of the real along with its determination to produce convincing theatrical artifice. In its adherence to authenticity, however, documentary theater risks charges of theatrical illegitimacy if not outright fraudulence: if theater is made of history, is it theater? In 1994, the Pulitzer Prize committee dropped from its lists of considered dramatic texts Anna Deavere Smith's solo documentary performance text *Twilight: Los Angeles, 1992*, justifying its decision on the grounds that the "language of the play is not invented but gleaned from interviews," and that the play "is not reproducible by other performers because it relies for *authenticity* on the performer's having done those interviews" (emphasis mine).[13] Smith protested the decision, noting that her earlier documentary solo piece *Fires in the Mirror* had been subsequently performed by a small company of actors.

But Smith herself has called attention to the fine line between creation and reproduction in her work, calling what she does "community work in some ways . . . a kind of low anthropology, low journalism; it's a bit documentary."[14] As Will Hammond and Dan Steward write in their introduction to a 2008 collection of essays and interviews on documentary theater: "The claim to veracity on the part of the theatre maker, however hazy or implicit, changes everything. Immediately, we approach the play not just as a play but also as an accurate source of information. We trust and expect that we are not being lied to. When this claim is made, theatre and journalism overlap, and like a journalist, the dramatist must abide by some sort of ethical code if their work is to be taken seriously."[15] At the same time, however, Smith makes a compelling case that her creations are theater, their construction and delivery processes driven by dramatic principles honed over her years of training and performance as an actor. Indeed, she has described the origins of her documentary series entitled "On the Road: The Search for American Character" as the search for an acting style to better reflect the nonnaturalistic alternatives of the contemporary theater; as she explains, it's not "psychological realism, . . . it's the opposite of that. What has to exist in order to try to allow the other to be is separation between the actor's self and the other."[16] In the search for authenticity in representation, then, documentary theater must balance the demands of the real with the determination to produce convincing theatrical artifice; the playwrights who create and the scholars who study this genre wrestle with the challenge of conveying this style of drama as drama rather than as history or sociology while maintaining the ethical obligation to accuracy called for by Hammond and Steward.

But the hybrid nature of the form does not and should not undermine the significance of this theatrical mode or prevent it from securing its place in theater practice or history. Documentary theater pioneer Peter

Weiss demanded both sociological and imaginative success for the form; while documentary theater "presents a selection which converges towards a precise and generally social or political theme," it is also the case that "the criterion which determines the editing of these cuttings from reality guarantees the quality of this dramaturgy of the document."[17] Indeed, the "editing of these cuttings" is a major element of the documentary text's constructed nature, as Laureen Nussbaum argues: "In order to be effective [documentary theater] has to transform its raw material into art. It does so by its critical selective activity and by the way it handles details of the language, rhythm, juxtaposition, flashbacks."[18] And, Carol Martin reminds us: "Most contemporary documentary theater makes the claim that everything presented is part of the archive. But equally important is the fact that not everything in the archive is part of the documentary. This begs the crucial question: What is the basis for the selection, order, and manner of presentation of materials from the archive? The process of selection, editing, organization, and presentation is where the creative work of documentary theater gets done."[19] Despite the legitimate claims made by Weiss and others about the artistic nature of these plays, their unusual relationship with the true story as it exists in the public record and the public imagination suggests that at their very foundation, these plays pose complicated challenges to truth and authenticity. Moreover, by frequently taking as their subjects very recent events, remembered by or even experienced firsthand by its audiences, documentary theater makes transparent its confrontation with existing records and memories of incidents that have often polarized members of a community or nation.

Documentary theater at its best is not seamless; it seeks not to cover over the gaps in meaning and understanding, but to expose them, and it achieves its efforts by way of a diversity of narrative and performative techniques. It highlights the impossibility of a coherent narrative, legal or otherwise, and although the documentary trial play incorporates documents first created for the courtroom, it juxtaposes them against nonlegal narratives related to the judicial proceeding but often outside the court's purview. It presents the legal case from unique, multiple, and multifaceted perspectives, serving as a useful resource that exists alongside the legal history of the case. Although enhanced perspectives and new insights may emerge from the creation of the documentary trial play, the theatrical performance of a trial cannot change the outcome of that proceeding. However, it can urge its audiences to closely examine the existing legal system in relationship to the community that upholds it, creating the possibility that such scrutiny will better prepare a society to meet the challenges of the next high profile trial. The next such trial might inch closer to justice, might provide more adequate recompense for injury. By facilitating the work of its audiences in renegotiating, imaginatively, a collection of conflicting texts, the documentary trial play prompts audiences to remember that every verdict or judicial ruling is decided by judges and juries faced with an equally diverse set of narratives. In reminding us that every trial is composed of a collection of narratives that may prove volatile when combined, it helps to undermine assumptions that judgment is easy or unambiguous.

As these performance pieces educate or remind audiences about significant moments in history, they have the capacity to contribute to the healing of social and cultural wounds caused by the original event; the staging may, simultaneously, have a quite opposite effect, stirring up old conflicts and the pain they caused by reopening the case, albeit in a representational version, and therefore provoking new disagreement about its controversial issues. The goal of presenting information while also engaging in the critical discussion of complicated issues and topics has been termed *stereopsis* by Laureen Nussbaum, which she explains as the combination of truth telling (providing history for those previously uninformed) with a challenge to the belief in truth telling; her claim is that this seemingly conflicting duality is essential to the documentary theater form.[20] Fraught with contradiction and with the impossibility of resolve, these theatrical confrontations with our past or our present (or both) are nonetheless useful in forging a clearer picture of the future, the multiplicities of meaning and belief laid plain through the forging of reason and emotion, law and language, legality and art.

Theater performance and trial share certain structural elements: similarities of stage and courtroom include the physical similarities of the spaces, each with carefully defined areas for participants and onlookers and with a raised area at the front of the space (bench in courtroom, stage in theater, although there are other possible configurations in theaters); prescribed speaking roles for participants, with scripted dialogue delivered stylistically; ritual movements on and off the stage areas of each space; dramatic reenactments and revelations; plot twists and possible surprise endings. Nussbaum notes that the court cases selected for dramatization in tribunal plays are likely to entail engagement with significant political issues, and that the first layer of enlightenment comes with the review of a recent occurrence that "constitutes a history lesson for the young or uninitiated."[21] As Weiss argues, the theater trial or tribunal "can also introduce the public into the heart of the proceedings, which is impossible in the real courtroom; it places the spectator on an equal footing with the accused or the accuser."[22] Weiss's suggestion that the tribunal play can take the public into the "heart of the proceedings" suggests that the performance not only provides access to the event's essential elements, but may also expose the emotional component of the proceeding and thus provide unique revelations about the cultural moment and its significance.

The ritualistic properties of theater and courtroom suggest further fruitful connections; dramatic texts that contain literary and theatrical enactments of the law point to both the theater and the courtroom as sites of potential resolution in a society brimming over with violence and racism. What Shoshana Felman says about a new paradigm of trial that emerged after World War II may also be true in part for the tribunal play that followed; it involves "conceiving of justice not simply as punishment but as a marked symbolic exit from the injuries of a traumatic history: as liberation from violence itself."[23] When we consider these texts as records of and reenactments of mass trauma, we begin to grasp the psychological ramifications of the events themselves. The documentary trial play, and contemporary American documentary theater of which the former is a subset, presents itself as a body of dramatic work that compellingly demonstrates the power of testimony and its role in psychic release. Felman notes that although trial and trauma were not linked for previous generations, these concepts have been more readily combined in contemporary social and political thought "ever since the Nuremberg trials attempted to resolve the massive trauma of the Second World War by the conceptual resources and by the practical tools of the law."[24] This new conceptual link provides the theoretical basis for an examination of the documentary theater and its potential for providing release from trauma caused by political conflict, racial hatred, gender discrimination, and other psychic wounds suffered by individuals and communities.

In her analysis of the connections between law and trauma, Felman identifies "the two poles of a dichotomy between private trauma and collective trauma."[25] Her study demonstrates, however, that the two poles of private and collective trauma "cannot be kept apart but, rather, keep reversing into one another."[26] The same can be said for most, if not all the trials dramatized as documentary plays, for even cases primarily involving individual crime and punishment can be widened and connected to collective values, schisms, and traumas in American culture. Most of these cases are noteworthy from the start, easily capturing the interest and imagination of the community. The actual trial segments staged as theater provide ways to connect trial with trauma and develop a reading of these performance texts that, in their success in getting "at the heart of the proceedings," serve as an emotional map by which we can interpret these social catastrophes and their psychological impact on our nation and its people. While we examine this theater from the standpoint of rationality and the law, we are moved by the emotional toll that these texts take on us; the documentary form provides an opening for legal narratives to supply information and opportunity for evaluation while also allowing for interpretive reactions.

It is no coincidence that the development of the documentary theater in the twentieth century has coincided with a proliferation of theories about public tragedy and community trauma. In a century of world wars, genocide, and, in the contemporary United States, violent political unrest spanning several decades, the turn to law and art, not to mention their intersections, have been simultaneous and significant. In explaining the "Theaters of Justice" that emerged in the decades following the Holocaust, Felman notes that our *vocabularies of remembrance* were, on the one hand, a trial report and, on the other hand, a work of art" (emphasis in the original). As she explains,

> We needed trials and trial reports to bring a conscious closure to the trauma of the war, to separate ourselves from the atrocities and to restrict, to demarcate and draw a boundary around, a suffering that seemed both unending and unbearable. Law is a discipline of limits and of consciousness. We needed limits to be able both to close the case and to enclose it in the past. Law distances the Holocaust. Art brings it closer. We needed art—the language of infinity—to mourn the losses and to face up to what in traumatic memory is not closed and cannot be closed. Historically, we needed law to totalize the evidence, to *totalize* the Holocaust and, through totalization, to start to apprehend its contours and its magnitude. Historically, we needed art to start to apprehend and to retrieve what the totalization has left out. (emphasis in the original)[27]

While Felman's discussion of law and art in the above passage is particularly focused on what is arguably the twentieth century's most significant global trauma, the Holocaust, the connections to the American documentary trial play and to American traumatic events are multiple, and what Felman argues about representations of the Holocaust might also be applied to traumas in contemporary American life: as she says, it is "precisely in this space of *slippage between law and art*" (emphasis in the original) that such events become accessible even as they continue to elude us. The same, I will argue, might be said of the American documentary trial play.[28]

The law's capacity for achieving justice for the masses who have suffered, and for diminishing the painful psychological residue left behind when riots or other kinds of violence have exposed tears or eruptions in the so-cial compact, has prompted scholars and artists to explore the ways that the law succeeds and the ways that it falls short in diminishing the lasting effects of traumatic events. The documentary trial play, in its attempts to take control of an event's varied texts and thereby direct participants to the "heart of the proceedings," stages excerpts from the collection of doc-uments, doing so in a combination of artistic and political purpose. While different documentary theater texts have different goals, a common pat-tern of composition uses the dramatic form for interrogating the complex legal and moral issues raised in the judicial or extrajudicial documents, for further understanding if not resolution of the issues that these texts bring to light. The audience has the opportunity to evaluate the witness testi-mony, attorney arguments, and judicial pronouncements and to reexamine statements, be they confessional or defensive, from the accused, providing "a frame of reference different from that in which the original action, and from that in which the tribunal took place."[29] Although use of verbatim testimony recreates segments from the actual trial in a very exacting way, the frame of reference is modified when the testimony is heard in a theater rather than in a courtroom, and audience evaluation may be strikingly different than that of the judge or jury in the actual case.

The perspectives facilitated by the change in venue provide for the pos-sibility of moments in which the tension between the judicial action and the action of the play collude or collide in order to reveal the shortcomings of each. In, using Nussbaum's term, its stereoptic nature, with truth telling and truth contesting occurring simultaneously, the documentary trial play interrogates justice and, in doing so, conveys the extent to which issues of justice pervade this theatrical form. The possibility of creating a space for multiple viewpoints about an event from legal history thus expands theater's purpose and serves as a motivating force for these courtroom-situated dramatic texts, as they provide a way to "question verdicts and established conclusions by means of an alternative vision."[30] The judicial proceeding and the dramatic representation of that proceeding are largely but never entirely identical, the theatrical version designed to examine the trial's most complex topics with the resonance of the actual trial pervading the atmosphere. The trial and the play are similarly structured ritualistic events, each working in its own way to wrestle with conflicting points of view and test justice in a democratic society; but, again as Felman points out, law is a "discipline of limits" while art is a "language of infinity."

The results of the real trial also contrast sharply with the outcome of a trial reenactment: significantly, the courtroom proceedings produce real-world consequences for the people involved. Pnina Lahav delineates this crucial difference: "When a character in a play is denied bail unjustly, the audience may become upset, may go through catharsis, and may learn about justice. But the spectators know that it is just make believe, and that after the curtain falls the actor (who was thrown into jail or released by the court of appeals) takes off her make-up and goes home. In a real trial, denial of bail means incarceration, at least for a while."[31] In his essay "Violence and the Word," Robert Cover speaks of the issue of punishment and the violence of sentencing, which he notes is "most obvious when observed from the defendant's perspective."[32] Cover goes on to make this assessment: "any account which seeks to downplay the violence or elevate the interpretive character or meaning of the event within a community of shared values will tend to ignore the prisoner or defendant and focus upon the judge and the judicial interpretive act."[33] Cover insists that "the violence of judges . . . exists in fact and differs from the violence that exists in literature or in the metaphoric characterizations of literary critics and philosophers."[34] In his delineation of the difference between the real and artistic illusion, Cover draws our attention to the limitations and protections of literature in order to differentiate it from the real violence of the court and its violent effects on everyone involved.

The trials that are reenacted in these plays, however, did take place, and the texts that were created in and around the courtrooms that tried these cases were composed in a legal realm prior to their release to the language of infinity that is art; they begin with legal narratives but do not end with them, and the journey they take us on has the potential to lead us to some further understanding of justice and authority in American culture. In an attempt to "explore the way authority is thought about and constituted in a series of texts, chosen from different cultural contexts and different generic types," legal scholar James Boyd White argues that an imaginative text, for which he uses the example of the *Crito*, can invoke an authority outside and perhaps beyond the law by "defining its own idea of reason, its own way of being with language and with others."

White continues: "The effect of this dialogue, like many, is not to offer the reader a system, a structure of propositions, but to disturb and upset him in a certain way, to leave him in a kind of radical distress."[35] As we shall see, the documentary trial play likewise takes us beyond the law to a place of "radical distress" and, similarly to the *Crito*, directs us first to the legal narrative as a source of authority before challenging us to enter more ambiguous territory. As White explains, the imaginative text offers us "contradictory and paradoxical movements of the mind" with the following effect: "Instead of an authority out there in the world—the law—and instead of an intellectual authority, a mode of reasoning that will proceed ineluctably from general principles to particular conditions, the [imaginative] text offers us a mode of thought that is inherently inconclusive and puzzling, and thus transfers the problem to us."[36] The documentary trial play draws from various kinds of legal proceedings for its inspiration and source material: criminal trials, civil trials, political trials, and government hearings. Many of these cases have been "tried in the press" concurrently or subsequently with the judicial action, and the journalistic attempts at pinpointing the face of justice or the rightful body of authority are also included. Extralegal first-person accounts further contribute to the creation of "inconclusive and puzzling" modes of thought about the judicial matter under investigation.

As a result, then, the documentary trial play does the work of the imaginative text as White describes it, for it "offers us the experience of incoherence partly resolved, then, but resolved only by our seeing that our own desires for certainty in argument, for authority in the laws—or in reason, or in persuasion—are self-misleading; that we cannot rest upon schemes or formulae, either in life or in reading, but must accept the responsibility of living, which is ultimately one of establishing a narrative, a character, a set of relations with others, which have the kinds of coherence and meaning it is given us to have, replete with tension and uncertainty."[37] However, by turning to law for inspiration, documentary theater becomes an art form whose verbatim use of documents unseats it from its imaginative limitlessness and therefore, to some extent, from its artistic authority, for it is circumscribed by history. At the same time, these performance texts pry law away from its disciplinary limits and its very different kind of authority. Once again Felman's assertion springs to mind, that it is ""precisely in this space of *slippage between law and art*" that traumatic events can be accessed and that our complex reactions to them can be examined.

Diverse disciplines have paved the way for this comparison of the real courtroom and the recreation of the courtroom on the documentary stage. The intersection of psychoanalysis with legal studies that Felman's work represents, along with the application of that intersection to literary and other art forms, has created a body of interdisciplinary scholarship with law at its center; several strands of this work, beyond what has already been noted above, provide useful insights on the documentary trial play and its connections to American culture that this study will explicate further. In her essay on the 1969 Chicago Conspiracy Trial, legal scholar Pnina Lahav sets out to "explore the question of what can be learnt about the law from the theatrical trial," her specific goal to shed light on the law by examining a highly publicized trial that contained some exaggerated and quite theatrical elements.[38] Not surprisingly, a discussion of the documentary theater reenactment of the Chicago Conspiracy Trial is included in chapter 2 of this book. Performance artist Lucy Winner writes of the connections between trial and theater that she and lawyer Jessie Allen explored in a course that drew from both dramatic and legal theories to analyze the function of the law in our society: they "considered how trials, like rituals, function as a way for the public to confront chaotic, painful, and contradictory social issues," and they designed an approach for their course stressing the three-way relationship between ritual, theater, and trial.[39] These critical models are particularly apt for a sustained examination of the documentary trial play: itself an interdisciplinary endeavor, the performance text teases out the artistic features of high profile law, drawing on law's philosophical and sociological elements, and it performs its own dramatic skirmishes while reporting details from history. It creates and presents a "humanities" experience, the artistic and expositional account of a public conflict re-presented as representation. It creates a new moment of legal imagination, an event developed as one that allows for creative space but that also exposes the law's parameters; it stipulates the end of freedom, marking the legal line that may not be crossed without the incurrence of punitive damages.

Notably, the primary focus in these essays is on the trial and on its significance to the democratic process, while the ritual of theater is invoked primarily to spotlight's law's theatricality. But the use of dramatic theory and the discussion of the performative aspects of the law can also point to the ways that the documentary trial play enacts artistic and democratic processes at once, enriching our understanding of the body politic while enhancing and expanding both the perceived and the real values of the theatrical experience. As legal scholar Peter Brooks argues, the "concept of narrative" can be used as a "vehicle of dissent from traditional forms of legal reasoning and argumentation. In this view, storytelling serves to convey meanings excluded or marginalized by mainstream legal thinking and rhetoric. Narrative has a unique ability to embody the concrete experience of individuals and communities, to make other voices heard, to contest the very assumptions of legal judgment."[40] With its unique connection of law and theater, the contemporary documentary trial play confirms Brooks's assertion about narrative, that it is "a form of countermajoritarian argument, a genre for oppositionists intent on showing up the exclusions that occur in legal business-as-usual—a way of saying, you cannot understand until you have listened to our story."[41] The story that the documentary trial play asks us to listen to is one that dismantles the seamless and seemingly rational legal account of the trial embodied by a verdict or a judicial opinion, and uses that narrative as part of a series of story threads, some majoritarian and some countermajoritarian, to reconstruct the trial in a more psychologically and emotionally comprehensive way.

This style of dramatic reconstruction has developed in step with critical interest in the emotion of law. In a 1999 volume called *The Passions of Law*, editor Susan A. Bandes begins her introduction with a deceptively simple assertion: "Emotion pervades the law." But she goes on to explain that in the "conventional story, emotion has a certain, narrowly defined place in law," confined to those without legal training and to a "finite list of law-related emotions . . . so that emotion doesn't encroach on the true preserve of law: which is reason." The essays included in the collection, however, as she explains, "tell a far more unruly, complex, and emotional story about the place of emotion in the law," and the essays do so in order to demonstrate that the "emotions that pervade law are often so ancient and deeply ingrained that they are largely invisible."[42] The volume is just one example of the recent contributions that emotion theory has made to legal studies, but it provides a way to frame the simultaneous development of the American documentary theater and its unique attempts to tell an equally "unruly, complex, and emotional story about the place of emotion in the law."

As each documentary trial play stages one or more historical legal decision, the emotional components of the law are enacted by witnesses, victims, defendants, and juries, with the dramatic heightening of spectacle serving to underscore the psychological outpourings of the high profile legal event. The theatrical representations of selected cultural crises contribute to a new understanding of our social systems, both legal and artistic, and their complex and overlapping roles in confronting and resolving explosive issues. We become aware of the extent to which the proceedings themselves, as well as the dramas that follow, often fail to resolve but rather stir up emotions and antagonisms. In doing so they remind us of the responsibility we bear for telling and retelling the traumatic stories of the past. For if we owe the connection between trial and trauma primarily to the Holocaust and to the field of study that has emerged from that dark period, we must also heed the pronouncement that has been linked to that horror: that we must not forget.

Moreover, we remember by recounting victims' narratives, which Dori Laub calls "the very process of bearing witness to massive trauma," which begins with "someone who testifies to an absence, to an event that has not yet come into existence, in spite of the overwhelming and compelling nature of the reality of its occurrence."[43] Documentation of these events in a form that is intended for repetition suggests that this kind of testimonial can bear witness to trauma repeatedly, even perpetually, and thus reduce its power for harm. The theater can assist in the witnessing thus created, because as Laub notes, while "historical evidence to the event which constitutes the trauma may be abundant and documents in vast supply, the trauma—as a known event and not simply as an overwhelming shock—has not been truly witnessed yet, not been taken cognizance of. The emergence of the narrative which is being listened to—and heard—is, therefore, the process and the place wherein the cognizance, the 'knowing' of the event is given birth to."[44] Thus does the value of continued turmoil, for "a journey onto an uncharted land, a journey the survivor cannot traverse or return from alone" asserts itself.[45] In the documentary trial play, the representations of these traumatic events chart these journeys and their need for vigilance, lest hatred and cowardice succeed in defeating national tenets of liberty and equality. Shifting focus to each play's legal elements and the cultural ramifications of the political conflict as drama provides an opportunity to explore the testimony and other forms of judicial language "at the heart of" each play, an attempt to multiply narrative meaning and its impact on theater, trauma, and truth.

The concentration on testimony underscores its role in achieving some relief/release from trauma, be that trauma of an individual or a community. Connections emerge between the trial testimony staged in these plays and the possible resolution for those victimized by violence and injustice in the real events. The development of the documentary trial drama in the United States in the last three decades of the twentieth century, among other things, exposes the diversity of pressures placed on individuals and institutions to negotiate successful relationships with the law and the legal system.

The topics taken up in all these plays themselves raise critical questions about the proliferation of documentary trial and tribunal dramatization in the contemporary world. How do the events chosen for dramatization uniquely raise and seek to resolve issues of justice, civil rights, and democracy? To what extent does this kind of theater reflect the unique challenges of the era that ended with the millennium while also forecasting concerns that would continue to provoke national interests in the 9/11 world?

These challenges to the justice system raise important questions about law, truth, and witnessing while revealing the links between the law and other ideological issues: race, religion, human and civil rights, individual and communal interactions, and so on. They demonstrate links between law and art, particularly the literary and theatrical arts, and they examine the role that representation plays in supporting or confronting the precept and execution of law and order in a democratic society.

Indeed, the trials and tribunals that have been most public and most publicized are, along with their attending social issues, readily represented here; often directly, in the form of legal discourse as dialogue, but occasionally in the personal testimony gathered in the wake of judicial actions. The parameters set by the focus on trial plays limit the discussion to explorations of truth and justice, law and performance, as well as the link between courtroom and playhouse. But the frequency with which trials are woven into documentary theater texts has resulted in a range of plays to be considered within this context, thus adding to a larger critical dialogue about the development and significant presence of documentary theater in contemporary times. The texts chosen lend themselves to diverse examinations of playwrights and performers whose work in this genre has brought them celebrity, plays whose power have convinced celebrities to commit to their causes, and plays that have remained underground but have nonetheless been a source of inspiration and theatrical development.

The documentary tradition is rooted in the public and the political, in its determination to privilege social, political, and historical conflicts over the personal conflicts often better suited to the tenets of dramatic realism. It is in our high-profile trials that the culture acts out the dilemmas that challenge our institutions. Even when such differences originate on the streets or in private homes, they are often resolved in open court. In this case, the open courts are presented to us on a stage; and, as documentary theater enacts the law, it provides the law a unique interpretative perspective just this side of imaginative experience. By connecting theater and the legal system on issues of religion, violence, mercy, kinship, love, madness, all are implicated, and as these issues are played out in dramatic texts, they raise complicated questions and point to tentative but nonetheless powerful answers about law and the execution of justice, about art and the resolution of emotion.

1

Judicial Identification: *The Trial of the Catonsville Nine* and *The Chicago Conspiracy Trial*

During his 1968 presidential campaign, Richard Nixon promised to end the war in Vietnam. But within a year of taking office, his pledge to decrease US involvement in Southeast Asia seemed to have been forgotten as reports of renewed and expanded military offensives surfaced. Details of the 1968 My Lai Massacre, the brutal mass murder of several hundred Vietnamese civilians by US soldiers, became public in November 1969, prompting global outrage and fueling existing domestic opposition to the American involvement in the war. On December 1, 1969, the first lottery draft since 1942 was held to determine the order of induction for men born between January 1, 1944, and December 31, 1950, and on the evening of April 30, 1970, President Nixon announced the invasion of Cambodia and the plan to attack and conquer this center of Viet Cong power. The announcement confirmed the continuation of national aggression on the battlefields of Southeast Asia and further accelerated and expanded protests on the home front. The day following the announcement, Friday, May 1, students on college and university campuses raised their voices in unison against the expansion of offensive military actions. But thousands of lives would be lost on the battlefield before a troubled peace brought an end to the protests that themselves would rain violent death down on some of the participants.

After the announcement of the Cambodia campaign, protest weekends were planned at universities around the country, including a schedule of demonstrations for the weekend of May 1–4 at Kent State University, with rallies to be held Friday and Monday on the university commons. After multiple disturbances on Friday night, Kent mayor Leroy Satrom and other city officials met to discuss the potential for trouble and asked the Ohio National Guard to set up a presence on campus, which they did, one thousand strong, on Sunday, May 3. By noon on Monday there were about three thousand students in the area identified for the rally, even though the university had announced the rally's cancellation. Some half of the crowd was spectators, with the other half a combination of several hundred committed protestors and a significant number of less strident supporters. The National Guard commander read an order to the crowd, demanding that the group disperse, but the guard's attempts to end the protest were met by shouting and rock throwing. As the troops, locked and loaded, retraced their steps up Blanket Hill, twenty-eight of the seventy present turned and fired on the crowd. Some fired into the air; some didn't. Over sixty shots were fired in thirteen seconds. Four students died, and nine were wounded.

Some forty years hence, the shootings at Kent State remain one of the most shocking reminders of the social upheaval that marked the 1960s: a reminder of the era's political divisions and a mark of the animosity in its citizenry that incited members of the US military to fire on unarmed American civilians. The event sparked the largest national student strike in history, leading to hundreds of closed campuses and motivating several million students to participate in protests and walkouts. On May 8, one hundred thousand people gathered in Washington, DC, and that number plus another fifty thousand came together in San Francisco to denounce US involvement in Vietnam and to rise up against the violence directed at students or at anyone else who called publicly for an end to war. Across the nation, ROTC buildings were targeted, and many burned as tension between the military and the country's youth accelerated. Between the years 1968 and 1972, Ivy League institutions responded drastically to student outcry against the armed forces and the subsequent decreased enrollments in the ROTC (Reserve Officers' Training Corps), in most cases by severing the connections between academics and military training. A 1973 article in the *Harvard Crimson* indicates the extent to which the death of ROTC had occurred in the Ivy League, for almost all programs had been eliminated or severely cut, with funding diverted and no new students admitted to programs.[1] At present, the ROTC is still absent from many of the Ivies, a leftover of antiwar sentiment that continues to reflect and project the divide between uniform and gown now etched onto our national consciousness as a result of those searing images from the Kent State shootings.

Elsewhere that spring, another act of violence had initiated a chain of confrontational incidents that left in their wake a legacy of distrust and division. On February 25, 1970, student protestors at the University of California at Santa Barbara stormed the Bank of America branch in the off-campus community of Isla Vista with stones and then set the building on fire. It burned to the ground and was soon rebuilt, but during the reconstruction, a student who approached the building site to put out a fire was shot by a police officer who suspected him of criminal mischief. On June 10, almost four months after the fire, a crowd of over a thousand people gathered at the campus community's Perfect Park to defy the curfew and protest the treatment of Isla Vista residents by the police. The crowd was tear-gassed, and four hundred protestors were arrested. This conflict and dozens like it dramatized the political rift that came to a head during the antiwar protests of the 1960s and 1970s, as what seemed to many to be unreasonable if not unconstitutional government actions sought to silence or contain domestic protest. At universities, the philosophy of civil disobedience spilled out of classrooms onto the quads, increasing the likelihood of violence, even in a cultural and legal framework that sanctions nonviolent forms of protest, and suggesting the extent to which the law was failing to preserve a space for the citizen activism deemed central to the success of the democracy. Not surprisingly, debates about freedom were acted out in courtrooms as the players on both sides sought support or resolution in statutes, precedents, and judicial rulings, and the wide range of narrative and dramatic representations that recorded or recreated these courtroom clashes suggest the enduring power of such clashes while providing an artistic catalog of this national trauma.

Neither the Kent State shootings nor the Bank of America burning became the subject of a documentary trial play, but two performance texts that center on activist efforts against the war and the criminal charges that followed were composed and staged: *The Trial of the Catonsville Nine* (*Catonsville*) (1970) by Daniel Berrigan, and *The Chicago Conspiracy Trial* (*Chicago Conspiracy*) (1979) by Ron Sossi and Frank Condon. These two plays share a number of elements and themes, not least among them the centrality of judicial representation and the dominance of the judge's voice as illustrative of and empowered by the rule of law. As writer Graham Burnett remarks in his meditation on jury service, what he and the other jurors "discovered directly about the real power of the state and its agents" was that "in the end there was, simply, the final power of the state," and furthermore, "there is nowhere to run from the state" as the people outside the courtroom or the prison cell "actually constitute the state itself."[2] While the two judges on the bench for the group trials of these protestors seem to have been very different kinds of judges and are very differently presented as characters and as individuals participating in the dramatic contest in which they are cast, in both cases, as judges, they stand for and convey the power of the court, not only to render a decision, but to dictate fit punishment.

As such, then, they are cast in these performance texts in the role that law professor Samuel H. Pillsbury describes as the "detached, principled— and dispassionate—decision makers," and as the "quintessential figure of American justice, the judge," who "dresses in a somber black robe, sits at a high bench, and employs universal principles of reason to surmount the self-interested passions of the litigants," thus "remaining above the emotional turmoil of the parties and their lawyers."[3] As legal theorist Paul Kahn argues, the "rule of law cannot appear as the empowerment of the judge as a particular subject. It cannot appear to be the rule of men, even if those men happen to be wearing judicial robes."[4] It follows, then, suggests Kahn, that when the judge is constructed as the state's primary spokesperson and agent, the individuality and subjectivity of the judge is suppressed. He goes on to note that when we pursue consideration of legal decisions as having been authored by a particular judge, we "approach law's product from a dimension other than that of law's authority" and "pursue, instead, history, biography, or literature."[5] Even as Kahn makes this distinction, however, he allows that the "rule of law is not pure," and "we continue to have an interest in the great judicial figure as a unique subject."[6] The representations of the judges in *Catonsville* and in *Chicago Conspiracy*, who in the first is designated only as "Judge" and in the second more specifically and historically as "Judge Julius Hoffman," convey two very different views of the judicial character and public demeanor, but each of these two theatrical embodiments of actual judges serves to dramatize, albeit quite differently, the complicated role that emotion plays in determining the demeanor and the decisions that emanate from the bench, the ultimate symbol of authority in the legal setting of the courtroom.

Despite the fact that these two plays were created a decade apart from each other, one in the immediate aftermath of the actual event and the other some ten years later, they share a commonality of subject matter that twins them, for both trials and therefore both performance texts have their origins and locate their dramatic power in community resistance to the war in Vietnam and take their subject matter from two famous cases of group prosecution of protestors. But they are also connected by the presence in each of a strong judicial figure, a character who dominates the theatrical action, represents the intersection of individuals and institutions, and is called on to mediate the conflict between the expression of dissent and public safety. Situated in the gap between the authorless judicial opinion and the robed man whose personality dominates, these documentary trial plays chart the tension between the legal and the literary, between decision and ambiguity, between justice and mercy; as Robert Ferguson argues, the figure who best exemplifies this paradox is the presiding judge, for "no other trial performer is equipped to think for everyone."[7] And so the trial performer best suited to embody the contradictions that present themselves during the contested courtroom proceeding becomes the primary focus in these two theatrical versions of high-profile criminal trials, as these performances borrow strategically from the historical record of what has already been decided in the actual courtrooms and embellish it as dramatic contest.

The first case, the trial of the Catonsville Nine, involves the destruction of draft records; the second case hinges, in part, on a group's failure to secure the appropriate documentation for an antiwar demonstration. *Catonsville* was written by a trial codefendant within two years of the arrest and prosecution of nine men and women who entered a Selective Service office in Maryland in May 1968, removed draft records, and set them on fire with napalm. The play was staged while the war, and resistance to it, continued and while its author was a fugitive from the law after going into hiding following the trial. The other case had its origins the same year as the Catonsville protest, during the Democratic National Convention that summer in Chicago. A group of radical defendants ended up in court, defendants in what would become known as the Chicago Conspiracy Trial, and they were prosecuted one year after the Catonsville defendants had been charged with and tried for the destruction of government property. However, the Conspiracy Trial was not adapted for the documentary theater until 1979, when it was first staged by the Odyssey Theatre in Los Angeles and since revived by the group numerous times, most recently in 2007.

In one of the first critical examinations of the contemporary American documentary theater, Dan Isaac observed the impetus that would serve to connect this developing genre to a series of high-profile legal trials over the next thirty years. Isaac, in his essay "Theatre of Fact," recalled its historical connection to another period of theater history before forecasting what would become the source of inspiration and material in this newest incarnation of the form: "like a fast sock in the jaw from the thirties, [the theater of fact] has forced its way onto the American stage again. But unlike its noisy brawling predecessor, the Living Newspaper, which was fathered by the Federal Theater out of the fertile discontent of the depression, this present brand of theater of fact has lowered its voice and grown more decorous. It has entered the courtroom."[8] Isaac's remark about the courtroom connection might have seemed at the time of his essay's publication in 1971 little more than the contextualization of a reemerging dramatic form, but it accurately predicted the direction this style of theater would take, for the courtroom and the trial have become one of contemporary theater's most effective frameworks for representing clashes between a government and its citizens, and for exposing the inconsistencies of a justice system designed to protect all individuals equally. In addition to their reflection of the cynical national mood of the 1970s, the decade during which they were composed and performed, the early contemporary trial plays *Catonsville* and *Chicago Conspiracy* represent a judicial trend that has continued to the present: staging the major courtroom battles of the past and the present, critiquing the American justice system, and illuminating the gap between the theory and the practice of American law and between the ideal and the reality of equality and democracy.

Catonsville dramatizes the federal trial of the nine Catholic activists who burned draft files as an explicit public protest against US involvement in the Vietnam War, an action that was made up of several symbolic or ritualistic elements. By using a crude form of homemade napalm to set fire to the files, they called attention to the use of napalm as a destructive weapon in Vietnam. As defendant David Darst explains during his testimony, which appears in part 3 of the longer of two printed versions of the play, in a section titled "The Day of the Nine Defendants," the group "felt it was fitting that this agent which had burned human flesh in the war in Vietnam and in many other places should now be poured on the records which gave war and violence their cruel legitimacy."[9] Defendant Daniel Berrigan, when reading to the court a meditation that he wrote just before the action, reminds audiences of napalm's significance as well: "Our apologies, good friends for the fracture of good order . . . the burning of paper instead of children."[10] Members of the support team had concocted this homemade form of napalm using a recipe adapted from a Special Forces handbook.[11] They also alerted the press before the crime so that their actions would be filmed and reported, and a video of the news footage that captured the burning on tape was shown in the original production of the play that followed.[12]

As the files burned, the group held hands and prayed as they waited for the police to arrive, and then they peacefully climbed into the paddy wagon. They were charged and subsequently convicted on three counts: destruction of US property, destruction of Selective Service records, and interference with the Selective Service Act of 1967. All nine defendants were found guilty on all charges and were subsequently given prison sentences ranging from two to six years. Although the defendants pleaded not guilty, they never denied removing or burning the files. Defense attorney William Kunstler argued in his opening statement for the invocation of the doctrine of nullification, which allows a jury to find a defendant not guilty if the jury agrees that the law invoked in the case is an unjust one. Kunstler announced as much to the jury: "We have what the defendants consider a historic moment, a moment when a jury may, as the law empowers it, decide the case, not on the facts at all, but decide the case on the principle issues involved."[13]

The judge did not allow the jury to consider the nullification doctrine, however, and the defendants appealed the case the following year on the basis of his refusal, as acknowledged in the appeal document: "The appeal is based on asserted error in the trial court's instruction to the jury. The appellants claim that (1) The trial court erred in charging the jury on the definition of criminal intent and the meaning of 'willfully,' and (2) That the trial judge should have informed the jury that it had the power to acquit the defendants even if they were clearly guilty of the offenses, or at least, that the court should have permitted their counsel so to argue to the jury."[14] The judge's refusal to allow the jury to deliberate on the moral principles that had compelled the defendants to burn the files had implications for the appeal historically, but the nullification issue also makes the case complicated and dramatic and thereby desirable as a theatrical narrative. That the nullification issue in this case stems from a debate about morality and conscience as both apply to the justness of the war renders the trial of these activists a particularly fitting selection for the documentary theater, as the latter concerns itself with staging contested events that evoke strong reactions from the realms of reason and emotion and pitting them against each other as part of the conflict to be acted out.

Indeed, the inclusion of this judicial issue becomes a primary component of *Catonsville*'s dramatic tension, and the treatment of the jury's basis of deliberation becomes a key and climactic scene in the performance text. In both published versions of the script, a debate about what the jury ought to be considering when it deliberates becomes a wide-ranging commentary on the law and on the extent to which personal principles and personal emotions play a part in the verdict the jury is asked to deliver. The Prosecution begins his closing statement with a reminder to the jury that "the government is not about to put itself in the position—has not heretofore and is not now—of conducting its policies at the end of a string tied to the consciences of these nine defendants." While allowing that the defendants have every right to believe that the war is "illegal, that it is immoral, that it is against religious principles" and that "any reasonable man could take that view," it is the job of the prosecution and, by implication, the jury, to decide if the act of burning the draft records was wrong. For prosecution, he insists, is the "government's response, the law's response, the people's response, to what the defendants did." The burning of government documents and the statute that forbids such destruction: that is what the case is about.[15]

The speech attempts to persuade the jury (and the audience) that while the nation's policies may be open to criticism, "our problems" will not be solved by people who "deliberately violate our laws, the foundation and support for an ordered and just and civilized society."[16] The position that the Prosecution argues makes the reasonable assumption that the law must be upheld because it is crucial to justice. This reasoned and reasonable argument is immediately juxtaposed in the script with the very different perspective of the Defense, whose speech follows. The Defense begins on a radically different note and in a different tone by calling for a "great measure of personal reflection" needed by all in coming to some understanding of the trial's significance, and a request that the jury pardon him for injecting a "personal note." He goes on to reveal that although he was trained in law school not to identify with prospective clients, he confesses that he has "come to love and respect the men and women who stand before the court."[17] His appeal to the jury, then, is for its members to ignore their own "training" as citizens instructed to uphold the law and to allow for a conscience-driven and therefore personal kind of judgment in deciding on a verdict. Although the Judge responds by reminding the Defense and the jury that "the law does not permit jurors to be governed by sympathy, prejudice or public opinion" but rather to "ascertain the truth" by means of facts, the scene underscores the difficulty of determining truth even in a case whose facts are undisputed.[18]

Another way we see this challenge to law's supremacy is in the way that the work captures the skepticism about the law and the distrust of governmental processes common during the Vietnam War era; as John Simon wrote about the play in his overview of the theater season in New York in 1971, the main point of *Catonsville* "emerges gradually with increasingly powerful clarity: the actions of these nine people are based on a reasoning and language totally different from the reasoning and language of the Law."[19]

As an early example of the contemporary American version of this genre, and one that happens to have been written by one of the trial defendants, *Catonsville* constitutes a unique contribution to the canon of documentary trial plays. Author Berrigan is a poet activist and a Jesuit priest who has devoted his life to protest and resistance, but his participation in the Catonsville incident has remained the most publicized of his many peace acts. His brother, Philip, was also an activist priest and a codefendant in the Catonsville case. No doubt the reputation of this incident stems from the collective fame of the most notable antiwar movement in our nation's history, but Daniel Berrigan's theatrical adaptation of the trial has also contributed to the ongoing legacy of this protest. His own comments about the intentions that guided his construction of the play as well as some details about his process shed light on his dual roles as participant in the events and, subsequently, as the dramatist responsible for adapting history for the theater.

In his introduction to the play, written at the time of composition and production and reprinted in the Fordham University Press copy of the text, Berrigan describes this process of transformation.[20] Working "directly with the data of the trial record, somewhat in the manner of the new 'factual theater,'" Berrigan claims to have been "as faithful as possible to the original words . . . making only those minute changes required for clarity or good sense."[21] But he goes on to argue for the artistic transformation of the material: "it was predictable that a qualitative change would occur, almost by the law of nature, as the form emerged." His hope, he goes on to say, was that not only would he "induce out of the density of matter an art form worthy of the passionate acts and words of the Nine, acts and words which were the substance of the court record," but that the work of art would succeed in reinstating the "firmness and clarity of the original deed."[22] By creating a work of art from the documents of law, he brings a new version of the legal case and its history back to the public, and to subsequent generations of citizens, for consideration.

Although the verdict of the actual case cannot change in response to a theatrical rerendering of a trial, the public's conception of and beliefs about the rule of law can be affected by the recreation, and by the conflict that arises when law would appear to fall short of upholding a culture's values: as the Defense in *Catonsville* acknowledges, the Prosecution is correct in stating that the defendants burned the records. But, he asserts, it is not "a question of records which are independent of life"; indeed, he argues that no other records "so directly affect life and death on a mass scale," for draft records "stand quite literally for life and death to young men."[23] The jury in the case was not persuaded to find the defendants not guilty, for doing so would have meant ignoring the indisputable factual evidence in the case; in this fact-based representation the jury in the play is similarly constrained. The play ends as the case did, with guilty verdicts for all. However, as a performance text presented to a theater audience, it creates a space for further deliberation of the issue, particularly as the issue calls attention to ongoing debates about law and morality. The patrons witnessing the reenactment of the trial may come to a personal decision that the strict adherence to law or to fact is not always the reasonable or right choice. The questioning of the reliance on fact is, ironically, instigated by a theater of fact, as this type of theater constructs a unique relationship between the details of a trial (the facts) and the passions of the issues (the emotions).

Whether or not Berrigan achieves his intended purpose of recapturing the "firmness and clarity of the original deed" is subject to differing critical opinions. However, as a writer working at the forefront of the documentary movement in the United States, his commentary on this style of playwriting serves as a valuable record of the process and the purpose of the documentary trial play, especially as conceived of and practiced in the earliest contemporary examples. Berrigan suggests that the text can potentially offer to the audience a new version of the trial, for the judicial event itself, burdened as it was by bureaucracy and procedure, had decreased the "intensity and passion" of the protest "in the obeisance paid to legal niceties and court routine, in the wrangling and paper shuffling." Thus does he infer that the documentary theater serves, at least in this case, as a revitalization of history as it is newly infused with intensity, moving us back through the trial documentation, which he claims has had a deadening effect, in an effort to reclaim the power of the "passionate acts and words" of the defendants. Rather than adhering to a conception of art as removed from reality and distanced from history, Berrigan posits that the documentary theater account of the trial "had but one purpose therefore: to wind the spring tighter."[24] That is, the play was intended to lend additional power to the act begun in the parking lot of the Catonsville Selective Service office in May of 1968, furthering the antiwar protest in a way that the trial, he seems to suggest, had failed to do. His inference, too, is that the crime and the trial, from the defendants' perspective, were both attempts at protest; the play that developed out of those historical events, particularly in its reconstruction of trial documents, might be seen, then, as the next step in the antiwar demonstration that began with the destruction of draft documents.

The timeline of the act of file burning, the trial, and the theater production of *Catonsville* did in fact allow for the performance to "wind the spring tighter," with all three events taking place within a span of two years, as the draft and the war continued to polarize and traumatize American citizens. The 1968 trial was transformed into a play that premiered in Los Angeles in 1970 and was then staged in several subsequent productions and adapted to film in 1972.[25] As a result of the play and film, the Catonsville incident became the most widely known in a handful of similarly ritualistic protests events involving Catholic activists. One year prior to the parking lot fire in Catonsville, two of the Nine, along with several other protestors who opposed the war, had seized records in Baltimore and splattered them with blood. One month before the Catonsville trial, a group known as the Milwaukee Fourteen destroyed ten thousand draft records with napalm. Several other similar incidents followed.

As *New York Times* reporter Philip Nobile wrote of these incidents, "The scenario was always the same: a swift seizure of Selective Service or defense property succeeded by fireside prayers and songs until the law arrived. Nobody tried to quit the scene of the crime. Otherwise there could be no tribunals, no jail sentences, no witnesses. So far, even the trials . . . seem to have followed a common script. Irresistible moral arguments were defeated every time by immovable legal principles which declared the war and conscience inadmissible evidence."[26] Nobile's description of the protests uses theatrical language, blurring the line between the scripted nature of the burnings and the scripted nature of the documentary trial play that emerged from the Catonsville episode. He also rightly notes the need for "tribunals" to follow the burnings by nodding to their public and performative nature. Although he is analyzing the connection between the burnings and their necessary legal epilogues, he seems to be indirectly describing and predicting the role of the documentary theater as well. An act of social protest is followed by a legal action, the latter prescribed by the rule of law and its "immovable legal principles," but in the case of Catonsville, the legal action is followed by a theatrical version of the action that may use artistic techniques to privilege the "irresistible moral arguments."

The creation and production of *Catonsville* might be considered, then, as one more scripted protest, but one that could be advertised in advance to attract an audience; that could be repeated as needed; that could enact resistance but do so without real arrests or convictions. While all courtroom dramatizations simulate judicial activities that in many cases mirror, more or less, the activities of an actual courtroom, documentary trial plays, by their very nature, take the notion of representation further by enacting a version of a real trial using the words first spoken in the courtroom. Paradoxically, however, it is in its very adherence to the trial's transcript that such a play reminds us of the differences between an actual trial and the trial represented in the documentary theater. For no matter how true to the experience it may be, it is not the same as being a witness or a juror in a real trial. It is but the shadow of an act of legal interpretation; the original act takes place, as legal scholar Robert Cover reminds us, "in a field of pain and death," for "legal interpretive acts signal and occasion the imposition of violence upon others." As Cover describes the process, it links the judge in particular to that violent imposition: "a judge articulates her understanding of a text, and as a result, somebody loses his freedom, his property, his children, even his life."[27] In the theatrical version of the trial, the "imposition of violence" is fictional; the anxiety a judge or jury might experience in delivering a guilty sentence or in the trauma that a defendant might experience at receiving that sentence is imitative of real anxiety, guilt, and pain but is not the pain itself.

However, information about the real trial and its outcome, commonly communicated to audiences by means of program notes, announcements, slides and videos, along with the reminder that the play belongs to the theater-of-fact genre, intervenes in the reception of the cultural text and may complicate both aesthetic and emotional responses. Carol Martin hints at this complication when she suggests that "documentary theater creates its own aesthetic imaginaries while claiming a special factual legitimacy."[28] This play of imagination and "factual legitimacy" may foster a complicated emotional reaction in audience members who are asked to revive their memory of or become familiar with the original trial as part of the experience of the theatrical and aesthetic event. The tension between imagination and fact helps to make documentary theater a singular kind of dramatic performance; in the trial plays, our conceptions and perceptions of the law exist in a liminal place between the imagined and the real, which is also the place where the rule of law resides, bound as it is by the abstractions of truth and justice on one side and the concrete prison wall on the other.

Likewise, the basic dramatic convention that allows for actors to stand in for people other than themselves is heightened significantly by the genre's use of actual words and actual situations. In the case of *Catonsville*, the notes in the acting edition of the play provide physical descriptions for each character that match the real defendants. A textual note explains that casting for the New York production was influenced by the fact that this is a play "about real people, all of whom (except David Darst) are still alive," and therefore "some attention was paid to the physical resemblances," although "what is more important is the essence and spirit of the characters and not physical likenesses."[29] As David C. Gild reports in his review of the Off-Broadway production, when the guilty verdicts in the play are followed by the screening of the actual defendants burning the files, the casting decisions made for an uncanny intersection of fact and fiction: "We see from the film strip that the actors on stage actually look like the real-life people involved in the real trial."[30] As Martin argues, in documentary theater "the technological postmodern meets oral-theater culture" and "the bodies of the performers as well as the bodies of those being represented in documentary theater are decisive in ways that overlap but are also different from fictive theater."[31] The casting decision had the effect, then, of tilting the performed trial closer to the real one, for the bodies of the dramatic personae served to shadow those of the defendants, offering a reminder that the state used its legal authority to confine the flesh-and-blood bodies of the Catonsville protestors, men and women in some sense "just like" the actors who recreated them.

During the play's first production in Los Angeles in the summer of 1970, the real defendants and their legal status were not only a matter of theatrical debate, for several of them at that time were evading the FBI and their sentences. Berrigan had gone into hiding, and so the show's director, Gordon Davidson, who claimed that his phone was tapped by the FBI during the rehearsal period, traveled to Boston to meet covertly with the playwright during rehearsals. Davidson claimed to believe that the FBI had staked out the theater, looking for Berrigan and hoping to take him into custody. In a 2005 lecture about his long career in the Los Angeles theater scene, Davidson said that he and Berrigan had recorded the latter addressing the theater audience. On opening night, when the tape of Berrigan welcoming the audience to the theater was played ("Good evening, this is Father Berrigan speaking to you from the underground"), Davidson noticed movement in the theater that he claims was FBI agents who had been assigned to stake out the theater in case Berrigan showed up and they had a chance to apprehend him.[32] Berrigan was arrested at a safe house in Rhode Island just days after the play's run ended, but not before the convicted criminal playwright-at-large had added an element of suspense to the production of *Catonsville*, one that underscored the work's factual origins in recent history and its dealings with a very real world of law enforcement and criminal imprisonment, particularly with the loss of freedom that accompanies the guilty verdict.

The play's return to Los Angeles the following year instigated a local controversy that threatened its production and once again called attention to the ways that documentary theater could engage in social protest, and mix politics with art. A group that called itself the Citizens Legal Defense Alliance appealed to the city's board of supervisors to halt the production of the play on the grounds that the Mark Taper Forum, which received public funds, should not be allowed to stage propaganda that supported liberal radical beliefs. The response of the board of supervisors to the request came from lawyers in service to the local government, who firmly stated that the board had no jurisdiction in the matter and no power to censor or prohibit the performance.[33] Not surprisingly, the controversy boosted advance ticket sales, and the show set a new record for tickets sold in a single day in the wake of this news report.

The play's political potency, evident from the citizens' group protest, emerged in part from the contemporaneousness of the play's staging: while the war in Vietnam continued; while the nation's divisions continued to gape wide; and at a time when the last of the defendants at large, Mary Moynihan, had not yet been apprehended.[34] In this case, the line between real trial and documentary theater trial was blurred, and the antiwar ideology presented in the play could not be safely ascribed to the artistic abstractions of form or content that insure a safe distance from representations of resistance or revolution. It is notable that the objections to the show and the attempt to block it came from the city's Legal Defense Alliance, and that the response from the Los Angeles board of supervisors was prepared by lawyers; thus did the matter become one of legal rights and legal authority, with the decision coming down firmly on the side of citizens' right to challenge the rule of law in a stage play, and for public funds to help support that presentation and that challenge. The episode and its publicity made evident the political nature of *Catonsville* and the extent to which this kind of theater could participate in shaping or disrupting the political ideologies of its time.

The intentional blurring of the real and its re-creation has, not surprisingly, preoccupied the critics in their evaluation of the documentary theater's artistic merits and has, ironically, often resulted in negative assessments that become intertwined with acceptance or rejection of the form's essential nature. The reviews at the time of production of *Catonsville* are typical of the difficulty critics were faced with when confronted with a theatrical style reliant on and demonstrative of the facts and documents used explicitly as the materials of construction. Clive Barnes, who called the Off-Broadway production of *Catonsville* "riveting" and a "wonderfully moving testament to nine consciences," nonetheless defined it as "a new kind of play that is the almost instant replay of a politically theatrical gesture" while bemoaning that there "may alas be more plays where this one came from."[35] Four months later, his review of the Broadway production typified the combination of respect and skepticism that continues to haunt the reception and evaluation of the documentary theater: he calls it a "dramatic document—which is less than a drama but more than documentary"; nonetheless, he adds, it is a dramatic document that "remains fascinating."[36] Simon also proclaims his interest even as he damns with faint praise by naming *Catonsville* at once "the best thing on the boards" while also "barely a play at all."[37] Faced with this new or, at least, this newly revived form of American drama and one that had been revised for the contemporary moment, critics were often unconvinced that the documentary theater even qualified as theater. It confronted them with issues of political intention, the nature of artistic creativity, the "truth" about history and the desire to stage a truth rendering right along with the impossibility of telling history's truth. What became the measure of the success of this kind of theater could not be separated from the discomfort it engendered with its participation in the current political and cultural environments out of which it emerged.

In reviewing the first Mark Taper production of the show in the summer of 1970, Dan Sullivan of the *Los Angeles Times* had been similarly dubious, writing that the problem with discussing the play "strictly as a theater piece is that it can't be done," and that "as drama the work is inert, suggesting an oratorical contest in some fully politicized high school."[38] But Sullivan was converted by the script as revised by Saul Levitt for its subsequent Off-Broadway run in January 1971, noting that "a thrilling thing" had occurred in the period since his first viewing: *Catonsville* "turned into a play."[39] When this shorter version returned to Los Angeles, Sullivan titled his review "'Catonsville'—Once a Sermon, Now a Play."[40] Dan Isaac occupied a middle ground in his assessment; for Isaac, the play evoked the "dramatic tradition of the Platonic dialogue, except that it has found a locus and conventionalized situation that polarizes and dramatizes its dialectic: a trial in an American court room."[41] By noting the appearance of documentary theater's subgenre, the trial play, he implies that the marriage of court and theater brings a coherence and life to the portrayal of history's stories done for the stage. Certainly the rituals of the court blend with the rituals of the theater to some advantage, as we learn more about and have a richer experience of both. Furthermore, the documentary theater takes courtroom drama to the next level with its use of the real courtroom drama, particularly its words, not just as inspiration but as verbatim material. It does not merely join court and theater, but inserts the trial itself and its documents into the performance text. It links the rule of law to the art form that recreates it, and takes the trial transcript back into the world for another, nonlegal and very individual kind of "verdict," one that can also allow for additional evidence or other extralegal materials to be placed alongside the court documents.

The justice system provides copious documents for its cases, and the records of such proceedings are commonly available to the public because of freedom of information laws. But the formal elements of the trial also prove appealing to this style of theater, as the cases selected for dramatization often produce, with various degrees of editing by the playwright or director, word-for-word speeches of compelling testimony: in some cases they are transformed into soliloquies, in others they become explosive dialogues that debate the values or the failings of American culture and American law. Because conceptions of who we are as a nation and of what we believe are diverse and often disputed, any theater piece that sets out to convey even some of that variety would need be a cluster of contrasting viewpoints. And the dramatization of legal cases proves no exception, for such criminal and civil proceedings regularly become the space where contested social or political issues arrive in order to be systematically examined. In describing the study of law in literary representations, legal scholar Paul Gewirtz reminds us that "at its best," a literary text about the law "can help to illuminate the legal world in distinctive ways by attention to literature's narrative particularity, its focus on kinds of human understanding beyond reason alone, its capacity for provoking an empathetic understanding of others' inner life."[42] The American documentary trial plays thus join law and theater by broadening the space for law in culture; the area of "human understanding beyond reason alone" applies literature or, in this case theater, to the creation of a more pliant view of the legal materials, whether that view is aimed at standard court procedures or abstract moral imperatives.

Derek Paget, in his discussion of the "'documentariness' of a cultural product," similarly identifies the tension between the record of a historical event and the cultural product that may be created from it and in reaction to it; he defines this tension as one of "two, distinct, but interlinked, structures of feeling: one is expressive of a faith in facts, grounded upon positivist scientific rationality; the other is expressive of a profound political skepticism which disputes the notion 'facts = truth.'"[43] Like the culture it reflects, the documentary product contains and highlights a rational belief system based on order and progress; in the case of the trial play, the judicial system stands in here for the "faith in facts," a certain inherent comfort in having court proceedings provide the structural foundation that satisfies our urge for and attraction to a rational epistemology. In its revisionist and relativistic techniques, however, the documentary theater proceeds in undermining its own presentation of fact.

The artistic composition and production, that is, the elements that make *Catonsville* a theater piece, encourage the audience to question the very notion that records can provide substantiation of events and their significance.

And indeed, assumptions about the contemporary theater or other contemporary art is that it likely begins from a position of subjectivity and relativity; furthermore, that it may very well call attention to this starting point, as subjectivity becomes central to both the formal and the thematic elements of the performance text and reflects such skepticism back on the systems represented. In documentary trial plays, that system is the justice system, one of the most pervasive and persuasive sources of the value and power of rationality.

Paget's discussion of distinct structures interlinked proves to be a common critical theme in the assessment of documentary theater. In her argument of the 1960s German version of the fact-based tribunal play and its stereopsis, Laureen Nussbaum explains that the "stereoscopic vision occurs when two two-dimensional vantage points are superimposed to create a three-dimensional, i.e., an in-depth image of reality." Applying this theory to the tribunal play, she explains: "The cases heard or tried are of a public, political nature. Within the play, first-hand evidence concerning an important occurrence of the recent past is reviewed. This factual material constitutes a history lesson for the young or uninitiated. It provides the first two-dimensional image. Superimposed is the second one derived from the tribunal's dealing with the case: the audience is encouraged to evaluate the pronouncements of the witnesses, attorneys, and judges along with those of the accused."[44] With *Catonsville*, yet another system of belief and law, a religious one, comes under scrutiny: Christianity, which in this case, is specifically and passionately Catholicism.

The Berrigan brothers and their colleagues in reality and in this script present a united front when expressing their beliefs and a direct connection between their religious principles and their actions; their rationalist grounding emerges from the "facts" of their faith, particularly as that faith echoes centuries of intellectual and philosophical thought about goodness. On the other hand, by breaking the law and by openly criticizing the policies and actions of the government and even, at times, of the church they represent, the defendants convey the kind of "profound political skepticism" in rationalism that Paget proposes is a necessary piece of "documentariness" and its tensions. In her study of the courtroom in popular film, Suffolk University law professor Jessica Silbey reminds us that "the trial is a ritualistic aspect of the law that is often overlooked (and, in fact, a *stage* in the litigation process that is rarely reached) but that is crucial to the law's binding of its practice with its ideals in culture" (emphasis mine). The trial, therefore, "for many people, is the *symbol* of law in action" (emphasis mine). [45] Law's structures, she implies, are representative as well as real.

The stage set in the documentary theater is often the sparest arrangement of tables and chairs, *Catonsville* and most of the trial plays that follow in this discussion using that sparseness to suggest, if not to fully reconstruct, a courtroom. The legal proceeding adapts easily to the theater space, and we find ourselves occupying a site common to ritualistic practices: a gathering place, with a structured seating arrangement and assigned places for the principals. The religious features of *Catonsville*, and the Phoenix Theater Company's Off-Broadway venue for the show, which was the Good Shepherd–Faith Church in New York City, further mark the play as a blend of different ritualistic experiences.[46] In a review of that production, David C. Gild describes the set and its intersection of church, theater and courtroom: "The raked stage is placed in the altar area and it contains a skeletal setting of a courtroom. . . . The jurors' box is placed at stage left, where members of the audience with stern, set faces take their seats in defiance of stage illusion."[47] This theatrical event about religious activists who challenge the secular power of the law combines the physical markers from three distinct institutional gathering places; this intersection of the three serves as a reminder that all these gathering places normally exist in separate spheres but that all function as sites for acting out ritualistic cultural practices. Simon argues for the effectiveness of the Off-Broadway production's ecclesiastical setting, claiming there to be "something particularly poignant about a pulpit's becoming the judge's chair, a pew's turning into the jury bench." He continues: "We are reminded that official religion (in this case Catholicism, but it could be any other) is on the side of the Law against its own saints (for that is what these nine are) as it always was."[48] But the making of *Catonsville* indicates that the law and the theater and the church, for that matter, might combine to convey a measure of cultural power in excess of what each institution can achieve when acting alone, not to mention the conveyance of the tensions and contradictions that exist within and across such institutions.

The conflation takes place at the textual level as well: the legal text becomes a dramatic text, and the legal text contains elements of a religious text. In his study of language, liturgies, and the law, Richard K. Fenn proposes that religion is "traditionally the court of last resort for the problems of authority poised by the ambiguities of human speech," and in its "prophetic language, then, religion places the world on trial, but in the course of secularization the trial is institutionalized in all areas of social life until even religion itself is tried and, on occasion, found wanting before secular tribunals."[49] The church is put on trial in *Catonsville* and found wanting, insofar as the Berrigan brothers and their colleagues represent religious doctrine, but Philip Berrigan also explains to the judge that the crisis of conscience being acted out in the courtroom is one that indicts both law and religion: "we have lost confidence in the institutions of the country, including the courts and our own churches. . . . We have lost confidence, because we do not believe any longer that these institutions are reformable. They are unable to provide the type of change that justice calls for."[50] Such words as spoken in another cultural context, the theater, words that Philip Berrigan used in court and that Daniel Berrigan included in his performance script, imply the possibility that if the church and the courtroom cannot "provide the type of change that justice calls for," perhaps the theater, which reflects important elements of the other two while also pursuing its own unique cultural project, can be the site for the reform that the Berrigans insist is needed.

That reform cannot come too soon, for the question that remains is "how much time is left for this country, this magnificent, frantic, insane, nation-empire to which God has entrusted so much of the future of mankind?" Codefendant George Mische follows this question with a possible answer: "Change could come if one judge would rule on the war. If one judge would act, the war could not continue as it does."[51] The judge responds that Mische misunderstands "the organization of the United States. One judge ruling on it would not end the war. Each judge must do his best with what comes before him."[52] The heart of the matter in this play and in this case is that decisions of national policy may be indirectly tied to the law courts and may ultimately be submitted to the courts for resolution, but the expectations of the defendants in this case are that individual actions can lead directly to judicial decisions that favor what they consider to be righteous rebellion against policy. What also becomes clear in the play is the challenge each side faces in a debate, even a theatrical debate, about human life.

The defendants argue that they burned the files because they believed that the crimes of the US government called for civil protest: as the character of Thomas Lewis protests, "I wasn't even thinking about the law. . . . The young men whose files we destroyed have not yet been drafted, may not be drafted, may not be sent to Vietnam for cannon fodder. My interest in going in there was to save lives. A person may break the law to save lives."[53] The conflict is not over actions; what happened is not in dispute, and in that respect this legal conflict is quite different from many that we see, not only in the courtroom but on the stage or in the cinema. The conflict is one between law and morality, and as Lewis suggests, the morality of saving lives overrules principles of national defense. The emotional reaction to death that prompts us to protect life, according to the defendants, is more compelling and persuasive than the rational directive of either war or the court that punishes illegal protest against it.

As Daniel Berrigan tells the Judge, "we are having great difficulty in trying to adjust to the atmosphere of a court from which the world is excluded, and the events that brought us here are excluded deliberately by the charge to the jury." He combines spirituality and morality by protesting that "our soul got us in trouble" and "our moral passion is banished from this court," to which the Judge responds with admiration for the defendant's skills as a poet while pointing out that such skills have not adequately prepared Berrigan for this experience: "Well, I cannot match your poetic language. You made your points on the stand very persuasively, Father Berrigan. I admire you as a poet. . . . I think you simply do not understand the function of a court."[54] This exchange seems to once again point to the gulf between the defendants and the judiciary, and as originally spoken in an actual courtroom, it would surely lend credence to the judge's authority as fitting and rightly expressed in the legal setting. With Berrigan's creation of *Catonsville*, however, this exchange has been moved from the courtroom to the theater, the Judge's dialogue, as well as Berrigan's, altered. That is, the two now speak, through actors, with words that have become part of an artistic performance, the words delivered and received differently as a result.

This exchange raises the question of whether the ideas presented in the play, wrapped in yet another layer of poetic speech, will strike the audience as believable or merely beautiful, as legally relevant as they are artistically relevant. However, as James Boyd White argues, these two things need not be distinguished from one another but may be one and the same, for "we can hope to find a point at which rhetoric and poetry are themselves seen to fuse, or at least be comprehended in a single field of vision"; where such fusion occurs, "the concerns of law and art, and of justice and beauty . . . can be seen not as competing or divergent but as one," creating an activity "that can serve as the center of life."[55] Although the differences revealed in this exchange continue to indicate a conflict of perspective, they are now a conflict between two characters, both of which are no longer real, but representative. When the jury in the actual case heard these words, it was required by law to consider them as a part of the legal interpretation of the case. Removed from an actual legal framework, the words have more free expression, and those who hear them have increased freedom of interpretation. The possibility White suggests, for the concerns of justice and beauty to act in concert, "not as competing or divergent but as one," locates the potential for this fusion in the documentary theater.

Thus does law's transformation into theater through the documentary trial play allow for multiple perspectives on legal decisions by placing a rational approach in conflict and in concert with a more emotional perception of and reaction to the legal narrative. Fenn suggests that a trial itself "consists of fragmented narratives and narrative multiplicity. To be sure, the skilled lawyer is always shaping the fragments and at least implicitly pointing to the whole." However, as he goes on to explain: "one side's narrative is constantly being met by the other side's counternarrative (or sidestepping narrative), so that 'reality' is always disassembled into multiple, conflicting, and partly overlapping versions, each version presented as true, each fighting to be declared 'what really happened'—with very high stakes riding on that ultimate declaration."[56] The documentary trial play provides further complications to such fragmentation by enhancing and calling attention to the "narrative multiplicity" and adding the uncertainty we have come to expect as convention in artistic versions of history. Here we have a script rather than a scripture, but they are similarly conventional, representing a vision of humanity tied to ritual and principle rather than merely to documented facts. In its work as theater, the documentary trial play also becomes an avenue for the promotion of social justice. As Fenn claims: "The trial, long before it became a model for the justification of God's words and for judgment on human language, was and is a social arrangement for closing the gap between language and reality."[57] So it is that the documentary performance text demonstrates the contradictions and the void between what we say and what circumstances exist in the world, and, more specifically, in our cultural and political institutions.

The longer Fordham script reminds us that Daniel Berrigan's primary craft is poetry, as portions of the text are displayed and read as verse, the speeches serving as stanzas. Texts by Pablo Neruda and Brecht, a quotation from *Antigone*, and a passage from Peter Weiss's *The Investigation* interrupt the flow of the action while contextualizing the Catonsville crime of resistance with artistic language from other revolts and other trials; the proximity in time of the latter quotation from Weiss's Holocaust documentary play to defendant George Mische's assertion that all Christians bear "the responsibility for having put those Jews in the ovens" ensures that we recall the literary and dramatic traditions of resistance literature to which *Catonsville* would now belong. [58] To further convey both the poetic and the dramatic forms in his play, author Berrigan structures the defendants' narratives as soliloquies, rhythmic and poetic. As he arranged them, they do not readily suggest a performance style, but Saul Levitt's production revision tightens the original script, blending various single testimonies together in order that they better stand in counterpoint to each other and demonstrate the contrast of the two sides, each one claiming to act on a moral imperative.

Neither version, particularly in the closing scene from which the sections quoted above are taken, remains strictly faithful to courtroom procedures, for in both of them the defendants, with only the occasional verbal rebuke, talk on without interruption. But it should be noted that this section of the trial is jury deliberation and therefore has no effect on the verdicts that follow. The exchange has come about because of the Defense's request to the Judge that the defendants "be permitted to speak frankly and openly with the court," a request met by the Judge with a respectful assent: "I want to hear the defendants. I do not want to cut them off from anything they may want to say." The trial testimony was unusual from start to finish in that it relied on and needed only two witnesses other than the defendants; the latter's testimony took up almost the whole of the courtroom time. The nine defendants were allowed to speak on their own behalf throughout, using their testimony to summarize their experiences and beliefs, and to explain as well as defend their actions at Catonsville.

The stage version takes liberties with the witness testimony by rearranging it and tightening it; as a result, the play becomes a terse and powerful script about civil disobedience and morality. The theatrical arrangement connects and highlights the similarities among the defendants' histories, how each of them came to recognize the corruption and injustice that the American government regularly perpetrated throughout the world as they served the church and its laity either in developing nations or in domestic urban centers such as Baltimore and New Orleans. How each of them came to perform acts of resistance in order to counter what they saw as the inequality and barbarism of the Selective Service System, indicative of the Pentagon's policies in Vietnam and throughout the world. How each of them "defends" a not-guilty plea by charging the government with crimes and raising a protest to them: as David Darst proclaims, "to stop the machine I saw moving and killing, to hinder the war effort in an actual, physical, literal way. To raise a cry, an outcry over what I saw as a very, very clear crime." What follows suggests that they do not consider themselves criminals, for Philip Berrigan explains that while they have violated the law, "the law is not absolute to us. . . . The point at issue for us personally when we went to Catonsville was not leniency or punishment, not being a danger to the community or a benefit to it, but what it means to be a democratic man and a Christian man."[59] Their personal narratives contribute to the emotional quotient of the play and to the emotional experience of this legal representation, the audience exposed to an unusual kind of logic and argument, a redefinition of what it means to be a man (or woman) seeking to enact justice in a community that has been traumatized by government-sanctioned violence.

In one final and powerful assertion of what the defendants see as the system's inequity and their determination not to capitulate to it in order to spare themselves punishment, Daniel Berrigan says to the Judge: "We want to thank you, Your Honor; I speak for the others. But we do not want the edge taken off what we have tried to say by any implication that we are seeking mercy in this court. . . . We do not agree with you, and we thank you."[60] He then acknowledges that the people involved, all of them, have goodness in their hearts, and he asks to finish with a prayer, the Lord's Prayer. The Judge and Prosecution, the latter who "rather welcomes the idea," readily agree and participate, and then a taped reading of the sentences concludes the play. The final words in both versions of the script are Daniel Berrigan's: "We would simply like to thank the Court and the prosecution. We agree that this is the greatest day of our lives."[61] The dramatic version of this trial proves to be quite civil and rather sedate, the documents in this case recreating a narrative in which the opposing sides honor each other even as they disagree. The most contested element of the conflict took place in the Selective Service parking lot, where the only casualties are documents and the symbolic significance of using napalm to destroy draft files is the closest these pacifists come to engaging in violence.

The emphasis on community and on the cohesiveness of vision are reflected in Daniel Berrigan's words: as he says, "I speak for the others." As both a leader of this group and as the writer responsible for this stage play, his choice of words in both cases exert dominance over the event and control over the performance text that recaptures the debates from the trial and reconfigures them as theatrical dialogue. As he emphasizes with his repetition of the word "we," he speaks in both cases of the group/for the group, reminding the audience of the values shared and the extent to which he has exerted power over the narrative by reproducing and editing it for performance. His statement is then extended by the verdicts, for all defendants are found guilty by the jury as those who have joined together in protest are united in punishment. The quality of mercy has not prevailed. Just prior to the return of the jury and the reading of the verdicts, however, when Berrigan asks if the court would agree to a group prayer, the Prosecution and the Judge both welcome this moment of communal reflection as the defendants form a semicircle and recite the Our Father, joined by others in court.

The trial, as we see through the performance, did not bring participants on either side, defense or prosecution, to a shared understanding about the legal system's role in mediating the conditions of social dissent when the dissenters overstep the boundaries of law. The defendants, for their part, sought arrest with the express purpose of bringing such a debate into the courts, and although they had their day there, they did not succeed in convincing judge or jury to set the law aside and find them not guilty. Although the Judge attempts to downplay the conflict that the trial brings to light, claiming that the "only difference between us is that I believe the institutions can do what you believe they cannot do," that difference is both ideologically and practically significant.[62]

For a belief in the power and success of institutional systems versus a belief in the failure of institutions can lead, as it does in *Catonsville*, to very different actions, and it can lead to a tacit support of war versus a criminal act of protest with its attendant punishment. The two sides also differ on whether or not the institution of law can change national policy, for as we have seen, defendant George Mische believes that "if one judge would act, the war could not continue as it does," a statement the Judge counters.[63] The Judge does concede that as a man, he himself would be "a very funny sort" if not moved by Mische's "sincerity on the stand . . . and [his] views." He goes on: "I agree with you completely, as a person. We can never accomplish what we would like to accomplish, or give a better life to people, if we are going to keep on spending so much money for war." But ultimately his personal agreement and his emotional reaction to the defendants and their argument (he is "moved" by both) are overruled by his belief in the law, whose basic principle, he argues, stipulates that we "do things in an orderly fashion. People cannot take the law into their own hands."[64] *Catonsville* puts forward two strikingly different views of law: that it is and that it relies on a structure solid and unmovable that nonetheless allows for the expression of alternate views through the trial format; that it is, respectfully, a fluid mechanism for (radical) change by ordinary citizens, be they defendants, jury members, or judges acting as men rather than as authority figures. In the end, this Judge justifies the guilty verdicts with a maxim that subtly underscores the difference between individual good and institutional strength: "Good character is not a defense for breaking the law."[65]

Bela Kiralyfalvi makes the argument that the Catonsville saga formed a trilogy of street, courtroom, and theater actions, thus joining the three most important venues of resistance during the era.[66] But the *Catonsville* stage play in production embraces yet a fourth arena of ritualized activity: the church. The centrality of the trial and the law in every arena of life, even religious life, Fenn reminds us, signifies that the "theme of the trial is coded in terms of a Last Judgment that lends significance to earthly trials in everyday life or in courts of law."[67] And in ritualizing the experiences of modern life through carefully scripted and rhetorically powerful arguments, the law provides the documentary theater with the raw material that can be transformed into the artistic expression of socialistic, political, and humanistic issues and concerns.

In staging religion and law, the documentary trial play highlights key thematic elements of the performance text and reminds us of the secular yet nonetheless sacred duties of judges, attorneys, and juries. The audience members, at once court spectators, theater patrons, and congregation, are asked to employ critical thinking skills to analyze the legal proceedings; aesthetic judgment to rule on the drama's artistic merits; and familial or cultural belief systems to decide the religious issues. All these perspectives weigh in on morality in one way or another. Pressed into service as American citizens, asked at least implicitly to reach a verdict about the legal outcome of the case, audiences are urged by the play to render a moral judgment on either the defendants or the state, while also being encouraged to look inward and evaluate their own moral stance on the war and on acts of individual and state-condoned violence.

Another documentary trial play that reenacts a clash between antiwar protestors and the legal system during the late 1960s and early 1970s, *The Chicago Conspiracy Trial*, was not staged until the latter decade's end, and its representations of the law, its depictions of proper courtroom behavior, and its commentary on civility or its lack in the high-profile criminal trial contrast sharply with what we have heard from the participants of *Catonsville*. The judicial conflict in *Chicago Conspiracy* is quite similar to *Catonsville* in its ideological components, as both plays stage cases that reflect polarized opinions about the Vietnam War and the civilian opposition it stirred.

The events that led to the March 1969 federal grand jury indictment of the defendants first known as the Chicago Eight, whose number shrunk by one after defendant Bobby Seale's case was severed from the group, had occurred one year earlier, at the National Democratic Convention in Chicago in August, 1968. Just months before the convention, Americans had been traumatized by the loss of two leaders brought down in violent assassinations, the Reverend Dr. Martin Luther King Jr. in April and presidential candidate Robert Kennedy in June. With Kennedy's sudden death, the Democratic presidential candidacy became an important focus of attention for various groups who were anxious to spur change and influence the political establishment, and several of these groups turned their attention and energy to the upcoming convention in Chicago. Two of these groups, the

National Mobilization to End the War in Vietnam (MOBE) and the Youth International Party (Yippies), as well as organizations such as the Black Panther Party, made plans to send representatives to Chicago to have their voices heard. Although these groups had different goals and agendas and did not usually work together on strategy and event planning, in the polarized atmosphere of the time they were viewed by many as a collective counter-cultural force that represented the counterculture's values. Indeed, several meetings organized by MOBE were attended by Abbie Hoffman and Jerry Rubin, two of the Chicago Eight and the primary organizers of the Yippies' "Festival of Life," planned for Chicago during the week of the convention.

The clash between some members of these groups and Chicago author-ities began when the Yippies requested that demonstrators attending the convention be allowed to sleep in public parks, but city officials refused the request and ordered police to post signs warning of 11 P.M. curfews for park use. As students and other activists began to arrive, the protest groups' radical leaders learned that a federal judge had denied the request for an injunction against the city's curfew. Conflicts between protestors and police escalated over the next few days, with the police releasing tear-gas grenades into groups who refused to exit the parks at curfew time and with activist leaders, including defendants Bobby Seale and Rennie Davis, publicly advocating for violent response to police attempts to interfere with their activities.

The federal grand jury indictment for conspiracy on March 20, 1969, and the trial that followed in the autumn of the same year were facilitated, ironically, by passage of the 1968 Civil Rights Act several months prior to the convention in Chicago. This legislation, which expanded the protective policies of the 1964 bill of the same name, was primarily concerned with in-suring equal housing opportunities to members of minority groups. But in the wake of the April 1968 urban riots that followed Dr. King's assassination, a rider was attached to the act; that rider, Title 18, made it a felony to cross state lines with the intent of inciting, promoting, or participating in a riot. The new statute allowed the federal government to become involved in the prosecution of the eight defendants and to charge them with conspiracy, which meant that the legal epilogue to the violence during the convention played out in federal court rather than in a local or state legal venue. This change in venue, combined with the challenge that the charges posed to civil liberties and specifically the right of assembly, contributed to the high profile of the case, and it would very quickly come to national attention as a legal proceeding that epitomized the generational and ideological divide that marked the close of the 1960s.

A letter to the editors of the *New York Review of Books*, published on June 19, 1969, provides evidence of the public reaction to the conspiracy charge. Signed by a group that called itself the Committee to Defend the Conspiracy and that included Norman Mailer, Susan Sontag, and Noam Chomsky, the letter declared that the federal indictment of the eight political dissenters was "one of the most ominous challenges to political liberty since the passing of Senator Joseph R. McCarthy"; the letter called, its writers continued, for a "clear and considered response from all who believed that the preservation of political dissent" is "crucial to the survival of democratic process in America." The letter went on to argue that the antiriot clause and the indictment in the Chicago Conspiracy case were legally and constitutionally dubious: "conspiracy—which deals not with act but with intent—is a vague concept at best." Since the prosecution for conspiracy requires no proof of the commission of a crime, nor even of an attempt, it "all too easily becomes political harassment of persons who hold dissenting ideas."[68]

This delineation of the nature of the conflict that we see dramatized in *Chicago Conspiracy* suggests the cultural importance of this case and helps to explain the impulse that led to the creation of a documentary theater text that recreates the trial. While the letter writers may or may not have sought legal advice to support their assertion that the antiriot law is constitutionally dubious, their position makes a claim for the significance of the case by the very existence of the letter. The indictment of the Eight propelled a group of public intellectuals to take a stand against the law and to do so by challenging its constitutionality. Significantly however, the challenge appears not in a courtroom setting but in a literary setting, so that even prior to the trial, the case was identified not only as a legal matter but as a cultural matter. By arguing for the vagueness of the "intent" component of a conspiracy charge and its misuse in this instance, the committee members claim that the law is being used to harass political dissenters, thus suggesting not only that the individual legal statute is a challenge to freedom of expression, but that the system itself may be using the law to silence difference.

The letter goes on to state in some detail the approach that the defendants plan to take in their defense, thereby nicely contextualizing the case in its historical moment. The defendants, the letter claimed, had set their path on challenging the charges not just legally, but politically as well, and were committed to focusing attention on the unconstitutionality of the antiriot act. Moreover, they intended to direct public attention to the "root issues that brought them and thousands of others to Chicago and the Democratic National Convention—the war, racism, the widening power of the military-academic-industrial complex, the enfeeblement of the nation's political process." The letter ended by inviting other Americans who are similarly committed to radical change in this nation to join *The Conspiracy*, by requesting "financial and moral support from other Americans invested in protecting constitutional liberty."[69]

What we can expect to find in the play, as suggested by the ideology of the defense here, then, are considerable parallels to *Catonsville*. We can expect that its speeches will not be confined to points of law, but will require audiences to grapple with constitutional issues of freedom and evaluate a proposal for radical social and political revision. We can expect that the morality of war will be debated, and that the right to protest against the immoral acts of a government will be upheld as not only good but necessary. We can expect that the defense will attempt to justify selected acts of destruction or violence as inevitable when countering an institutional system that fails to protect its own citizens. We can expect that the defendants will use their courtroom appearances to make the plea that all Americans ought to join in the fight against injustice. We do in fact find these elements, as forecast in the letter quoted above, in the case dramatized by *Chicago Conspiracy*.

What we also find, however, is a radically different presentation of a very similar ideological conflict to the one enacted in *Catonsville*. The prosecutorial and judicial stance of the latter, reflective of the perceived link between reason and law, maintained its stark opposition to the emotion-driven morality asserted unapologetically and in "poetic language" by the defense. That stance, one that held up law as the ultimate authority when a crime has been committed, remained strong even in the face of the judge's revelation that he experienced a sympathetic personal alignment with the position held by Daniel Berrigan and codefendants. In *Chicago Conspiracy*, and in the actual case out of which the performance text emerged, the courtroom proceeding features a colorful and chaotic collection of defendants and an outrageously idiosyncratic judge, thereby dramatizing a legal face-off that could not be more different in tone than the staid and respectful arguments of *Catonsville*. *Chicago Conspiracy* draws solely and directly from the transcript of the infamous trial, and so it is that in this version of the documentary trial play we are confronted with an actual legal proceeding that bore little resemblance to the orderly process we expect to find when we witness a courtroom event of any kind. That this play is taken from the transcripts as it happened and reproduced as a performance is emphasized in the way that its authorship is recorded: the cover of the published edition of the play does not list authors but rather claims to have been "adapted by

Ron Sossi and Frank Condon." The title page furthers this impression of an adaptation by calling the work "A Theatrical Arrangement of the Original Trial Transcripts."[70]

Although there are other verbatim dramatic or film versions of the trial that precede this adaptation by Sossi and Condon, the play is the first American version of this trial that stages this unusual and notorious judicial case.[71] The pair created and presented it as members of the Odyssey Theater Ensemble in Los Angeles, which Sossi founded in 1969; he has served as artistic director from its inception. *Chicago Conspiracy*'s original run, extended multiple times, was a record-breaking fifteen months, from March 1979 through May 1980, and it was adapted for the screen as an HBO Special Presentation in May 1987. It has since had numerous revivals at the Odyssey, and for the most recent revival in October 2007 at the company's current home on Sepulveda Boulevard in Los Angeles, which I attended, the audience was required to wait in a dimly lit parking lot adjacent to the stage door in order to witness and participate in a preshow performance. A group of long-haired, jean-clad youth waved signs that proclaimed "End the War," while a guitarist led them in a round of protest songs. Spectators heard a speech by an actor portraying a member of the Black Panther Party and were invited to sign a petition protesting the trial of the eight men on conspiracy charges for inciting violence at the Democratic National Convention. If the response to the singers and speakers was not as fervent as one might expect at such a rally, it may have had something to do with the fact that almost forty years had passed since the trial and the conflict that had led to it had taken place.

As theater patrons were ushered into the Odyssey Theater Ensemble Playhouse, the emotion and spontaneity of the preshow shifted, at least temporarily, to a subdued atmosphere reflective of a courtroom. Indeed, members of the theater audience spoke to each other with trepidation as glaring "bailiffs" patrolled the theater and appeared ready to enforce order if necessary. The bailiffs' suspiciousness was particularly directed at the actor-protestors from the parking lot; after the audience was seated, the actor-protestors planted themselves in the aisles in visible resistance against the structure of the space. Archival video footage from the time of the events, including some scenes of violent confrontation during the Chicago convention, began the show, recalling the past while connecting the impending representation of the legal proceeding to both the live demonstration enacted outside and to the scenes of conflict that resulted in the government's decision to prosecute the alleged conspirators. The bailiffs had no trouble inducing the audience to rise as actor George Murdock, reviving the role of Judge Julius Hoffman that he originated in 1979, entered and took his seat on the judicial bench. What became the focal point of his authority, however, was not the massive set piece he settled into but what he wielded, a gavel that he banged loudly at every opportunity in deafening accompaniment to his verbal proclamations.

Two tables flanked the bench, and at them prosecutors and defendants gathered: the former, in gray suits, on the right; the latter on the left, enlivening their side with colorful clothing and hair in excess. The lawyers for the defense were costumed in rumpled corduroy jackets and pants, attire more commonly associated with liberal academics than with officers of the court. The stage was full to overflowing with actors, all men, and as reviewer Julio Martinez noted about director Condon and his work on the 2007 production, he "impressively choreographs an impassioned 36-member ensemble."[72] In the persons of the actor-defendants were represented some of the most notorious and outspoken radicals of the period: Abbie Hoffman, Tom Hayden, Jerry Rubin, Bobby Seale. An actor playing Allen Ginsberg appeared as a witness for the defense. And while characters from both tables and the judge himself displayed emotional behavior during the play, the costumes and gestures as well as the action established a consistent contrast that differentiated the presentational, not to mention the representational differences between the prosecution and the defense. Procedural adherence served to limit the prosecution attorneys and other government employees present, while excess and emotion visibly drove the defense and resulted in a higher decibel range and much chaotic movement from that side of the courtroom.

No event of the era, legal or otherwise, so represented and recalled the political divide that marks the period. With this performance text we have a narrative that signifies the age in its struggle for freedom and equality for so many in the midst of an increasingly corrupt and conforming system. Although the disillusionment with government brought about by Watergate was still several years away, the establishment and the radicals had already become entrenched in distrust on both sides of the cultural divide. In the director's notes, published with the script of *Chicago Conspiracy* in 1979, Frank Condon calls the actual trial a "courtroom battleground for the two opposing forces representing individual conscience vs. government policy," a cultural seismic shift that emerged when "a climate of fear apparent throughout the nation" met a "heady atmosphere of a renaissance" expressed in language of change and revolution. One other detail of the historical case that Condon notes is the defendants' prosecution under the "'conspiracy' provisions of the newly instituted Civil Rights Act."[73]

Although the clothing, hair, and hippie lingo of the defendants set this work squarely in a historical moment that would have been a familiar but distant memory for some audience members and the recreation of their parents' era for others, a standoff between citizens calling for peace and officials spouting government doublespeak seemed to be all too familiar to the 2007 audience of *Chicago Conspiracy*. As reviewer Steven Leigh Morris argued in his review, the production caused a "queasy sensation of how the world has changed in 40 years, and of how little it's changed." Morris continues: "*The Chicago Conspiracy Trial* offers a discomfiting if not painful reminder that the toxic brew of paranoia and aggression has a far more constant and forceful place in American history than democracy or anybody's constitutional rights."[74] As this comparison indicates, the revival of a documentary trial play can serve at once to recall for the older theatergoers an incendiary event from their youth, to inform a new generation about such a time, and to lead members of both groups to reflect on the connections and similarities between the past and the present.

Also forging this link is the description of the Odyssey's 2007 production included on the theater company's website at the time of the production: "Now, in a new century, is passionate political debate and dissent still part of our national fabric, . . . or is it 'unpatriotic,' 'anti-American?'" That probing question is followed by an invitation to join "Abbie Hoffman, Jerry Rubin, Bobby Seale, Tom Hayden and the rest of their band of clown activists in this amazingly timely revival."[75] Almost thirty years since its premiere, which occurred almost ten years after the genre of documentary trial play had emerged as a compelling way to revive and revise contemporary history, *Chicago Conspiracy* recalls a period of contemporary American history that was contested in its moment and is contested in its memory. It serves also as a jolting reminder that law and justice do not always coincide, and that legal decisions do not always follow from judicial examination of facts and events. Finally, as the letter to the editors of the *New York Review of Books* suggests, the legal conflict over conspiracy is complicated by the "root issues" that had convinced the defendants and scores of other protestors to go to Chicago that summer: to publicize and theatricalize their dissatisfactions with "the war, racism, the widening power of the military-academic-industrial complex, the enfeeblement of the nation's political process." In other words, it was not only crimes but values that separated the defense from the prosecution, as well as a chasm of difference in the amount of faith in the system and its processes that each side brought into court.

The examination of such fundamental differences proved relevant to 2007 audiences, for the Odyssey Theater chose to revive the play during another era of cynicism and ideological division among Americans that raised challenges to the institutional integrity of the government in all areas: executive, legislative, and judicial. Unpopular wars and their price tags, bureaucratic limitations on freedom, an embattled political process, and the rise of new strains of racism were issues of concern all too familiar to post-9/11 Americans. The continued relevance of topics raised in this documentary trial play, a play first staged a generation ago, demonstrates that the critique of systems, even systems that are nonetheless considered crucial to stability and order, make for recurring conflicts that can be as dynamic in the theater as they are in the courtroom, and that the artistic renderings of such conflict can hold history and current events in a single hand. *Chicago Conspiracy* also serves as a reminder that while criminal indictment might bring a single defendant or a group of defendants to court to answer the charge, some such proceedings (both the real and its dramatized version) may result in the system being put on trial in conjunction with and in counterpoint to the individual defenses. For example, some testimony selected for inclusion suggests that the lack of cooperation from Chicago mayor Richard J. Daley and his city officials, which may have bordered on suppression of free expression, was as much to blame for the outbreaks of violence as alleged riot plots may have been. Such was also the case in *Catonsville*, and such is the case in many documentary trial plays.

The Chicago Conspiracy trial was, in every way, a public spectacle, a media event, a theatrical moment, readily adapting itself to the stage with little need for intensification of the drama. As Lahav suggests of the actual trial, putting it in representational terms: "the mise-en-scène is itself a Rorschach test of America in the later 1960s. Culture and counterculture collide. The government and judge stand for order, convention, and self-control; the defense for a mix of individualist philosophy and communitarianism, reflected by their overt camaraderie and solidarity. Race, gender, and class are present."[76] The trial and its participants symbolized the gaping generational divide, and in choosing to "adapt" this particular court transcript for the stage, Sossi and Condon drew on a courtroom drama with high-powered, built-in theatrics.[77] As fitting for what the two call an adaptation, the director's note explains that the performance text is a condensation of the five-month trial and its transcripts, and the result a "docu-drama representation of the event." Although "every word is taken directly from the transcripts of the trial," there are some exceptions to the verbatim nature of the piece: "some of the Government's witnesses' names have been combined for structural unity," and "purely for structural reasons the chronology of some events has been rearranged."[78]

While the intentions of such alterations may have been structural, the playwrights' attempts to tighten and heighten the drama do make for a performance piece staccato and confrontational in nature, composed as it is of many short scenes that often end at the moment of the sharpest counterpoint or agitation. Such a structure calls attention to the moments when the Yippies and the government representatives are serving up their most pointed attacks in value-laden observations and retorts. What occasionally comes across as thoughtless and obstinate behavior from both sides has defendants and prosecutors engaged in an ideological battle that has, to some extent, been transformed into broad-stroke comedy. On the other hand, the extremity of the theatrics that occurred during the actual trial proceeding, echoing the street theater and other forms of dramatic protest that defined the antiwar movement, has insured that the trial has continued to attract commentary from scholars of various disciplines: law, media studies, and political science. The times, they were outrageous, and the Chicago Conspiracy Trial has proven to be of significant interest to historians and theorists who focus on this period in their work.

Like *Catonsville*, *Chicago Conspiracy* lays plain the defense's attempt to indict the government: as Kunstler notes in his opening remarks in act I, scene 2, "this prosecution which you are hearing is the result of two motives on the part of the Government" and the "real conspiracy in this case is the conspiracy to curtail and prevent the demonstrations against the war in Vietnam and related issues." As he continues: the "real conspiracy is not against these defendants as individuals," for the "real attack was on the rights of everybody, all of us American citizens," to protest "in a meaningful fashion." The justification for the attack, in his estimation, was "protecting property, or protecting law and order, or protecting other people." He finishes the speech by noting the possibility that this justification led to the temporary demise of a crucial right of the people that is also supposed to be protected but that he suggests has not been, and that may not be revived: "Dissent died here for a moment during that Democratic National Convention. What will happen in this case will decide whether it is dead."[79] The inclusion of this speech asks theatergoers to consider the delicate balance between freedom and law; that while the two often depend on one another, they can also be in contest. This speech demonstrates a repetitive pattern of conflict in the performance text, with prosecuting attorney Schultz objecting to Kunstler's statement of counsel for the defense, the third such objection in less than two pages of dialogue, followed by the judge's third decision to sustain the objection. As this pattern continues throughout the play, it makes for increased frustration, outrage, and disbelief from the defense and fuels the heightening of emotion that quickly takes this theater piece to a dramatic fever pitch.

Another pattern determined early on is the punctuation of the action by frequent scene breaks. The text is divided into two acts, the first act with twelve scenes and the second act with eight. Not all scenes end with a blackout; several of them do, and beyond that there is a pattern of scene conclusion that is relatively consistent. The most common scene endings feature judicial rulings or proclamations: fifteen of the twenty scenes end with a statement from the judge, two scenes end with dialogue from the prosecution or a prosecution witness, and three scenes close with a comment from either a defense attorney or a defendant. The final words of the play are spoken by defense attorney Kunstler, after a brief exchange that suggests the extent to which the judge has dominated the proceedings as we see them enacted in the theater:

> KUNSTLER: Your Honor, couldn't I say my last words without you cutting me off?
> COURT: You said you had nothing to say.
> KUNSTLER: Your Honor, I said just a moment ago we had a concluding remark. Your Honor has succeeded perhaps in sullying it, and I think that maybe that is the way the case should end, as it began.[80]

As we see above, *Chicago Conspiracy* refers to the judge in this case, Julius J. Hoffman, as "Court" in the script. That designation distinguishes him from all the other speaking characters, who are referred to by name, and connects the judge with the law, or at least with the power of the court, while seeming to disconnect him from his subjectivity, a separation that is considered an important and necessary component of judicial impartiality. Paul Kahn notes that the kind of disconnection that is implied when the judge dons a robe, ascends the bench, and is then referred to as Your Honor serves to bring attention to the "distance . . . between what the judge knows as individual subject and what he or she knows as a judge." The character of Judge Hoffman as portrayed in the performance text, referenced in the script as "Court" and therefore as the location of the trial rather than as a member of the proceedings, may have been intended to highlight "the division the rule of law strives to maintain between the person of the judge and the judicial function," but in this case the behavior of the judge counters this attempt, his actions only accentuating the "Court's" departure from impartiality.[81]

The face-off between the black-robed symbol of authority and the shaggy protestors is an apt contest from the era it recalls, and it has a recognizable set of clear oppositions, but as the matter is dramatized by Sossi and Condon, both sides emerge as irrational. The personality of this judge is not suppressed when he dons the judicial cloth and raises himself above everyone else in the courtroom; if anything, he takes this opportunity of authority to exert his individual viewpoints in all their emotional tenor. There is a stark contrast between Hoffman as represented here and Kahn's insistence that the "judge is responsible for maintaining and articulating the rule of law."[82] Actor George Murdock's revival of the role he had originated included a most striking audiovisual choice: he banged the gavel excessively throughout the action, subverting its function as a tool of order and transforming it into the most disruptive element of the proceeding. As demonstrated in the script, the judge in the play is also quite verbally disruptive, cutting off the defense lawyers at every turn and arguing directly with defendants. The representation of the figure who, whether in the actual courtroom or in the documentary trial play, ought best to exemplify the rationality and equality of the legal system, proves least likely to say and do what is needed to keep order and to pursue justice. He is also primarily responsible for promoting a high-pitched atmosphere in which a reasonable assessment of the events in question proves impossible for audience members.

The theatrical Hoffman also uses language sloppily, and because the play imports verbatim the language of the trial, we have reason to believe that the real judge had done as much. His linguistic slips may be, and may be interpreted as, purposeful if passive acts of control; he mispronounces or misspeaks the name of the defense attorney, Weinglass, in what appears to be an attempt to annoy or intimidate the side he treats as his opposition. Whatever the source of these slips, however, they reveal a stark contrast between *Chicago Conspiracy*'s "Court" representative and the respected and respectful judge dramatized in *Catonsville*. The striking difference between these two judicial portrayals stands in sharp relief to the similarities of crime, of motive, and of time and place.

When one of the defendants in the *Catonsville* proceeding asks to end the trial with a prayer, judge and members of the prosecution team readily agree, calling the idea a most welcome one. At the opening of act 2 of *Chicago Conspiracy*, on the other hand, when defendants ask to read the names of the Vietnam dead in order to commemorate them, and defendant David Dellinger requests that the court observe a moment of silence, the prosecution objects to the suggestion, and Hoffman replies that there is no need to object because "I forbid him to disrupt the court."[83] Prayer comes as a welcome salve to the inadequacy of the verdict in the first play, after the judge, constrained by the law, cannot do justice in a case that seems to call for an other-worldly or at least an extralegal resolution. Prayer manages to sooth hearts where justice failed to do so, bringing both sides together, albeit briefly, in an earnest embrace of a common humanity, and that connection is welcomed by all. In sharp contrast, Dellinger's request in *Chicago Conspiracy* for a moment of silence, a secular substitution for prayer with a similar goal, is rejected by Judge Hoffman and considered a "disruption," to be noted as such in the trial transcript.

The isolation of *Chicago Conspiracy* defendant Bobby Seale and his subsequent removal from this trial makes for a striking example of the play's delineation of judicial intolerance and evidence of the judge's refusal to provide a neutral day in court for the defense. The purely coincidental occurrence of the absence of Seale's attorney due to illness, just prior to the opening of the trial, places Seale in a position of legal limbo: in court as a consequence of the procedures that had indicted him, but unrepresented and unprotected by his attorney. Defense attorney Kunstler, compelled by the other attorney's absence to file an appearance for Seale, finds himself in the difficult position of being compelled by the judge to speak for Seale even though Seale wishes to defend himself. Kunstler refuses to "compromise Mr. Seale's position" and then says: "I want the record to indicate quite clearly that I do not direct Mr. Seale in any way. He is a free, independent black man who does his own direction."[84] In the next scene, Hoffman agrees to hear Seale's motion demanding to represent himself and requiring release from custody in order to interview witnesses and do research. As procedure dictates, Seale depends on the language of law to make his case: "I, Bobby Seale, demand and move the court as follows. . . . Because I am forced to be my own counsel and to defend myself, I require my release from custody. . . . I know we've gotten some attack from the Government saying that we're playing games over here, but I'm not playing no games with my life."[85] Despite the justification that Seale provides for his release, the prosecution calls the request a "simple obvious ploy" and argues that the defendants could be seeking a mistrial, for they know, prosecutor Schultz allows, that because Seale is not a lawyer "there would be reversible error and there would be nothing we could do about it."[86]

Seale's challenge to the court and the prosecution's response to that challenge dramatize the atmosphere of suspicion about conspiracy on both sides that pervades this case and that contributes to the reactive stance each side maintains throughout. In the next scene, Seale demands to cross-examine mayoral administration officer David E. Stalh, claiming the right to speak and to have his "rights recognized," following that claim with the tautological statement: "that's my constitutional right to talk in behalf of my constitutional rights." He also asserts his ability to defend himself in the face of what he believes to be the perceptions of the court: "You think black people don't have a mind. Well, we got big minds, good minds, and we know how to come forth with constitutional rights." During this exchange, he repeats "rights" or "constitutional rights" nine times, demonstrating at least a rudimentary knowledge of law and employing the force of repetition and reassertion to attempt to dominate this courtroom exchange.

But the court officials refuse to engage with him at the level of legal argument, choosing instead to use their authority to dismiss and silence his speech. The marshal says, "Mr. Seale will you sit down"; the judge: "Will you be quiet?" and "Are you going to stop, sir?"[87] The judge also asks the re- porter, "Are you getting all of this, Miss Reporter?" reminding the audience of the transcript that was composed during the trial and whose contents are being repeated here, while subtly threatening the defendant that all he says goes on the record and may be held against him. Although Seale does not cave to the intimidation, saying in response, "I hope she gets it all," he becomes increasingly frustrated and begins to speak more frankly and less formally to the court, referencing the "jive letter" he was accused of sending to a juror, which he calls "a lie," and "that jive letter you know damned well I didn't send."[88] He refuses to rise as the judge departs for the day, and his codefendants join him in this action and sit in support of Seale's rights.[89] Five scenes later Seale again demands to question witnesses and to "speak out on behalf" of his defense; at that point Judge Hoffman finally sets in motion the punishment he has threatened Seale with several times already: to be bound and gagged.

It is just prior to this order to physically restrain Seale that the defen- dant's protests shift explicitly from the treatment he is receiving as an individual man of color to accusations of institutional racism that indict the American government of the present and of the past. When the judge responds to what Seale calls his "request again—demand, to cross-examine the witness," the judge responds, "I will issue the orders around here." The charge that Seale answers with goes beyond his claim not to "take orders from racist judges" to an indictment of a system that has supported vio- lence against black men and women: "We protested our rights for 400 years and we have been shot and killed and murdered, brutalized and oppressed for 400 years."[90] At the court's threat of punishment for this outburst, Seale continues to indict the judge for representing "the corruptness of this rotten, fascist government for 400 years," dismissing the notion of judi- cial censure by asking, "What can happen to me more than what Thomas Jefferson and George Washington did to black people in slavery?"[91] On the judge's order, the bailiffs remove Seale from the courtroom and "deal with him as he should be dealt with in this circumstance."[92] In production, the physical seizure and removal of Bobby Seale, combined with the horrific image of his return, bound and gagged, calls up the very dangers that Seale has just referred to and that still threatened black men at the time of the first production: lynching and other forms of punishment and containment imposed on the black man historically, as Seale says, "for 400 years."[93] The scene thus succeeds in highlighting the trial's failure to pursue justice in an orderly fashion and to use procedure rather than violence to achieve resolution.

It also raises the specter of possibility that racism contributed to the legal decision to sever the trial of Bobby Seale from the Chicago Eight case and thereby segregate him from the fellowship and power of the group. Of the scene in the original trial, Lahav describes it as follows: "with the exception of the Eichmann Trial, where a defendant was put into a glass booth and was thus under the total control of the government, I cannot think of a more powerful scene that depicts the defendant as an 'other.'"[94] Certainly the physical restraint that Seale suffered alluded to a prison system that in the contemporary period became increasingly and disproportionately populated by African Americans, one that has strapped hundreds of black men into electric chairs or onto gurneys to die in a system that in many cases have denied their rights or interfered with their ability to defend themselves. The last speech Seale makes before being physically subdued reveals his disdain for the court and its proceedings: "You have done everything you could with those jive lying witnesses up there presented by these pig agents of the Government to lie and condone some rotten fascist, racist crap by racist cops and pigs that beat people's heads . . . and I demand my constitutional right—demand, demand, demand!"[95]

Lahav calls the image of the bound and gagged Seale "rough theater, frightening and grotesque at the same time. It is also a powerful commentary about the law. . . . I cannot think of a scene more stunning than a bound and gagged defendant, trying to communicate, through his gag, his demand to have his constitutional rights recognized, while the judge and the prosecutors pretend to continue business as usual."[96] Her purpose in examining the courtroom proceeding is to illuminate the theatrical side of the law, while mine is to consider how the impact of those historical details becomes a point of central dramatic conflict in the documentary performance, one that highlights the imperfections of the legal system and poses the question of how a theatrical reenactment might redress or at least call attention to the imbalance.

By the end of act 1, the judge has found Seale guilty of contempt and declared a mistrial in his case alone, separating it from the case of the remaining seven defendants. This occurs in the face of but despite numerous attempts from the defense and the defendants themselves to have Seale released from bondage. At one point, for example, Kunstler moves "for the removal of the irons and the gag on the ground that Mr. Seale was attempting to assert his right to self-defense under the Constitution." The judge's response is to insist that the "measures have been taken to ensure the proper conduct of this trial which I am obligated to do under the law."[97] Both sides, then, claim to inhabit the legal right and, in doing so without allowing for modification or compromise, suggest the very different visions of procedure, not to mention justice, separated by an indelible line down the middle of this stage courtroom. The impossibility of either side reaching across the divide with a view toward resolution underscores the nature of the disputes of the age, be they war or race, individual freedom or institutional governance.

In response to the judge's decision to sever his case, Seale questions him: "What kind of court is this? Is this a court? It must be some kind of fascist operation like I see in my mind, you know—I don't understand you."[98] A scuffle between Seale and the marshals ordered to remove him recreates the physical confrontations that marked the antiwar protests of the period. Defense attorney Kunstler calls the removal of Seale "an unholy disgrace to the law," and defendant Abbie Hoffman entreats the judge to leave the bench and "come down here and watch it, judge. It's the same thing that happened last year in Chicago, the exact same thing."[99] The legal proceeding, in this theatrical version, has been conflated with the public skirmish that had created a need for it, and this conflation suggests that the demarcation between street and courtroom has diminished, the latter as dangerous a place for the demarcation of difference as the protest site. Neither location, despite the constitutional stipulations that the first ought to serve as a platform for peaceful dissent and the second as a public theater for conflict resolution, has, in this case, provided the safety and security they were designed to support.

The court prevails in its determination to remove Seale by the end of act 1, and as supportive as the other defendants have been of Seale and of his position, the play's structure indicates the remaining defendants' ability to move ahead without their African American colleague. A renewed sense of solidarity among the accused marks the opening of act 2, which begins with the defendants' observation of the Vietnam moratorium. Of the original trial, Lahav notes that "Seale is formally administered justice, and yet he is visibly different from any other person in the courtroom, including the other defendants."[100] Seale's impassioned pleas to defend himself proved too judicial for the left's position and too often put the court and the defense at a stalemate that ultimately seemed to prove tedious to the other defendants. Abbie Hoffman's narrative, reflective of the often privileged Yippie philosophy and lifestyle, includes his proclaimed residency in "Woodstock Nation," in his mind and "in the minds of my brothers and sisters," a nation that "does not consist of property or material, but rather of ideas and certain values." Hoffman's status as a white man, even one marginalized by his position on the war and his activities in the alternative movements of the time, allows him the freedom to discuss abstract ideas and promote values such as "co-operation versus competition."[101] Seale, on the other hand, is forced to defend his very body against assault, his claim of rights falling on the deaf ears of the justice system, at least as represented in the play.

As the trial continues in act 2, the other defendants speak out of turn in order to argue with or challenge the judge, but they are not removed, nor are they bound and gagged. When Hoffman accuses a member of the defense team of laughing at him, defendants Hoffman and Hayden each attempt to take the blame, but as the judge tells them, "I can't ask you to leave. You are at trial."[102] The judge's insistence on keeping the white defendants in the room despite their disruptions, and the juxtaposition that Sossi and Condon have created in the performance text by placing this statement by the judge in such close proximity to the scene of Seale's expulsion, means that the specter of the eighth defendant continues to hang over the remainder of the trial as we witness it in this documentary trial play format. The testimony of defendants Davis and Hoffman is followed by that of defense witness Allen Ginsberg, which is then succeeded by the defense attorneys' attempts to question Chicago mayor Richard Daley and Wisconsin Democratic delegate Donald Peterson. Although objections by the prosecution do not permit the latter two witnesses to testify for the defense as they have been called to do, the defense team and the defendants dominate the action and the dialogue in act 2, and only one scene that occurs just before closing arguments allows for the prosecution to take over the court in its rebuttal case. While the sequence follows standard procedure, the effect of it in this theatrical version is to impart to the audience a contentious atmosphere throughout. In the first act, Seale's regular outbursts put the focus on him and his demands and thus diminish the attention to the information that the prosecution provides about the conspiracy charge. The judge's attempts to control the proceeding, whether with his rulings, his expulsion of Bobby Seale, or his gavel pounding, ultimately do little to contain the rebellious, even anarchic behavior enacted by the defendants. Five of the seven are found guilty of violating the antiriot act in the play's final scene, but even this news does not have a sobering effect on the Chicago Seven.

Chicago Conspiracy raises more questions than it answers, consciously, of course, but perhaps unintentionally as well. The two sides represented here, the center and the fringe, are both as alike and as different as possible. Each captures one end of an extreme moment in time, when the moral and social line between the right and the left was particularly visible and required a particularly striking choice on either side. In the context of Kahn's assertion that the "judicial role is a paradigm of the meaning of citizenship under law," what happens under the watch of Judge Julius Hoffman, at least in this case, would seem to reflect that paradigm's opposite.[103] The play's final moment conveys a strong sense that the trial has been in vain, for it concludes with one last verbal battle between the judge and Kunstler, the latter asserting that "maybe that is the way the case should end, as it began."[104] Although Kunstler may be referring specifically to the judge's insistence on interrupting him throughout, in the context of the dramatic action witnessed, the defense attorney's remark serves as an apt summation of what has gone before, leaving characters and audiences alike in a position of stasis, without insight, without resolution, with a tearing down of the justice system in a particularly absurd case that may represent the tensions of the age but sums up little else.

Paget asserts that what he calls the "True Story" is at times "a subversive form, at times profoundly subservient to the hegemony," playing "an important role in disturbing one of the most treasured myths of the twentieth century, that 'facts = truth.' It is through such myths that a society recognizes and confirms its collective model of itself." In these two plays, we see both influences, a culture recognizing a "model of itself" that nonetheless challenges the myths that order our collective existence. Paget also reminds us that "'hard facts' are never likely to be in dispute," but the "really interesting facts are those most buried, concealed, or disputed."[105] Although the trial transcript might at first thought seem a transparent document of undisputed facts, it can be transformed into a complex display of values and systems.

2

National Investigation: *Inquest* and
Are You Now or Have You Ever Been

In the years immediately following World War II, the Palace of Justice in Nuremberg, one of the only courthouses in Germany that had survived the war, hosted a great tribunal organized by the consolidated power of several Allied nations. Representatives from these countries collaborated in planning the tribunal, whose objective was to bring to justice the major war criminals of the European Axis. In the first Nuremberg trial, which lasted almost one year, twenty-two defendants were indicted (one of the twenty-two, who could not be located and was believed dead, was tried in absentia) on at least two of four separate counts: conspiracy to wage aggressive war, waging aggressive war, war crimes, and crimes against humanity. Three of the defendants were found not guilty; the other nineteen received sentences ranging from ten years in prison to death by hanging. Twelve other trials of war criminals were held at Nuremberg over the next several years, bringing the total number of defendants charged with war crimes to slightly over two hundred. Although the first trial was conducted collaboratively by the four most powerful Allied nations, the twelve subsequent trials were prosecuted by the US military tribunal and presided over by judges from the United States.

The Nuremberg tribunals had originated with an agreement between Franklin Roosevelt, Winston Churchill, and Joseph Stalin in February 1945 at the Yalta Conference held several months before Germany's unconditional surrender; the leaders vowed then to bring "all war criminals to swift and just punishment." In the immediate aftermath of the war, representatives of fifty countries that had declared war against Germany and Japan met in San Francisco to sign the United Nations charter, designed to prevent future wars and to foster communication and peaceful negotiations among nations. In addition, the United States, the Soviet Union, the United Kingdom, and France formed the Allied Control Council to rule over defeated Germany; they divided the country and the city of Berlin into zones, each zone presided over by the military of one of the four nations. In August 1945, the Allies signed the London Charter, which established the International Military Tribunal, and it was this body that created the conditions of and procedure for the Nuremberg court. At the Soviet Union's insistence that the trial ought to take place on Soviet-occupied territory, the first trial convened in Soviet-controlled East Berlin, where the indictments were handed down, and then the trial adjourned to Nuremberg. The joint governance of Germany by the nations represented on the Allied Council contributed to a renewed tension between the East and the West and, most pointedly, between the United States and the Soviet Union, as each nation sought to promote its political and economic systems in the reconstruction of Europe. The Cold War between the two countries, a decades-long period of mutual antagonism that did not end until the 1990s, was marked by an arms race, multiple attempts to control vulnerable or resource-rich nations through force or coercion, and extensive espionage, all of which created a culture of fear and a stridently ideological atmosphere in postwar America.

This international rivalry and suspicion had a profound effect on US domestic policy, for as the government sought to protect its citizens from the possible annihilation of a nuclear attack as well as from more insidious attempts at Soviet control or influence, it waged internal as well as external battles against the perceived Communist threat. Two of these battles were waged in the courtroom or hearing room and subsequently became the subject of contemporary documentary trial plays in the early 1970s, several decades after the events themselves had become part of the period's legacy of accusations and prosecutorial intimidation. The opening night of the first play, *Inquest* (1970) by Donald Freed, preceded *Catonsville* by several months; and the second, Bentley's *Are You Now or Have You Ever Been* (1972), appeared two years later. *Inquest* dramatizes the FBI's investigations of Julius and Ethel Rosenberg, and the trial that followed, *United States of America v. Julius and Ethel Rosenberg*. The couple was indicted in January 1951 on charges of espionage in connection with a Soviet spy ring. *Are You Now* reenacts the investigations and hearings conducted by the congressional House Un-American Activities Committee from 1947 to 1956, on assignment to expose Communists and former Communists that might pose threats to national security.

The two trial plays created from the extensive documentation of these proceedings dramatize a central government in opposition to its citizens, with federal law investigation and enforcement empowered to root out Soviet infiltration. Substantial support for the government from the public sphere, as well as the law-and-order atmosphere of the 1950s, reflect for the most part a shared national resistance to Communism that enabled the central government to make unilateral decisions about international security. In part, the concentration of power was facilitated by citizens who supported or who did not object to heightened defense tactics that included the investigation and detention of American civilians; additional authority was bestowed by informants and witnesses, some willing, others coerced, who testified when faced with the alternative of their own arrests and interrogations and in doing so helped to justify more arrests. The law temporarily assumed increased power, placing the interests of "justice" above the values of due process, outside the expectations that the accused is to be presumed innocent until proven guilty. The judged culpability of the accused and vulnerability of the accused would come to depend on the level of threat, real and apparent, that the American people perceived from both internal and external forces.

Although Freed and Bentley wrote and staged their trial plays during the same decade as *Catonsville* and *Chicago Conspiracy*, *Inquest* and *Are You Now* look back to an earlier era and its documents for inspiration, situation, and information. The two former plays focused the selected trial documentation on the courtroom judge as the representation of central authority and his relationship with the defendants, thus placing emphasis and attention primarily on the judicial branch and its legal powers. However, *Inquest* and *Are You Now* shift the spotlight to the legal authority of the prosecutorial arms of the executive and the legislative government branches; as a result of this shift, different elements of law emerge, and unique competitive interests stand in opposition to each other. In *Inquest*, the government is represented by Irving Saypol, and the character description in the script makes clear that, as the *"senior attorney for the Government in the great espionage cases of the fifties,"* the character of Saypol represents the federal prosecution in this case, a prosecution powered by the government's executive branch, under which the investigating organization, the FBI, resides.

However, as we learn here that Saypol "was subsequently made a judge," the play makes visible that the judicial branch of the government is key to the prosecution and punishment of the defendants. The stage directions for the prologue of *Inquest* convey this connection as well, for the judicial branch ultimately decides the death-penalty appeals in the case. The theater audience views the judicial representatives in the prologue, with a full screen of the *"Supreme Court yearly pictures with entire area blue-gelled except for circle surrounding the head of Justice Felix Frankfurter"* as Frankfurter's "voice" is heard: "To be writing an opinion in a case affecting two lives after the curtain has been rung down upon them has the appearance of pathetic futility. But history also has its claims."[1] The documentary trial play sets out its purpose very specifically as one that is "writing an opinion," but not one to be upheld by law, for the curtain has already "been rung down upon them." That the case was decided two decades before the theater curtain rose on the case does not change the fact that "history also has its claims" and that we have our claims on history: namely, the right to make ongoing challenges to what has been recorded and remembered.

The trial of Julius and Ethel Rosenberg, who were convicted of conspiracy to commit espionage, concluded with a guilty verdict and a death sentence for both defendants, and the couple was executed two years later. *Inquest* playwright Freed included his essay "The Case and the Myth: *The United States of America v. Julius and Ethel Rosenberg*," published and reprinted with the play, and in it he argues that for him and for many other Americans, "the meaning of a case like *The United States of America v. Julius and Ethel Rosenberg, et al.* does not turn on guilt or innocence, but only on the astounding and unprecedented death penalty exacted by a panic-stricken and twitching majority."[2] The case remains an unsettling example of the government acting on what appear to be misguided ideas about right or wrong; it stresses the conflict between the need for national security and the guarantee of individual liberty, and it examines the influence that public opinion can have in a culture already seeking conformity as a shield of protection.

Inquest was produced twice in 1970: the first staging, a held-over performance in Cleveland; the second, a twenty-three day run at Broadway's Music Box Theater. Like *Catonsville*, *Inquest* was produced in two versions of different lengths, and it was performed originally under the title *The United States vs. Julius and Ethel Rosenberg*, the latter title clearly underscoring the work's documentary and legalistic origins. The text notes its debt to two published texts on the Rosenbergs, *Invitation to an Inquest* and *The Judgment of Julius and Ethel Rosenberg*. In his essay, Freed claims that all "exponential numbers, facts and figures, names and dates and places are necessary even to begin to come close to the phenomena of our time: the death camps, the great purge trials, the Triple Revolution and most of all the atom bomb."[3] In the acknowledgment of this indirect source material, as well as the indication, conveyed in performance via screen message, that "every word you will see or hear on this stage is a documented quotation from trial transcripts and original sources or a reconstruction from actual events," *Inquest* tests the limits of the documentary form.[4] In his review of the Music Box Theatre production, Walter Kerr describes his reaction to this information provided before the play and notes the confusion and distrust it generates for the reviewer: glass panels in the theater lobby that were covered in typescript, Kerr tells his readers, provided more information about the use of reconstructions, prompting him to conclude that although the reconstructions draw from letters and reports, they are nonetheless invented, serving truth rather than the truth itself.[5]

Kerr's challenge to the author's equivocation with facts is justified, especially given the particular way that Freed mixes fact and conjecture while championing the perception that the play represents an improvement on the existing historical record rather than the more commonly accepted attitude that dramatic license allows for the blending of facts and fiction in the service of narrative coherence. A frequent approach to "true" stories has been to loosen the narrative's adherence to fact; doing so often enhances dramatic potential, but it has tended to produce narratives that viewers approach with a skepticism appropriate to what are accepted conventions. When audiences are told that a story is "based" on a real event, for example, they have expectations of learning more about a historical event, but these expectations are tempered by the shared understanding that liberties have been taken with the facts. Freed's disclosure, while necessary, confuses rather than clarifies the play's documentary identity. Further complicating the difficulty of parsing out the facts as presented in this particular documentary trial play, and therefore problematizing the critical assessment of this performance text, is the knowledge we now have that the charges brought against the Rosenbergs were constructed from facts that have since been disproven, and that the untruths presented in court and in the press were both general in nature and specific to the accused couple. In a blatant example of the former, Judge Irving R. Kaufman stated during sentencing that the Rosenberg crime was "worse than murder," telling the defendants that "by immeasurably increasing the chances of atomic war, you may have condemned to death tens of millions of innocent people all over the world."[6] This statement, beyond its inflammatory generalization about any actual threat of nuclear attack, was simply not true: government officials at the time had already determined that the Soviet Union's successful development of the atomic bomb did not depend on information obtained from the United States.

The documentary theater in this case, then, recreates a case whose documentation is fraught with many suspect or disproven details that had initially been put forward as facts; they were disputed by the defense at trial, and the play includes some of those examples taken from the actual proceeding. Thus does Freed's reenactment of the case provide an example of the way that documentary theater engages with what Robert Ferguson calls the "master narrative," a critical perspective that Ferguson applies in his own examination of the Rosenberg trial:

> The execution of the Rosenbergs became a certainty when the prosecution's account held narrative desire for the long moment of the trial. The state's master narrative was exciting and deceptively simple in its denial of all other possibilities. It covered contingencies that the Rosenbergs could answer only through mundane claims about their normal existence, but the daily lives of the accused would prove less than satisfying in court and in media accounts. As told, the everyday has no narrative. It has no structured beginning-middle-end to define itself, and it was no match for the story of a nation plunged into peril.[7]

Ferguson goes on to note that the "truly fascinating thing about the prosecution's untrue master narrative is that it dominated the country as well as the court."[8] Within the context of Ferguson's comments on narrative, specifically legal narrative, Freed's statements about the text he created as well as the text itself serve to make visible the challenges and the consequences of the documentary trial play and its relationship to legal history and American history.

Freed composed *Inquest* from a distance of twenty years, and the interim provided some perspective on the paranoia and fear that gripped the nation in the postwar decade and fueled the prosecution's persuasive powers. But his essay makes clear that this degree of distance may be compromised by the fact that the "atom spy ring" was his "political baptism," an event that was, he writes, "the start for many of us in the fifties of what was to become known in the sixties as 'the movement.'"[9] He likened the events to a mythic struggle that cast the Rosenbergs as antiheroes and involved a government that "dominated the stage with its federal agents, lawyers, judges, Congressmen, and armies of functionaries." As the years passed, he explains, this attitude shifted for him and for others as "books, opinions, journals, authorities from all over world, were beginning to be univocal about the conduct of the judge, about the plaguelike atmosphere of what was already being called (somewhat unfairly) the 'McCarthy Era,' as 'The Case' became 'The Scandal.'"[10] It is within the context of these tensions between history and national mythology that *Inquest* was created.

The stage directions inform readers that the action of the play "takes place in: The Courtroom; The World; The Past."[11] Images projected on screens point to the validity and to the contemporary nature of the performance text and its documentation, "The World" represented through slides and videos, and, in the original version of the script, through spots with "The Man in the Street," who, "*like a survivor of an atom bombing, speaks.*"[12] He is both one and many, it would seem, and his speaking part allows him to offer the multiple opinions of the masses; regularly, however, that opinion is "No comment," which suggests the extent to which the authority of the government and the fear of the era had silenced ordinary citizens. His attitude is also a response to the atmosphere that the screen information provides, for he is bombarded with information about the dangers of the atomic age, and his lack of commitment indicates the difficulty if not the impossibility of forming opinions in the face of such a barrage.

This scene provides an example of a power that proves oppressive, as its visuals feature an atom bomb exploding, juxtaposed with smiling Japanese children. The sound effects, the stage directions tell us, should include Geiger counters and the noise of "*four engines of plane blunt-cut with country-side bird noises for delivery sequence followed by noises wind and bomb.*"[13] The power of the state has never been more destructive than it is at this moment of history, and Freed's play conveys the extent to which civilians are subject to possible devastation as a result. If a government can wipe out hundreds of thousands of its enemies in a blast of fire, an ordinary couple stands little chance of surviving the state's wrath, ironic in the fact that the Rosenbergs will be destroyed by their proposed connection to atomic bomb production rather than the effects of its detonation.

Two stages provide contrasting and complementing spaces for dramatic action, while a complex and constant slide show connects the performance to the trial's history with photos, sketches, film, and original or previously documented text. On Stage A, portions of the criminal proceeding are acted out, while Stage B presents private scenes and other contextual events.

While the two stages reinforce a separation between the public and the private spheres, the divide is not as clear-cut as it might first appear, for "Government" tableaus are enacted on Stage B as well, and their place in that realm suggests the intrusion that the state and the law have made into the personal and familial lives of the defendants. Stage B allows for some additional documentary segments, with journalists and federal agents, but it is primarily the space set aside for family scenes and for relationship scenes. These scenes compose the bulk of the "reconstructed" sections of the text; although they are clearly not taken from the public record, they are not entirely fictionalized either, but draw from the texts Freed credits as well as other information made public about the Rosenbergs and their lives. The courtroom scenes on Stage A form the central focus of the performance, for naturally the trial has come to dominate the lives of the Rosenbergs in their final years, transforming them from private citizens to the representatives of perceived Communist collusion. "The Past" unfolds on Stage B, dramatizing the Rosenbergs' lives together before and during the arrest. Thus does the play, structurally and visibly, counterpoint a system of reason (the law in the present) with a strain of emotion (the marriage scenes from the past), recalling Paget's theory of documentary theater's "two, distinct, but interlinked, structures of feeling": a rational one of crime and punishment, and an emotional one of a marriage tested, family loyalties broken, and children abandoned.

At the end of the prologue, after the red alert wail and the visual of atom bomb detonation, a barrage of media items assault the theater patrons: "The mushroom clouds, the contorted faces, the mountains of rubble, headlines in ten languages, wave after wave of incredible human suffering and destruction. The shock waves of sound reverberate together with sirens, screams, moans."[14] Freed writes in his essay about this element of the play in production, with its "series of aural-visual souvenirs" prepared by designer Ken Isaacs, all of which remind or inform viewers of the "sights and sounds of the Cold War past," as everyone "from Milton Berle to Joseph McCarthy" take the audience back in time, jog their memories and make them recall that it all happened."[15] As the historical perspective provided by films and slides and speeches ends, a comment by defense attorney Emanuel Bloch reminds us of the outcome while suggesting that the truth about the case may be unknowable: "I had no idea what was waiting for me. They were arrested in August 1950 and executed in June of 1953—in between was the trial. That's all I know. (*Pause.*) I was the defense, but I can't tell you what really happened to those two human beings. Let me put it to you this way—the future determines the past."[16] The elements of the play thus combine to suggest that although history has its limitations, doubts and uncertainties do not exempt the documentary theater audience from assuming its adjudicating duties.

Just as the prologue ends, the stage directions indicate that in the darkness, "the juror selection drum begins to glow and spin."[17] The spinning drum implicates the audience in the judgments to be made here, even as it emphasizes the randomness of decision making. The legal framework draws the audience into the play by demanding that it serve as trial jury; the Clerk spins his juror drum, and the screen image sets an exact time and place for the proceedings: the District Court of New York, Southern District, on the sixth morning in March, 1951 at 10:30 A.M.[18] Asked to literally sit in judgment on two fellow Americans and decide after the fact (and after the deaths) whether execution was warranted, theater patrons experience a discomfiting dimension when taking on this role that *Inquest* has assigned to them. The shaking drum is a concrete reminder, too, of the inevitable role of fate that comes in communion with a particular group of individuals at a particular moment in American history. Even with a twenty-year separation between the trial and the performance, theater historian Gad Guterman argues, the theater audience would most likely enter the performance space with a preconceived opinion of the Rosenbergs and a predetermined decision about guilt or innocence: "Most of the jurors here had already tried the case: in their heads, in their homes, in their hearts. *Inquest* should have proven easy. Instead, reliving the trial as theater, this time literally playing the jury, the audience faced a difficult situation, particularly because Freed's play confronted them with something unlike any article, pamphlet, or book ever had: a live performance."[19] As the audience is pressed into service, it also comes under the control of the "state," for the Bailiff delivers multiple orders to the crowd: "No talking, please, or reading or gum chewing. Please rise. Hear Ye, Hear Ye: Facing the flag of our country, acknowledging the principles for which it stands." His words charge the group to obey instructions and to recognize its place in the state's institutional system while also steering the audience into the present of the trial. Kerr provides important first-hand information about the way the audience received what Guterman describes as a "difficult situation," for on the night Kerr attended the show, he witnessed an audience challenged to understand its place in this re-creation. As the actor playing the clerk of the court requested the "jury" to rise and pledge allegiance to the flag, Kerr reports that only about a third of the audience rose to its feet, doing so as if ordered to in court. The remainder of the audience stayed in their seats but "tittered audibly." Thus was the event split, Kerr writes, "shattered in its essence, torn between treating the stage as a courtroom or as a stage, the play as fact or artifice.[20] Discomfort prevailed, both physical and psychological, as the theater audience is asked, at least implicitly, to act as one; even before the show and the trial begins, however, the decision is "split." The play takes one additional step in merging the players and the audience, planting actors among the viewing crowd who speak out as jurors and thus implying that all those seated with them are of the same group, all of them called to serve the state in evaluating guilt or innocence.

Engaging the audience thusly is exactly what Janelle Reinelt recommends in her "Notes for a Radical Democratic Theater," for, as she argues, "live theater enacts one of the last available forums of direct democracy, gathering an assembly of 'citizens' in the tradition of civic republicanism, related to the small assembly, town meeting, church social, school board meeting, or neighborhood block party. Spectators are, at the least, an implied community for the time of performance—even if riven with antagonisms and contradictions that make *community* a weak signifier" (emphasis in the original).[21] Reinelt's list of forums readily accommodates the addition of "trial," a crucial act of "civic republicanism," an act that connects a group of people and calls to them to participate and cooperate in an act of "direct democracy." And, indeed, *Inquest* demands a high level of audience participation, the price of a theater ticket bringing with it an opportunity and an obligation to share in an enactment of radical democratic behavior that reminds them of their responsibility to the network of cultural traditions and relations that creates and binds a society's members.

The dramatic presentation of the events in *Inquest* includes previously unheard narratives that add new dimensions to the legal proceeding. In the Rosenberg case, these unheard narratives are particularly significant because, as Ferguson argues, "narrative control is always a vital key, but successful narrative control in a courtroom always enjoys the extra proof of the decision reached and, as such, it can instigate widely held belief."[22] And, as Martha Minow claims in her examination of law's stories, "stories seem to work, when they do, on many levels; they can produce an experience, an insight, and one or more emotional responses."[23] In this case the stories not previously told or insufficiently known or understood, Freed reveals, are the upbringing, marriage, and family life of the Rosenbergs. These narratives flesh out the couple's legal chronicle, adding insights from their personal struggles to this room of judgment, this stage of revelation, even to this system of faith in the American Dream.

Inquest, with its personal reconstructions enacted on Stage B that form the emotional component of the play and its alternative "structures of feeling," has the capacity to add a new dimension to the public legal narrative that dominated the actual trial and sentencing. Minow reminds us that with "any given story, some people get it and some people do not. Some of those who get it do not like the experience and are troubled by it." She goes on to explain that the "experience of a response to the story is itself troubling because it occurs on levels not easily summarized by principles, logical analysis, or other specific modes of reasoning that seem more generally accessible or rationally defensible. . . . It raises questions about the accessibility of a given form of rational argument in a world of human and group differences."[24] In an example of the kind of knowledge that such stories can provide us, the character of Julius Rosenberg constructs a solo moment as he narrates a letter to wife, Ethel, recalling that his union activist father, "a garment worker, was on a long strike against sweatshop conditions" and therefore "was blacklisted and had quite a pull to make ends meet." The detail connects Julius to a Communist past, as the son of a union worker on a long strike; he might be expected to have inherited some feelings of anger and resentment toward the system that had held his father and then himself hostage economically. His words trail off in a memory, as he ends by saying that the "constant battle against rats and vermin is still vivid."[25] Although his forthcoming testimony on the benefits of the Soviet government reveals a lukewarm attitude toward Communism, the private moment in which Julius recalls his father's struggles against a system unsympathetic to the "underdog" establishes his loyalty to the proletariat even during the prosperity of the postwar years. In the reading version of the play, Freed describes Julius as "*a man of the Depression. Idealistic and a failure in his one business attempt.*"[26] Rosenberg admits on the stand that he believes that the lot of the underdog has been improved by policies in Soviet Russia.

In the dark years of the early 1970s during which *Inquest* was composed and produced, this skepticism about capitalism would have likely garnered some agreement from audience members, and Guterman suggests that Freed "saw his play as an attempt to make a viable break with an oppressive past by attacking the present." The Freedom of Information Act facilitated the release of documents to Freed after the play's production, and they indicated that he and his play were under watch at the time; also, as Guterman points out, the "grand spectacle" of the Chicago Conspiracy Trial had exposed audiences to a "very public and contested legal battle, one that, following the 1968 revolution, pitted not only marginalized minorities against dominant, white America, but also a younger generation against an older one."[27] *Inquest*, with its appearance at a time when the justice system was under attack from previously underrepresented groups identified by ethnicity and class as well as by age, serves as its own kind of protest against a legal system that marginalizes diversity among its citizens and punishes civil protests in what some believed were kangaroo courts. So while Freed's play could not overturn the verdict carried out on the Rosenbergs some years prior, it may have provided information and motivation for the ongoing defense of civil liberty, influencing public opinion and policy about the state's power and inspiring citizens to guard against unreasonable procedures passed off as safety precautions. In this sense, then, the audience's "verdict" in the Rosenberg case could be far reaching, suggesting the possibility that individuals can protect individual rights in part by interrogating past judicial decisions, by identifying injustice, and by instigating needed reforms in its institutional systems.

Knowing that the Rosenbergs were executed for their alleged treason may either alleviate or add to the burden for the audience/jury; whatever individual feelings they have prior to or subsequent to their viewing of *Inquest*, they cannot alter the fates of the real-life defendants in this case, who died at the hands of the government via state-sanctioned execution. What had been represented as a morally torn judicial representative in *Catonsville*, the judge who recognized and sympathized with the ideological aim of the nine defendants but who could not side with them legally, has become in *Inquest* a powerful legal system with the judge named and with the highly individualized characters of the prosecuting attorneys. These symbols of the state are out in full force to convict the innocence-protesting Rosenbergs, and the investigative perspective, represented in the play most significantly by the character of district attorney Roy Cohn, contrasts sharply with the emotional weight delivered during the family scenes. Screen images and text provide further historical documentation and link the two worlds, public and private. The presence of the government is represented as hulking and unsympathetic in this staged version of the trial; its representatives dominate the proceedings and every level of the law is visible in the cast: investigator, evaluator, and executioner. Furthermore, as is common in the documentary theater, actors play multiple roles, and the prosecutors Saypol and Cohn also appear as agents of the government, which means that the actors who play them appear on both Stage A and Stage B. Their appearance in connected but different roles and their presence on both levels of action reinforce the perception that the defendants are surrounded by figures of a pervasively present and powerful legal bureaucracy.

The FBI represents the power of the government that prosecutes the suspects; indeed, the dramatic reconstructions in which FBI agents are featured are titled "Government," with those words flashing onto the screen just prior to them, and they connect a courtroom scene to two investigative scenes during which Roy Cohn reveals evidence that the screen labels as "Government's Exhibit 8." This sequence, between the pretrial investigation and the judicial revelations of that investigation, highlights explicitly the federal government's interest in this case, and its role in prosecuting Julius and Ethel Rosenberg. But the responsibility for the conviction and execution of these two Americans is not only spread out to agencies of the federal government; it shifts closer to the average citizen. The public sentiment for protecting the nation from Communism is strong, and extreme action on the part of our elected or appointed officials may seem warranted. The play thus implicates its jury, the audience, it could be argued, by highlighting the expansive prosecutorial approach to the case, for such power originates or is supported by citizenry in its craving for protection for themselves and its attachment to what is considered a superior way of life that must be preserved.

These scenes thus expand the perspective on events that occur in the courtroom scenes and call attention to the court's power. The increasingly bullying questioning from the agents recalls the government's insistence at this particular point in history that the nation and its people were threatened by the dangerous outside forces of a radically different ideology. As the checks and balance of resistance to the law are undermined by the fear and paranoia of the age, the condemnation of the defendants is put into place; it is total and devastating, ultimately depriving them of life. Nonetheless, the moral superiority of the defendants is conveyed in *Inquest*, not only by Freed's composition of the documents and re-creations at hand, but, in Kerr's estimation, by the skill of the actors portraying Julius and Ethel Rosenberg in the New York production. Kerr insists that "as the shards of evidence fly off into space," the actors playing the accused couple, George Grizzard and Anne Jackson, are so sympathetic in their portrayals that audience members may decide that the Rosenbergs are innocent because of the power and believability of the portrayals.[28] For as Guterman reminds us, in the theater, the "imagined figures" of Ethel and Julius "were replaced by the real presences of actors Anne Jackson and George Grizzard. These effigies 'fashioned from flesh' could literally body forth the absent, electrocuted couple."[29]

Guterman then goes on to claim that "it is the presence of live actors that can energize documents and facts as well as push the audience to new limits from which preconceived notions may be tested and the task of judging may be advanced."[30] Carol Martin provides further explanation of the way that the documentary theater creates characters from documents: "In documentary theater, the performers are sometimes those whose stories are being told. But more often than not documentary theater is where 'real people' are absent—unavailable, dead, disappeared—yet reenacted. They are represented through various means, including stage acting, film clips, photographs, and other 'documents' that attest to the veracity of both the story and the people being enacted."[31] In the case of *Inquest*, there are ample documents offered up, but many of them challenge rather than attest to the veracity of the story. And it is the actors' skill in bodying forth the absent couple, combined with the reconstructions of the Rosenbergs' life together created by Freed, which may have swayed the audience/jury: not the facts of the case, but the emotional resonance of the script and the actors' performances.

Inquest foregoes documentary distance in its attempt to persuade viewers of the Rosenberg's innocence, the acting method yet another way that the performance of this documentary theater text departs from the conventions of the genre in order to convince audiences of its antigovernment viewpoint. Taking issue with the blend of "fact" and "reconstruction," Kerr argues that this example of the Theater of Fact has backfired both ways, and that no persuasive play has been written because we are witnessing fact, not theater, but in this case fact has been "compromised by the normal liberties, and the normal hazards, of playmaking."[32] The critique smacks of the standard objection to the documentary theater: that it cannot be two things at once. It must be either factual or imaginative. But Freed's attempt to balance the two might be considered a striving for synthesis in which the real and the fictional, the rational and the emotional, can join together in order to convey a range of experience, a diversity of narrative, a multiplication of perspective. Such synthesis may be difficult or impossible to achieve in a courtroom, but it may succeed in a theatrical space that allows not only for a mix of performance elements and altered conventions, but also a space for the real and the recreated to take part in reconstructing history.

The alternation of courtroom scenes with background and other personal information may reveal the liberties and hazards of "playmaking," but these narratives that imagine everyday lives of the defendants remind us that all the narratives, including the judicial sections, are constructed and even fabricated, as time would eventually tell, not only in their form but also in their content. Just before the first act comes to an end, the actor signified as the "Government" makes the following statement, which demonstrates the extent to which the state, in its legal capacity, makes claims on certainty and truth: "The evidence will come from witnesses and you will see and hear that the witnesses are telling the truth as each link in this chain is forged and put into place, by testimony, by *documentary evidence* which will point conclusively to one thing and one thing alone—the guilt of the defendants" (emphasis mine).[33]

In reality, however, the legal statements in this case, even when they are taken directly from the public record, are written and planned and delivered very similarly to the dramatic scenes in the family homes. Both kinds of scenes are driven by convention and ritual, include or omit details, employ a system of words and actions to convey complex meaning. This particular documentary trial play, in its dependence on both document and dramatic reconstruction, makes explicit the way that the imaginative elements of theater are complicated by the conventions of the documentary form. The cross-cutting of short scenes that play out on alternate stage spaces make the studied contemplation of conflicting facts particularly difficult if not impossible. Freed's attempts to show that the Rosenbergs were railroaded by an oppressive government stipulates that the script address this injustice, but the use of court documents may also inadvertently register the prosecution's use of repetition as a component of its master narrative.[34]

As Clive Barnes describes the action of *Inquest*, the entirety of the law-and-order system is accounted for, "from the first polite legal exchanges to the final electric flashes of society's revenge."[35] Indeed, neither the verdict nor the sentencing brings the play to its conclusion; rather, it is the scene of execution that brings the curtain down in an apt reminder that this case from history involves two deaths, and that threat of atomic war seemed to warrant the government's decision that two Americans had conspired to aid the enemy and therefore deserved to die. Just prior to the onstage executions in the expanded version of *Inquest*, various cast members representing the "Man in the Street" are polled about the "atom spy trial." Asked the question, "Do you approve of the verdict in the atom spy trial?" their responses are either "No Comment" or "Guilty"[36] No one who is polled challenges the verdict, and no citizen speaks out against the death penalty. The agents and the zealous prosecutors have dominated and driven the action with their insistent questioning and their mountain of damning details. The play moves toward an ultimate day of judgment and a scene of execution. In a tonal turn, however, the final scene is not solely focused on the state's power: rather, it contrasts the convicted couple's spiritual and political fates. It brings us to the end of two lives that have been horribly ruined by the fabrication of their crime, but the conclusion also acknowledges the redemptive qualities of prayer and faith, of community and morality.

In fact, the execution is attended by a number of officials, clergy, and medical personnel, but also by all the acting company, who are *"present as witnesses.*" The Rabbi, the Doctor, the Executioner, the Chorus (the company), and the Defense all speak. Only one line is spoken by a state's representative, the Executioner, and it is a question: "Want another [shock]?" The Rabbi recites the twenty-ninth psalm as Julius is strapped to the chair; three shocks follow, with a dimming of lights, a shaking chair, and a *"puff of yellow smoke from the head."* The Rabbi then sings the Hebrew lament for the dead, with the Chorus making explicit the threat this event represents for all "future traitors," who "should beware/They too will burn within the 'chair.'" It is the company who acknowledges that traitors will not be tolerated, even going so far as to repeat the final line as they are exiting the stage, "They too will burn within the 'chair.'"[37]

The action in this concluding scene contrasts with all that has proceeded it, for while the group onstage has gathered to serve the will of the state, the dialogue is dominated by the Defense. The final speech is spoken by defense attorney Emanuel Bloch, who decries that in thirty years as an officer of the court, he had "seen nefarious practices in the criminal courts, but basically [he] believed in the administration of justice and in the integrity of most officials sworn to uphold it."[38] No more, however, would he put his faith in such an administration of law, and particularly in the "officials of the Department of Justice." He argues that the justice to which he had devoted his life was not served up in the court that tried the so-called spies. The play serves as a revelation of citizen culpability as well as government culpability, and Guterman suggests that the mixed reception of the play may have had something to do with *Inquest*'s indictment of the press for its part in helping to convict the Rosenbergs publicly before the verdict was reached.[39] The emotional material and the convincing performances added significant depth and meaning to this documentary trial play, and the dramatization of personal testimony and circumstances provided a counterpoint to the injustice that marred the trial. The multiplicity of perspectives that the performance text presents and the utilization of two stages offer the viewers a complicated version of the trial that ended with two Americans dead and that raised larger questions about a system and a public primed to disregard truth in the name of safety.

As the war tribunals in Europe brought hundreds of Nazis to court to account for their actions during the war, and as FBI investigations rooted out real or perceived Cold War espionage on the home front, many more Americans were called on to defend their national loyalty and disavow their political past by appearing before a House of Representatives committee whose role was to gather information about subversive activities. Although this committee, serving under other names, had been convened at various periods since 1918, in 1945 it became a standing committee known as the House Un-American Activities Committee (HUAC); serving in this capacity until 1975, it is most commonly remembered for the hearings it conducted over nine days in 1947 to investigate Communist activity in and influence on the motion picture industry. The committee's goals were to expose Communist party membership in the Screen Writers Guild and to demonstrate that these alleged Communists inserted pro-Soviet propaganda into films they made. Friendly witnesses, not under suspicion, appeared before the committee and read statements detailing what they knew about Communist activity in Hollywood. Nineteen unfriendly witnesses were named, and of that group, eleven were called to testify during this first round of hearings; ten of them appeared but refused to answer any questions. Dubbed the "Hollywood Ten," the latter were all held in contempt, served time in jail, and were subsequently "blacklisted" by the film community. Over the next four years, several waves of hearings were held and more than three hundred Hollywood directors, actors, and screenwriters were blacklisted for refusing to testify before the committee or for refusing to name names or provide information about themselves or others in the entertainment community that were under investigation. The majority of these artists were never able to revive their careers, and some left the country to seek work elsewhere.

The narratives of interrogation and the subsequent blacklisting of playwrights, directors, actors, and others who worked in producing cultural documents would go on to provide ample material and motivation for print or performance texts, fact or fictional, that excoriate the committee's actions and explore their repercussions, many careers and lives ruined. In her study of "dramatic representations" of the HUAC, Brenda Murphy discusses the texts of resistance whose origins coincided with and followed this period; these performance texts confront issues of rights, freedoms, and the state's authority. She notes the "fundamentally forensic structure" of so many of them: "They involve cultural institutions of interrogation, and many use the trial as a structural principle for the play's action. Reflected at the center of these theatrical representations, in other words, was HUAC's major weapon, the Committee hearing, which was in reality a trial without a proper system of defense, a jury, or even, in many cases, evidence against the accused."[40] Murphy calls attention to the source and execution of government authority for these hearings: for the questioning, or, in the case of those who refused to testify, the nonquestioning, originates with a legislative body but in its system of inquiry becomes a visible arm of the law, punishing its offenders for either cooperation or noncooperation and doing so, Murphy suggests, in a way that exposes its movement beyond the rule of law or at least the rules of evidence.

Among those works that Murphy dubs as "dramatizing directly" the years of the investigations is Eric Bentley's *Are You Now or Have You Ever Been*, a documentary trial play fashioned from the voluminous records of this congressional committee and its investigative work during this period. No question mark ends the infamous quotation used as title, even though this incomplete sentence is familiar as part of the question posed to witnesses called to testify at the hearings. It makes for an unusual prompt in an investigation, for it does not ask about actions, it asks about being; it asks not what individuals have done but who they are. It asks about the past and about the present, and implies that being (and, in this case, being a Communist), rather than doing, is a reason for indictment. Bentley himself wrote, in the preface to another play in the collection in which *Are You Now* appears, that "everything I want to say in the three plays of this book is implicit in the title of the first one—*Are You Now or Have You Ever Been*—especially if a question mark be added thereto. I wanted to make each spectator ask himself if he existed, and, if he didn't, had he ever existed."[41] The answers to this question as posed by the committed varied, as one might expect: some "are now," some "had been," and some refused to say. The connection between law and existence is made plain before the play begins, emphasizing the significance of the legal institution in establishing a key cultural paradigm, and tying existence to one's place in the justice system, a public evaluation of individual presence and worth in society. The title also reminds its audience that the government can exert its right to question citizens and ask them to identify themselves according to belief system, and that despite the expectation of ideological freedom that citizenship carries, Americans may be indicted, questioned, and even punished because of values and beliefs, even when those values and beliefs are not acted on in ways that are dangerous or destructive to society.

Even the most rudimentary knowledge of the committee's activities includes an acknowledgment of the atmosphere of repression and resistance that prevailed during the era following World War II, as the HUAC hearings posed particular challenges to individual rights because of the nature of the indictments and questioning. To some extent both the Catonsville Nine and the Chicago Eight defended their right of resistance by arguing their crimes should not be crimes or that the criminal acts were necessary for calling attention to the larger state of injustice: government's crimes against its own people and against the Vietnamese. The Rosenberg trial was more traditional, with the defendants presenting a plea of not guilty to the charges of conspiracy to commit espionage leveled against them. HUAC, however, is a legal proceeding that subpoenaed individuals and required them to defend themselves against vague charges of anti-American sentiment and activity, and, perhaps even more insidiously, pressed witnesses to implicate others in subversive activities. It remained to those who came before the committee to register resistance by refusing to answer questions and thereby undermining the power of the congressional body, but the refusal to testify or the refusal to cooperate led to contempt citations and in some cases to blacklisting and subsequent career demise. The "crime" is thus often enacted during the interviews, as it was for many the refusal to cooperate that led to charges being brought against them; significantly, then, it is in the reenactment of the proceeding through the documentary trial play that we are able to witness such crimes taking place. We also see and hear what the government considers patriotic and unpatriotic during this period: cooperation was defined as a patriotic act, while the refusal to cooperate, even as an expression of personal liberty, was not.

Bentley's documentary trial play based on these hearings is a theatrical performance explicitly engaged in questions of freedom of speech and of belief. Stephen Farber, in the *New York Times*, quotes Albert Maltz, one of the Hollywood Ten, in 1975, when *Are You Now* was staged in Los Angeles: "'I have no regrets about the stand I took. We were trying to block the Committee from inquiring into the political beliefs of American citizens.'"[42] The protest is not one enacted by the crowd in the parking lot of a Selective Service office, or in a public park. The protest is registered in a hearing room, the result of and party to the legal proceeding. Witnesses argue with the interviewers about the legality of the questions they are being asked; the issue of whether they are guilty of being or having been a Communist becomes a secondary issue to the larger ones of justice and individual rights as they conflict with the protection of national interests.

Although this play was performed twenty years after the proceedings, the link between the hearings' investigation of the movie industry and the stage life of Bentley's play allowed for old regrets and resentments to erupt; there appeared to be a particularly personal sense of affront in this case that found its way into staging decisions and acting choices. In his review of the original Yale production, Mel Gussow reminds us of the "added factor that the witnesses were artists and entertainers, and, as Bentley acknowledges in the introduction to the play, in some of the testimony there is a measure of performing—people performing for their lives."[43] The immediacy of the material to the community who performed *Are You Now* made for a unique relationship between performer and audience, text and personal history, imagination and reality.

And, as Farber explained in his newspaper piece on the play, attitudes in the 1970s about what had happened during the HUAC years continued to include anger and resentment against the committee and against those witnesses who had cooperated in the government's efforts to root out Communist sympathizers: "for the people who were directly involved in the HUAC hearings, the old wounds have not yet healed; blacklisted actors, writers, and directors still shun the informers."[44] Some audience members whose lives had been affected by the hearings saw the production as an opportunity for healing, however, and for increased knowledge of a dark moment in American history. Garrett Parks, whose father, Larry's, testimony anchors the first half of the play, is quoted by Farber as having responded thusly to the Los Angeles production: "I came away very proud of my father, proud of his humanity. I know the subject is still very painful to a lot of people, and it was to us. But it happened, and you can't run away from it. The hearings are a part of history that America should not be proud of. I'm glad the play was done."[45] One possible effect of the documentary trial play comes with its exposure of the wounds and scars left behind after periods of cultural tension and strife; Parks's statement underscores the fact that some of the most successful performances, both critically and financially, are the ones that take place close to home and engage the locals who lived the events.

Bentley's role as playwright here works in concert with his other writing work in editing and journalism. Indeed, the three plays contained in the published volume in which *Are You Now* appears share a forensic structure as well as an interest in revisionist history, and so he takes up events from history that cross centuries and cultures.[46] Bentley's interest in HUAC is also evidenced by a book he had previously written and published on the subject, *Thirty Years of Treason*, in which he presented excerpts from thirty years of HUAC hearings. In the preface to *Are You Now*, he describes his role as a historian who uses public sources of information to construct the play, reminding readers that the earlier book had provided the testimony in a broader context. As Murphy indicates by way of evidence from a press clipping of the original Yale performance, the production has the "harsh reality of the hearings, which were held amid popping flashbulbs before a nation watching on television."[47] Photographs in the lobby and copious slide projections during the production re-create the black-and-white era of the Communist scare while also noting the kind and volume of documentation available on these proceedings, recorded as they were by the government and by the press. Admitting to having his own "opinions and commitments," Bentley nonetheless "tried to be fair" in his treatment of the events; his aim was "not, lawyer-fashion, to make an overwhelming case for a client."[48] At the same time, he sends readers elsewhere for other more scholarly examinations of the HUAC years, including his own; those interested, he says, can turn "to my longer book or even the HUAC records as printed in extensor by the government."[49]

Contextualizing his work while also providing a vision of the documentary trial play as it is intertwined with other versions of history, the preface to the play explains that what he hopes "to have captured in this shorter treatment is a story, a newspaperman's 'story,' and a writer's, even perhaps a playwright's story: a dramatic Action."[50] The "dramatic Action" is an investigative one as well, and despite any attempts on Bentley's part to be fair, it is an action that shows the government imposing its power on citizens in an unreasonable way, not only pressuring them to appear and incriminate themselves, but pressing them to identify other people who could or should be investigated for anti-American actions. Brenda Murphy would also have us see *Are You Now* as Bentley hoped it would be seen, as a creative piece, a "playwright's story." The only difference, says Murphy, "between Bentley's task and that of the playwright who works from imagination and personal experience is the source of the material."[51] Bentley's relationship to that material is not as personal as Daniel Berrigan's, nor does *Are You Now* seem as stridently intent on righting a wrong as *Inquest* does, but there are nonetheless some dramatic choices that cast a positive light on the witnesses, and especially on those who resist the efforts of the state.

Just as Berrigan omitted names of the prosecutors and judge in his re-enactment of *Catonsville*, Bentley foregoes the individualized identities of the congressmen who did the questioning and creates a composite, labeled the "Investigator." The choice makes for a single figure of interrogation that Murphy says constitutes "an anonymous antagonist for the witnesses, which functions simply as the Enemy, or more precisely, the Persecutor."[52] The similarities with *Inquest*, in having a generalized "Government" doing the questioning, make the side of authority very difficult to personalize and therefore to sympathize with. As Bentley describes it, he has created the image of "a single Committee in session throughout, presided over by a single Chairman, assisted by Investigators," even though he acknowledges that in reality the room "was not always the same" and "was not always even in Washington, DC." But, "for the imagination," he writes, "a single room will suffice," he says, just as a single Chairman or Investigator will do, the room "looking like any courtroom, or better, like any larger room in a government building."[53] With these choices, then, the play presents a bland

and centralized setting and interview structure with faceless investigators questioning the witnesses. The side whose guise or purpose it is to protect national security is presented and performed as soulless and aggressive. There is no individuality or personality for those who are acting on the authority of the state. Bentley edits the transcript significantly, shortening the more than four thousand pages of testimony and choosing representative witnesses for dramatization. With the "creation" of the characters who are called to testify, he believes that he has "credible and interesting human beings," and although some of the characters in *Are You Now* "pass too quickly across our line of vision to be portraits in any detail," several of the witnesses "whom the Committee held on to for hours (though here reduced to minutes) revealed themselves abundantly, more abundantly, in some instances, than they'd have wanted."[54]

As Bentley notes, "unlike many historians I am not using sources that the average person wouldn't have access to. On the contrary, I have used a record published by the United States government." And, in a footnote to his preface that describes the amount of transcription done by journalists for the *New York Times*: "scores of correspondents covered the proceedings, which took place before 30 microphones, six newsreel cameras and blazing klieg lights."[55] Not only did the pressing face of the media record and analyze the hearing, their presence drew attention to the hearings' focus on people in the entertainment industry, many of them extremely well known before they ever appear before the Committee. When the witness is a movie star, Bentley makes this suggestion to the companies producing the play: the "Chairman may have to ask press photographers to be less obtrusive" or a "witness may himself object to the use of TV lights and cameras."[56] Documentary and performance are brought together in these comments as Bentley plays with the duality of his text as the enactment of factual events and exact testimony that nonetheless draw audience attention to the formation and sublimation of individual character. "Such is the transaction—the drama—known as Investigation," Bentley reminds us. But it is the investigation not just of freedom of expression and belief; it is an investigation also of the way that history both shapes and records the individual experience as part of itself and as something it needs to control or otherwise determine. The tension in this duality helps to create the "transaction" embedded in this drama. It is a give-and-take rather than a one-way track of identity.

Are You Now consists almost entirely of question-and-answer testimony, punctuated at times with announcements or with the reading of other documents or news reports. Seventeen witnesses represent the numbers called before the committee; some of the names are well known for their fame as well as for their involvement with HUAC, such as Elia Kazan. Not all witnesses called have equal stage time, for Bentley cuts liberally from the transcripts to suit his dramatic and thematic needs. He includes a long interview with producer Abe Burrows, who "names names," and the scene makes a considerable impact, particularly in a short speech by Burrows during which he encapsulates the internal conflicts prompted by the call for self-identification that the hearing necessitates. To the question by the Committee Chairman, "Would you call yourself a Communist?" Burrows responds as follows: "Not in my own heart, sir. But I'm here to tell the truth, the whole truth, and nothing but the truth, and there's an element of truth in the statement that I was a Communist. *Pause.* There's also an element of untruth."[57] This documentary trial play not only dramatizes what makes cultural and political history difficult or impossible to excavate from the past; it demonstrates that personal history is also a challenge to reconcile as time and circumstances change the individuals whose historical moments, lived as personal experience, become the stuff of public debate.

Other than the questioning of Larry Parks, whose interview takes up the most stage time and sixteen pages of text, Burrows's testimony is the longest, and it best demonstrates the struggle that witnesses faced when attempting to resolve their past and their present. The challenge exists in no small part because the generation of Americans who endured the committee's investigations had come of age in the 1920s and 1930s, when public disputes about the merits of democracy and questions about its survival were commonplace. The economic woes of the Depression helped to prompt interest in alternatives to capitalism, and the American Communist Party attracted thousands of men and women, many of whom attended meetings or even carried cards only to abandon the new allegiance as events in Europe developed or the ideas expressed in the groups they had joined no longer seemed viable; the war would reunite many with their "patriotic" views, and in the aftermath of the Allied victory, their brief communion with Soviet philosophy was but an interlude that many argued had proved their patriotism by demonstrating their fervor for good governance.

Although the freedom to verbalize such challenges is always central to the democratic process, the postwar climate of suspicion that these witnesses experienced put the Hollywood Ten and the other witnesses who were called to testify before HUAC in the position of defending activities that they had considered patriotic endeavors and that they had believed would increase equality and prosperity for all. By the 1950s, even former membership in the American Communist Party had come to be seen by many government officials to render someone a threat to national security.

The filmmakers and actors who testified had become politically and culturally suspect because they had been politically active in their youth, a time when, as Larry Parks says in the play, being a Communist "fulfilled certain needs of a young man who was liberal in thought, idealistic, who was for the underprivileged, the underdog."[58] Many of these former Communists, including Abe Burrows, had broken with the party years earlier, as what had previously been presumed to be a collective global plan for political and civil reform had come to be recognized as the squaring off of two nations engaged in a postwar grab for supremacy, both domestic and international.

Despite the fact that many of the witnesses had put their political activism behind them, they struggled with how to make sense of it or defend it in the present moment and within a context of interrogation, and Burrows's testimony in *Are You Now* makes it clear that such a struggle weighs heavily on a man. In coming to the committee as someone with self-acknowledged prior Communist Party involvement, Burrows invokes the judicial oath as reasoning for why he must admit his dalliance with Communism. He prefaces that confession, however, with a plea based on his emotional truth, by claiming that in his heart he does not call himself a Communist. Legally, however, he understands that his commitment to truth goes beyond his own personal resolution of a past allegiance; that oath calls him to account in both a fuller ("whole truth") and a sparer ("nothing but the truth") way, thereby acknowledging one of the major dramatic conflicts of Burrows's situation and of the text: the nexus of emotion and law. More specifically, the extent to which the personal truth—which regularly pairs with feelings and with the psychological perceptions that color our views of ourselves—creates conflict when it comes into contact with legal jurisdictions, legislated loyalty in the form of oaths or other agreements to defend or at least cooperate with government efforts to protect the citizenry or uphold the documents that define the nation.

The aim to secure or maintain the power and influence of the Allied victory in World War II became a primary preoccupation of the postwar period, and the literary, cinematic, and theatrical products that many of the HUAC witnesses were involved in became an integral part of the packaging of American life during the 1950s, both for domestic consumption and for the export of our ideals abroad. In an era fueled by fear and paranoia, these products and their creators became subject to moral and legal investigation. Fears about the possibility that former American Communists might advance an agenda of Communist propaganda helped to support the power of the Motion Picture Production Code (also known as the Hays Code), the regulation in place from the 1930s to the 1960s, which sought to insure that film patrons had access to morally sound entertainment and could make their viewing choices wisely. The code relied on legislation of what could be included or what must be included in a film (due punishment for criminal or socially abhorrent acts, for example) and on the condemnation of films that questioned what had come to be seen as shared values.

The language of the code's legislation provides clear signs of the link between prosperity and morality, for as the code explained its purpose, it asserts that "industrial democracy can no longer be taken for granted" but "must be strengthened." While the national economy needs to be supported by "enterprise and freedom in industry and in business," there are significant "equivalent responsibilities—moral, social and economic" that must be considered.[59] The claim of responsibility calls for the imposition of standards, and the regulation serves as a version of our "self-government," encouraging the belief that the norms upheld have been agreed on by all. As claimed by the statement of purpose, the "alive and responsible public opinion is the guiding force in this, as in all systems of self-government," and that it is a "universal public attracted to the motion picture theatre by a vast variety of clean and artistic entertainment." As social mores continued to shift throughout the 1960s, pressure on the laws governing cinematic censorship relaxed, and the prohibitive restrictions of the past became recommendations about acceptable films for various ages of maturity. But the impact of the code was significant, artistically and socially, for it helped to determine representations of sexuality, the family, and familiar institutions, including the government itself. The influence of Hollywood was no small factor in determining public taste, and therefore the code had an impact on behavioral mores, for its officials regularly revised the content and thus the meaning of popular films, preparing them for national distribution by insuring that their messages were consistent and that adult life was best spent coupled in a marriage with children.

Although the production code and the careful restrictions it placed on film content in Hollywood was not dependent on government enforcement, it was strongest and most influential during the war years and immediately following the war, thereby paralleling HUAC's focus on preserving what were presumed to be shared cultural and political values. As these codes related specifically to the political content of films being produced in Hollywood at the time, the instigation of the hearings made evident that the studios, and particularly the producers who funded the films, were committed to cooperating with the government. In a Universal Newsreel from October 1947, Eric Johnson, president of the Motion Picture Association, made the following statement:

> We're accused of having Communists and Communist sympathiz-
> ers in our employ. Undoubtedly there are such persons in Holly-
> wood, as you will find elsewhere in America. But we neither shield
> nor defend them. We want them exposed. We're not responsible
> for the political or economic ideas of any individual. But we are
> responsible for what goes on the screen. We guard that with great
> care. If Communists have attempted to inject their propaganda
> into the motion picture, they have failed miserably. We will never
> permit them to succeed.[60]

Johnson's statement suggests the dangerous assumptions that the producers
and HUAC made: that there are Communists to be exposed, and that these
Communists are most likely guilty of trying to spread their ideals through
the movies. So far as the difficulty of proving these charges goes, what is
left to do instead is to uncover Communist affiliations of the past, during
a time when such affiliation was more likely and could be demonstrated by
records or by personal testimony about party meeting attendance.

The period that the investigators are asking the witnesses to recall is one
in which emotions about politics ran high, so it is not surprising that when
the very people who participated in theatrical programs such as *Waiting
for Lefty* went to Hollywood to make movies, both the industry itself and
eventually the government would become involved in making sure that
these artists would not have unchecked influence on cultural production.
Little wonder, too, that the performers who had come of age during the
Great Depression would appreciate the economic complexity of the situation many of them faced during the years of the HUAC investigations, when
family support and reputation (several of the witnesses mention having
children and wanting to protect them) was so dependent on their continued livelihood in Hollywood, which depended on staying off the blacklist.

Fittingly, if rather ironically, many of the most effective theatrical voices
likely to use their creative talents in Hollywood in order to promote Communism had initially spoken out against the hypocrisy of institutional governance while supported by the United States government. That they did so
during the 1930s in the form of documentary theater also makes Bentley's
1972 documentary trial play, in which some of them appear as characters,
a particularly poignant twist of history and art. For example, in 1935 the
Federal Theatre Project's Living Newspaper stage productions, modeled on
European developments in documentary theater, were staged for American
audiences, presenting citizens with information through dramatic enactments of current events. The project's director, Hallie Flanagan, employed

journalists as well as theater practitioners as the government-funded company of performers presented audiences with scenarios that depicted the problems of Depression-era America, supplying news accompanied by the emotional thrust of theater. The theatrical style that Bentley adopted for his interrogation of the HUAC period is the same one that had energized Kazan and others when they were first starting out as writers and actors.

The first Living Newspaper composed, *Ethiopia*, an account of Mussolini's invasion of that African country, went into rehearsal but never opened, for the federal government issued an order prohibiting the impersonation of heads of state onstage. Although productions of some of the company's subsequent texts went forward and garnered modest critical and popular success, within three years, the Federal Theatre Project would come under the investigation of the newly formed House Un-American Activities Committee that began, in 1938, to monitor American Communist activity. Congress cut the funding for the Federal Theatre Project the following year. The Living Newspaper Unit, in its brief life, served as a milestone in the subsequent development of contemporary American documentary theater and its dramatization of political events in their own words. It helped to define a generation of young Americans who saw themselves and their goals as integral to domestic peace and prosperity, instilling in some of them a zest for reform that would end with them speaking at a microphone not in a theater but in a hearing room.

As the speech from Burrows reveals, the conflict between a witness's past and his present may put into play a tension between truth and untruth, as Burrows puts it, or at the very least a certain ambiguity of identity that leads to character development, perhaps, or at least to character complexity. But there is another source of conflict, very clearly legal conflict, that emerges early in *Are You Now* and sets the emotional tone of the play. It is the tension between the committee's activities and its existence that becomes apparent during the brief appearance of Edward Dmytryk, which immediately follows the opening testimony of Sam G. Wood, the latter serving in an advisory capacity for the committee because of his membership in the Motion Picture Alliance for the Preservation of American Ideals. Wood testifies to alleged infiltration by Communist sympathizers into the Screen Directors Guild by John Cromwell and "the assistance of three or four others who "tried to steer us into the Red River." After naming the others, one of which is Dmytryk, Wood specifically targets "Communists" who "maintain schools in Hollywood for the purpose of training actors or writers," claiming that "any kid that goes in there with American ideals hasn't a chance in the world."[61] In this very brief scene a clear conflict is introduced: between "ideals" and subversive "training," between "preservation" and being without "a chance in the world." Wood's words suggest how the vaguest of accusations resulted in the committee's request for an interview, for Wood does no more than mention Dmytryk and his alleged role in the promotion of Communism in Hollywood before Dmytryk appears on the stage.

His testimony contrasts sharply with Wood's speeches: the latter's is cooperative while Dmytryk pointedly exemplifies the legal and emotional tensions raised when the hearings shifted from friendly to unfriendly witnesses. Rather than answer the committee's questions, Dmytryk challenges the right to ask them, relying on a common man's knowledge of rights, having "first learned about the Constitution in high school." He is persistent but not specific in his objections to the committee's questions, raising "a question of constitutional rights," and claiming to be answering "by saying I do not think you have the right to ask—," the line ending incompletely and thereby opening it up to production interpretation, for it may be performed as an inability to conclude or as an interruption from the Investigator that ends with the witness being excused. The inclusion of Dmytryk's appearance before the committee enables Bentley to introduce the emotional and traumatic effects of these hearings, for this character's few lines convey both a declaration of feeling and an accusation of division: "I feel these questions are designed to—," he tells the Investigator, to which the Chairman responds, "It is not up to you to 'feel' what the design is. It is up to you to be responsive to the questions." A moment later, the witness charges his questioner with trying to "bring about a split in the [screen] guilds at a time when we've just succeeded in getting unity between them."[62] Dmytryk's thwarted attempts to speak and to assert the rights of the individuals is also reflected in one of the two epigraphs that open Bentley's collection of three plays, the volume notably titled *Rallying Cries*, taken from the writings of William O. Douglas, the longest-serving justice on the Supreme Court (1939–1975): "The struggle is always between the individual and his sacred right to express himself on the one hand, and on the other hand the power structure that seeks conformity, suppression, and obedience. At some desperate moment in history, a great effort is made once more for the renewal of human dignity."[63] An advocate for First Amendment rights, Douglas was known for his support of liberal causes, particularly advocating for the rights of accused Communists; he became involved in the Rosenberg case when he granted them a short-lived stay of execution.[64] The epigraph invokes the individual's "sacred right" of expression as part of a "desperate moment in history" to restore freedom and self-fulfillment.

It also reminds readers of the struggles between a system of power that can be oppressive and the individual that attempts to fight that oppression, an individual that witness Larry Parks repeatedly calls "the underdog" when he takes the stage to testify in the play. While reminding us of the "power structure" and its efforts to achieve submission among its citizens, the epigraph solidifies Bentley's interest in the kind of desperate moment when "a great effort is made once more for the renewal of human dignity." The call for conformity is one heard loudly and powerfully during the paranoia of the postwar decade, and Sam Wood's testimony reminds us that there were many citizens ready to do what they considered patriotic duty. While such acts do not usually require betrayal of other citizens, particularly when that betrayal comes about without direct evidence that those citizens have acted against the best interests of the nation, the pitting of American against American that Bentley's play presents proves unsettling even when the viewer or reader knows the history and its context of fear. It may be more disturbing twenty years or even sixty years after the fact than it was when the hearings occurred, for the long-term effects on individuals' careers and families, not to mention the role the proceedings played in fostering cynicism about government, were more recognizable when Bentley's play appeared than they were at the time of the hearings.

After Dmytryk is excused, Ring Lardner testifies next, and, like his predecessor, he protests vehemently against the questioning, being "concerned, as an American, with the question of whether this committee has the right to ask me." This time when the challenge is cut off mid-sentence, the Chairman insists that the committee members "*have* got the right, and until you prove we *haven't* got the right, you have to answer that question" (emphasis in the original).[65] Once these three witnesses have appeared in quick succession, the action continues with the testimony of Parks, whose representation of a man ruined by the power structure connects him to the quotation from the Supreme Court's Justice Douglas that introduces Bentley's play collection.[66] During his extended interview, Parks objects to the questioning by challenging its judicial fairness: "I don't think this is a choice. I don't think this is sportsmanlike. I don't think this is American justice for an innocent mistake in judgment, if it was that, with the intention of making this country a better place to live."[67] Like the testimony of many other actors, writers, and producers, Parks's testimony reveals anguish, confusion, and naïveté. His use of the term "sportsmanlike" demonstrates his unawareness or his unwillingness to acknowledge that the committee in general cared little about upholding traditional standards of fair behavior. Gathering information was the goal;

honor seemed irrelevant when indicting differences in perspectives about notions of patriotism.

In *Inquest*, the legal system and the theatrical structure of the trial drama came together in a confluence of reason and emotion peculiar to the documentary style. In *Are You Now*, we can also identify the tension between the thought and the felt; here, it manifests itself primarily through the two different modes of language that came into contact with each other originally at the hearing, and which are then emphasized and the difference between them heightened in Bentley's text. Since the government representatives are already unspecified, they become not only more interchangeable and less individual, but their abstract personas tend toward the unemotional, stripped as they are of the personal traits that reveal humanity. In this trial, as in *Catonsville*, there is a disjunction between the information that the prosecutorial side demands and the identity-shaping narratives that the defendants/witnesses want to supply.

Larry Parks's testimony offers multiple examples of this disjunction, especially as he attempts to explain himself and his ideals as reasoning for why he participated in party activities for some years prior:

> MR. PARKS: No counsel, what I say is that the few people I knew are as loyal to this country as you.
> INVESTIGATOR: And if every witness were permitted to take that position, the extent of the investigation would be *limited* by the attitude of the witness, wouldn't it? [emphasis in the original]
> MR. PARKS: These people were like me, and the most you can accuse them of is a lack of judgment. *Pause.* I say none of this in apology for what I did, because a young man at twenty-five, if he's not full of idealism he's not worth his salt. If you make a mistake in judgment like this, I don't believe it is serious!
> INVESTIGATOR: Yes, but if every witness would be the final judge of when a thing was serious and when it was not, how could the Committee carry out its statutory duty?
> MR. PARKS: I'm asking that—
> INVESTIGATOR: And I'm asking that you see the other side.
> MR. PARKS: I do see the other side.[68]

In this exchange, Parks attempts to impress on the committee the values of those who joined, even briefly, with the Communist Party. He uses words such as "loyal" and "idealism," he attributes their "mistake" to a "lack of judgment," the better to see their decisions as minor character flaws rather than potential acts of treason.

Parks also emphasizes the similarities of the indicted ones to himself (a human being before them rather than a name) and to the government representatives, saying, "These people were like me," and going so far as to compare them to the investigator himself: speaking of the people he knew being "as loyal to this country as you." In his assessment of the situation, all citizens are part of a community that values idealism and patriotism; there are no real differences between the human beings who sit on opposite side of the table in the hearing room. When he mentions the harm to his career, the Investigator claims not to understand the "reference to the possible destruction of your career," to which Parks replies that he "has no career left." The issue of blame emerges from this exchange, with the reason for career destruction contested: The Chairman asks if Parks thinks that the "damage occurred when you became a member of an organization which advocates the overthrow of every constitutional form of government in the world" and Parks's own "act in affiliating with that organization." Parks's rather simple response does not account for the right or wrong of the organization but rather for his own change in attitude: "When I was younger, I felt a certain way about things" and "this organization appealed to me. I later found it would not fulfill my needs. At that time, I don't even believe this was a mistake in judgment." As Burrows will also do when he appears in the play, Parks distinguishes between a past self and a present self, but is more forgiving than the committee is of decisions made with good intentions, going so far as to conclude that now, as a father, he would rather have his sons "make the same mistake I did than not feel like making any mistake at all and be a cow in the pasture!"[69]

The testimony reveals the pain of being asked to speak against colleagues and friends, and we see in Parks the broken informant who is serving as one of the symbols of this period of the moral malaise. In this case the committee overpowers the reluctant but ultimately complicit witness. At one point Louis Mandel, attorney for Parks, suggests to the Investigator that, "in view of the feeling of the witness—I don't mean to rush you, but this whole thing being so distasteful—I wonder if we can proceed a little faster so he doesn't suffer so much."[70] After seeing the Los Angeles production of *Are You Now*, a wife of one of the Hollywood Ten remarked that although she had gone to the show thinking she would have no sympathy for Parks in performance, she was very moved by the character and his narrative. The play provides an opportunity to hear in the actual testimony Parks's concern for others and the anguish he experienced as a result of his broken convictions. Although court documents were used to construct this theater text, they become in Bentley's piece a signal of the humanity that sometimes stands in opposition to the institutions that order our society.

Parks demurs from naming individuals at first, saying that those who held meetings for the Communist Party, to which he had already admitted membership, were "small-type people" who have "done nothing wrong, ever."[71] If they have done nothing wrong, replies the Investigator, then naming them hurts no one. Parks switches tactics, allowing that the names he could name would be of little or no use to the committee. But he allows for something else at that moment; he allows for a belief that "to be asked to name names like this is not American justice. We as Americans have all been brought up to believe it's a bad thing to force a man to do this."[72] Forcing a man to report on the doings and the beliefs of other people is contrary to a national value of self-determination, for it is with the right we have to construct ourselves along a whole range of religious, social, racial or ethnic, and political positions or systems that comes the right to live according to those constructions without fear of control or coercion.

The committee, on the other hand, is concerned about the procedure to be followed and the responsibilities of their assignments: the investigator worries about the "extent of the investigation" being "limited" by witness attitudes. Thus do we see a distinction between examination and opinion, between fact and feeling. The "statutory" duties that the committee is determined to uphold conflict with another line of questioning, one that might lead to a better understanding of how people might follow their highest instincts for goodness even though reason tells them that change may be as problematic as complacency. Parks continues to insist to the committee, which questions him extensively and specifically about a whole list of suspected Communists, that being called for questioning is not "sportsmanlike," it is not "American justice for an innocent mistake in judgment, if it was that, with the intentions of making this country a better place to live."[73] He speaks for the right to resist the government but the Committee Members and the Chairman wear him down. He is, he says, a ruined man asking for mercy from the committee and from the public that judged him and may judge him again when watching an actor perform him in the play. Or, the feeling he conveys may in this context, with this audience divorced in time from the age of paranoia, earn him respect or at least absolution for what many colleagues judged harshly at the time.

At the other end of the spectrum, however, Bentley includes an example of testimony in which the witness adheres to judicial procedure in order to protect himself. While Larry Parks's testimony anchors the first half of the play, Paul Robeson's appearance before HUAC brings the play to its close and provides a counterpoint to the emotional tone of the earlier section. While Parks pleads for mercy or at least for sportsmanship, calling for an abstract brotherhood of American patriots and a swelling of emotion for the shared humanity, the character of Robeson takes a very different tactic, opting instead to demand his legal freedom. Peppered throughout his testimony in a kind of staccato repetition is his invocation of the Fifth Amendment, accompanied by challenges to the legal operations of the hearings: "Could I protest a reading of this?" he asks in response to the written testimony of one of his accusers, and "Why don't you have these people here to be cross-examined? Could I ask whether this is legal?"[74] Robeson's objections to the proceedings are not that they are inhumane, but that they violate due process.

Robeson's attorney asks that the "photographers take their pictures and then desist," but the star says it is not a problem, although as far as smiling goes, he points to the Investigator and says "I can't smile when I'm talking to *him*." He goes on to challenge the Chairman quite aggressively, asking for his name, his position, and even his family and corporate lineage, then ironically proclaiming him "a great patriot" who has authored "bills that are going to keep all kinds of decent people out of the country."[75] While Parks attempts to draw parallels between the loyalty of his colleagues and the loyalty of the investigating congressmen, Robeson's approach is to contest the standing and legality of the hearings and thereby establish himself and his choices as appropriate in a free society. His narrative particularly focuses on equality and race, and he readily admits that "when I am abroad I speak out against injustices against the Negro people of this land."[76] Comparing himself to Frederick Douglass and Harriet Tubman, he makes a claim for a universal justice to be recognized throughout the world, no matter the nation or its system of government, and he says that he stands in front of the committee "struggling for the rights of my people to be full citizens in this country."[77]

It may be, however, that his call for racial equality falls on the same deaf ears that Parks's pleas do, and that justice cannot be served as long as we continue to ignore the traditions of expression and egalitarianism that these two witnesses defend. While Parks looks backward to a more civilized set of values, Robeson looks ahead to the principles that will be championed in the civil rights movement to come. But in the world of the play, they both remain trapped in present circumstances that value accusation and blame, and that seek to accomplish their goals through rigid and impersonal interrogation. Robeson ends the play by saying that nothing "could be built more on slavery than *this* society," and that the hearing the

Chairman adjourns in lieu of allowing Robeson to read his speech should be adjourned "forever."[78]

Bentley's documentary trial play was originally produced just as the political darkness of Watergate descended on the nation, and it may be no accident that the show found its largest audience in a Los Angeles production of 1975, a particularly low point for American confidence in government and official morality. Of the Los Angeles production and its timing, Gale Sondergaard, an actress who had been blacklisted by the committee, remarked, "I think Watergate has stimulated a great deal of curiosity about other scandals in recent American history."[79] While this later production surely benefited from its Los Angeles residency, it also played to a house made more cynical by the Watergate hearings and Nixon's resignation. In this and in other dramatic renderings of the HUAC period, audiences continue to be shocked and horrified by the blatant disregard of individual rights that was permitted under the guise of national security; on the other hand, this documentary play reminds us that disregard for personal safeguards continues to be a contested judicial issue in our own age, as time has proven that the erosion of freedom is possible whenever the appropriate political climate conditions prevail. We know from the early-twenty-first-century perspective that such hearings and other similar investigations will not be adjourned forever in the immediate future. The American government continues to operate under a system of law as a way to achieve justice. But it also continues to set the law and the constitution aside when it claims such exceptions are warranted by danger to the national agenda, and the documentary trial play, formulated for American circumstances and American culture in the 1970s, has endured as a theatrical form most apt to convey such conflicts to a public without answers or any clear solution but nonetheless still in need of witnessing the questions. And the question of identity—individual, social, legal, political: "are you now or have you ever been?"—remains a most potent one.

3

Ideological Confrontation: *Execution of Justice* and *Greensboro (A Requiem)*

As the 1970s turned into the 1980s, the war in Vietnam was replaced by the culture wars at home. The violent clashes in the fights for civil rights for minority groups, women, and gay men had ended, but the tensions that arose during the development of an increasingly heterogeneous public sphere continued to reflect the often polarized nature of American identity politics. An executive order for affirmative action had been signed into law by President John Kennedy in 1961, promoted by Lyndon Johnson in the mid-1960s, and extended in scope and offered to additional underrepresented groups throughout the next two decades. Successful challenges to social and political hegemony resulted in diversity across college campuses, in media representations, and in politics, as women and people of color entered the university and the workforce in record numbers. The Summer of Love had brought thousands of people to the golden gates of San Francisco, and many of them had become permanent residents, changing the city's demographics as they partnered with natives or fellow urban immigrants, bought homes, and joined neighborhoods and neighborhood associations. Cities and city politics long dominated by well-established ethnic groups of European origin were transformed by the influx of new populations, be they Cambodians escaping the chaos of Southeast Asia, or native youth from suburbs or from the many small industrial centers across the country that had begun to show signs of economic rusting. Voting blocs shifted as San Francisco's Castro neighborhood became an enclave of radical gay life, and as the population's diversity ratios rose and elections became increasingly representative of a multiplicity of values and needs.

Artworks such as the Untitled Film Stills by contemporary photographer Cindy Sherman, a project begun in 1977 that extended into the next decade, challenged normative notions of gender and sexuality in their masquerade portraits of female types. Performance art of all types likewise reflected the cultural shifts that had occurred or were occurring, bringing into focus a wide-scale preoccupation with the construction of identity and recording the multitude of alternative voices raised in declarations or explanations of contemporary American life. Two documentary trial plays that explore such cultural developments within the context of law were brought to the stage by playwright Emily Mann, and her collaborative dramaturgical style, a philosophy she brought to script and production development, contributed significantly to the documentary trial play's maturation process. The theater company's role was already crucial in this genre's development, for the style may not have survived and thrived without the faith and skill of actors, directors, and production crews who brought their creative talents to it. But Mann's work in the documentary theater helped to demonstrate that reliance on and collaboration with actors and other members of a production team could uniquely shape the documentary theater action and spectacle.

What Dan Isaac had, in 1970, called the "Theatre of Fact," a term that recalls the staccato and static, often emotionless Living Newspaper style of the documentary theater, becomes for Mann a "theater of testimony," a change in nomenclature that signals the development in the genre that underscores its ties to trauma and trauma resolution and suggests that these texts often concern themselves explicitly with the psychological ramifications of conflicts and their legal aftermaths. Furthermore, her trial plays, *Execution of Justice* (*Execution*) (1984) and *Greensboro (A Requiem)* (*Greensboro*) (1996), deal with historical events that were overlooked nationally or that never took hold of the cultural consciousness to the extent that other legal contests had. In the case of the 1979 Greensboro Massacre, for instance, the event that inspired the later play, media dissemination of the details were limited or ignored when another newsworthy event, the Iranian hostage crisis, began, the day after the killings in Greensboro, gripping the nation and the world and dominating public attention for months to come.

Despite a lack of widespread or sustained news exposure or long-term historical investigation, however, the conflicts that Mann dramatizes are significant in the understanding of challenges posed to the shifts in national consciousness about race and gender, her plays serving as a reminder to her audiences that despite the entrance of members of previously restricted groups into politics and the workplace, equality was not and, arguably, still is not, guaranteed to all. While career and personal opportunities and freedoms for women and members of minority groups had multiplied in each decade of the contemporary period, having a lasting and positive impact on American life and American institutions, forward strides were just as often halted by resistance and violence. Mann's plays offer two views of the hostilities that continued to simmer and, with some regularity, erupt, as the promise of a better, more equitable life for everyone remained elusive in reality if not in concept. As documentary trial plays dramatize these hostilities, they represent the ways that the legal system is consistently confronted with challenges about how to address the conflicts that result when strides in social and political change come up against more conservative and entrenched values of stratified race, class, and gender systems. Mann's documentary plays examine historical events that involve an outbreak of violence against members of one or more minority groups, and in charting the developments in this theater through the contemporary period, it becomes evident that the cultural and social advances of the 1960s and early 1970s had contributed to the development of alternative narratives of American identity, even if the plays themselves go on to demonstrate a parallel measure of continual cultural resistance to the idea and the implementation of equal rights.

In chapters 1 and 2, we saw priests, Yippies, Jews, and former Communists in the defendant groups: fringe populations, relatively speaking, perhaps, but, with the exception of Bobby Seale in *Chicago Conspiracy* and Paul Robeson in *Are You Now*, these individuals prosecuted were white men and women of the middle class. If these defendants saw themselves or were seen as outsiders to the dominant culture, they had, with the possible exception of the Rosenbergs, chosen to consciously set aside the safety they had enjoyed by privilege of birth, by committing to strident religious principles, by self-identifying with revolutionary or radical factions, by joining or at least sympathizing with the Communist Party. To some extent, then, the legal troubles in which they became embroiled were brought on by their ideologies rather than by their identities. Despite their protests against government policies and the disenfranchisement they experienced as a result of these protests, the prosecuted figures that appear in the American documentary trial plays up to this point had chosen to separate themselves from the mainstream and thus risk exposure to legal problems that may come with beliefs or actions that are considered subversive. That they made these choices based on moral grounds and with sincere beliefs that these choices would serve a greater good seems most likely, and that they suffered injustice because of their ideals is evident in all the plays analyzed in previous chapters. But what Mann's works demonstrate, in subject matter and staging methods, is that we can expect to find (and we do) that the documentary theater of the 1980s and 1990s, and, more specifically, its documentary trial plays, increasingly include defendants or victims who are either targeted by the legal system or unprotected by it because of biological realities rather than ideological beliefs.

While the two previous chapters included perspectives on judges or government investigators representing the state's position as one in opposition to that of the defendants called into courtroom or hearing room, Mann's plays construct the conflict as one centered in the populous by focusing on "agitator" types drawn from the citizenry, characters either immersed in the struggle for civil rights or in the fight for class equality or equally committed to blocking such changes. The struggle eventually enters the courtroom, but the agitator figure or figures, situated at the intersection of conflicting attitudes or priorities, become embroiled in legal matters as a victim or perpetrator of the violence that erupts in the community. The agitators, like the judge and the investigator, play an important role in the way documentary trial plays order the legal experience theatrically, and as Mann's performance texts map the courtroom landscape, they provide space and structure for a variety of characters that challenge a system ill-equipped to deal with the diverse and often discordant voices of the community in conflict. The agitator may represent a source of friction that drives or orders the action, and this figure may exist in multiple forms in a single play and may work to advance either the prosecution or the defense. These characters thus explore the ambiguities and complications of our national beliefs and aspirations, especially as the latter are supported or thwarted by the rule of law.

Execution and *Greensboro* both feature ideologically based crimes and punishments; they expose the problematic nature of justice and the extent to which documentary theater recreates the trauma of the events and of the trials. *Execution* stages the 1979 trial of Dan White, the former San Francisco police-officer-turned-politician who was charged with murdering

Mayor George Moscone and city supervisor Harvey Milk. *Greensboro* recalls the deadly clash, in North Carolina in 1979, between Ku Klux Klan members and union demonstrators as well as the trials that followed. These texts forefront the contentious nature of the "testimony" that Mann places at the center of her dramaturgy, and Felman's explorations of the connection between testimony and trials illustrates in theory what Mann does in practice. As Felman argues, "in the courtroom situation—testimony is provided, and is called for, when the facts on which justice must pronounce its verdict are not clear, when historical accuracy is in doubt, and when both the truth and its supporting elements of evidence are called into question."[1] The judiciary proceedings that form the theatrical core of both of Mann's plays come about because of the kinds of contests that Felman outlines, but the trials that follow the events fuel rather than snuff out the differences that first created the need for the legal proceeding. The performance texts that Mann constructs from the documentation thus become a means by which some additional resolution might be achieved.

Felman goes on to explain that the "legal model of the trial dramatizes, in this way, a contained, and culturally channeled, institutionalized, *crisis of truth*. The trial both derives from and proceeds by a crisis of evidence, which the verdict must resolve" (emphasis in original).[2] Indeed, our reception of and perceptions about these trials are "culturally channeled" and "institutionalized," originating as they do in crisis. Felman calls on the judicial verdict to resolve the "crisis of evidence," but *Execution* and *Greensboro*, each in its own way, demonstrate the impossibility of complete closure while arguably producing a space for partial resolution; this process will involve community engagement, for the reconciliation, as we shall see, cannot occur without the participation of all. Ryan M. Claycomb provides a useful outline of four ways to understand the nature of community in documentary theater, calling the latter "staged oral histories."[3] He separates out and identifies various community groups endemic to the documentary theater text, a useful delineation for considering the trial structure and its impact in Mann's plays: the community of all voices; smaller communities formed by shared ideology or perspective; the community of actors who represent those first two communities; and finally, "the community of audience members and actors who together experience an individual theatrical event."[4] As we consider the impact these plays have on their communities, then, we come to recognize the fractures that these various communities experience as a result of the events dramatized in these works; the agitator figure also becomes central in manifesting the chasms within and between the communities represented.

In 1978–79, a local political struggle rocked San Francisco and challenged the advances made in civil rights battles fought across the nation. It led to a murder trial that became notorious for its use of what would thereafter be called "the Twinkie defense," and whose outcome prompted a change in California's penal code. Tensions had risen throughout the decade as gay and other minority activists began to impact voting results and wrench local power from the Irish-Catholic stronghold that had prevailed in the Bay Area for decades. The 1975 election of Mayor George Moscone marked and directed this changing political climate in San Francisco, for he represented liberal attitudes and policies; two years later, Harvey Milk, a community leader from the Castro Street gay community, won a seat on the city's board of supervisors, becoming the first openly gay elected official in the United States. Elected that same year to the board, Dan White, a youthful representative of the old guard and a former police officer, pledged to clean up the city and restore its working-class values and community. Just one year after his election, Dan White resigned due to family and personal economic pressures but quickly experienced a change of heart and asked to be reinstated. Moscone initially promised to reappoint White but then reversed that decision and appointed someone else to take on the representation of the Third District in White's stead. Upon hearing the news, and having become convinced that Supervisor Milk had influenced the mayor's decision, White took a loaded gun to city hall and shot Moscone and Milk, killing them both. He turned himself into the police almost immediately following the shootings and quickly confessed to having committed the crimes.

In May 1979, White's trial on two counts of first-degree murder began; although the defense team acknowledged that he had shot and killed the two city officials, it argued that he suffered from manic depression and had therefore acted out of "diminished capacity." Although it became known as the "Twinkie defense," the ingestion of junk food was secondary to the argument, a symptom of mental illness that, according to the defense position, prompted an otherwise upstanding citizen to kill two people in cold blood.[5] Argued before a conservative and mostly female jury, the psychiatrically based explanation led the jury to return a verdict reduced from first-degree murder to two counts of voluntary manslaughter. White spent five years in Soledad prison before being released; eighteen months later, he committed suicide in a gas chamber of sorts, dying by carbon monoxide poisoning in his ex-wife's garage in San Francisco. Beyond the tragedy of three senseless deaths and the ruined lives that accompanied them, the murders and the trial that followed polarized San Francisco citizens and called into question the strides the city had made toward creating a diverse and tolerant urban community. Harvey Milk's murder had a significant negative impact on the gay population, locally and nationally, and the outward show of grief in San Francisco began on the night of the shootings with a candlelight procession that flowed down Market Street from the Castro District to city hall. Six months later, however, grief turned to anger: on the night the verdict was handed down, protestors stormed city hall, breaking windows and burning police cars. Later that night, police descended on Castro Street and attacked homosexuals in the streets and in the bars.

Just two years before she created *Execution*, which dramatizes Dan White's trial, Emily Mann's interest in staging trauma was evident in her 1980 play *Still Life*, a meditation on violence in America that focuses on three people she met in 1978, one of them a Vietnam veteran. In her note for the earlier play, Mann explains that she uses the documentary form "to ensure that the reality of the people and events described could not be denied. . . . One cannot deny that these are actual people describing actual events as they saw and understood them." She goes on to say that "a specialist of the brain and its perceptions said to me after seeing *Still Life* that the play is constructed as a traumatic memory. Each character struggles with his traumatic memory of events and the play as a whole is my traumatic memory of their accounts."[6] As Naomi Siegel writes in a review of Mann's 2007 play *Mrs. Packard*, "Ms. Mann has tried consistently to give a 'voice to the voiceless.'" Siegel continues: "*Greensboro (A Requiem)* dealt with the civil rights movement; *Execution of Justice*, with gay rights; *Still Life*, the legacy of Vietnam; and *Annulla, an Autobiography*, the Holocaust."[7] John Istel writes in *American Theatre* that Mann's performance texts "form a theatrical treatise that details how human beings in the twentieth century have survived the most emotion-numbing, psyche-scarring acts of violence."[8] Attilio Favorini concurs with this viewpoint: "So engaged is she with historical course and documentary voice, with managing the tangle of archive and testament, that taken together her plays form a metanarrative of history and memory, based in key traumatic themes of the twentieth century."[9]

In Mann's corpus, then, we have a theatrical manifestation of the central place that testimony and witnessing have assumed in contemporary society; in *Execution* and *Greensboro*, more particularly, much of the testimony is from one side or the other of a legal conflict, and the witnesses, traumatized by the violence in the community, bring their agitation with them into the courtroom. The focus then becomes a consideration of whether and how the trial can serve as an adequate destination for the traumas that the two plays re-create. With *Execution* and *Greensboro*, Mann has composed documentary trial plays that intertwine personal testimony and legal testimony but that often show them at odds with each other as they work separately to convey truth. Thus does what Felman calls a "crisis of truth" lie at the heart of Mann's theatrical project, and the playwright's identification of that work as a "theater of testimony" signifies the link this style of performance has forged to historical traumas that have marked the contemporary period. Mann's trial plays provide significant evidence of the strength and significance of this connection, while also offering audiences the opportunity to explore further the emotional and rational interplay that emerges from this blending of history and art.

Execution was commissioned in 1982 by the Eureka Theatre in San Francisco, which had previously produced *Still Life*, and it was developed over eighteen months and subsequently premiered at the Humana Festival of New American Plays in Louisville, Kentucky, in 1984, where it was a co-winner of the Great American Play Contest. Its Broadway run premiered on March 13, 1986, with the playwright directing the production, and the show was nominated for the Drama Critics Circle Award as best new play of the 1985–86 season.[10] Although its long and diverse production history has subsequently attested to its widespread appeal, the play's genesis was local, and Favorini reports of Mann telling him in a telephone interview that she agreed to the Eureka commission provided that the new work would be specific to the San Francisco community.[11] Mann's stipulation is significant to a consideration of the play as a reenactment of events, for it underscores the fact that the trial itself had taken place mere miles from the site of its stage recreation.

During the months of play development, Mann conducted her interviews with those involved in or witness to the events, and, as she explained, "when a huge public event happens, and it's traumatic, it elicits a 'huge spectrum of response'"; she has said in an interview that she is "interested in that collision of different points of view," for by getting lots of viewpoints, "you might get close to what's really going on."[12] She goes on to say that "all [her] plays are dealing with trauma of some kind, or some kind of traumatic event" and therefore deal with the question "How does the human being, and how does this society, deal with traumatic events?"[13] Although several years had passed since the murders and the trial, *Execution* makes it clear that some Bay Area citizens had not yet come to terms with events that had torn the city apart and thus exemplifies the documentary theater's commitment to confronting recent history at its source. The goal of this kind of dramatic investigation stands to benefit both local and national audiences, providing healing and increased understanding about public trauma, its causes and effects. In this case, Mann's choice to dramatize a controversial trial demonstrates the abiding link between theatrical performance and the law and, more specifically, underscores the way that the documentary trial play interrogates the rule of law and its effects and aftershocks through theater's representational strategies.

Reviewers of the early productions of the show made note of this connection: William Kleb's extended review of the Louisville production that appeared in *Theater* is titled "You, the Jury," and he argues that the script and the set suggest that "not only is the audience meant to share the playwright's traumatic response [to the interviews she conducts], it actually seems to participate in the testimonial—as confessor, psychiatrist, juror, special friend."[14] Mel Gussow begins his assessment of the Broadway production (he had reviewed two earlier versions of the play) by using legal imagery to describe the work's purpose, saying that "the case of the People vs. Dan White is on trial in the court of theater and is found guilty of a miscarriage of justice."[15] David Richards draws a distinction between this play and other courtroom dramas, for although the latter may suggest that surprises are in store, it is common for such narratives to make "order out of disorder" and resolve the case. Mann's play, however, ends with questions, Richards says, not about White's guilt, but "about a society that can produce such profound fissures."[16] Richards' focus on the "questions" and "fissures" not only underscores a significant difference between *Execution* and more traditional courtroom dramas, it points to one of the key tensions between the real trial and the one staged in *Execution*, and more broadly the one that becomes apparent between trials and their documentary representations in the theater.

The documentary nature of this play is conveyed in its minimal staging and its use of actual footage of the events surrounding the trial and its aftermath, and the author's note in the published text makes clear that all dialogue in the play has been gathered from "trial transcript, interview, reportage, the street."[17] The first of two acts, "Murder," opens on a bare stage with white screens overhead, and the first things the audience sees are projected images of San Francisco, "*punctuated with images of Milk and Moscone.*" The stage is then populated with the acting company representing a "*maelstrom of urban activity.*"[18] On the screen overhead, footage of then city supervisor Dianne Feinstein announces news of the shootings and, in a strategy that establishes a link between the screen action and the narrative that is woven throughout the performance text, the crowd onstage produces "gasps and cries" before freezing in shock upon hearing that Supervisor Dan White is the suspect.[19] Other documentary footage and still images appear on the overhead screens throughout the play: photographs of the victims, documentary footage of the candlelight procession on the night of the murder, images of city hall stormed and police in riot gear after the verdict is announced. After a brief sequence in which Dan White confesses to his wife that "I shot the Mayor and Harvey," followed by Mary Ann White's collapse at the news, an actor playing the court clerk announces the trial to come: "This is the matter of the People versus Daniel James White."[20] These first few intense moments of the play thus contain many of its most significant elements: clear evidence of the work's documentary nature, its high emotional pitch, and the overriding presence of the legal proceeding that begins just before the lights change. These elements merge here, as they do throughout this performance text and in other documentary trial plays, to create a unique experience of history, law, and theater.

This introductory section is immediately followed by a contrasting pair of representative figures who share the stage as they recite monologues that are nonetheless intertwined: the stage directions state that the two figures "are very aware of each other but never make eye contact."[21] The first to enter and speak is the character known only as "Cop," who immediately refers to what he's wearing, and does so defensively: "Yeah, I'm wearing a 'Free Dan White' T-shirt, / You haven't seen what I've seen— / my nose shoved into what I think stinks. / Against everything I believe in."[22] As Sister Boom Boom enters, described as *"nun drag; white face; heavily made up; spike heels,"* the Cop continues his speech: "Sometimes I sit in church and I think of those / disgusting drag queens dressed up as nuns and / I'm a cop / and I'm thinkin', / there's gotta be a law, you know."[23] For her part, Sister Boom Boom's speeches indict Dan White, his attitudes, and the Twinkie defense, mockingly imploring her "gay brothers and sisters" to break "this cycle of brutality and murder" with "love, understanding and forgiveness" even as she laughs about the possibility that "some angry faggot or dyke who is not understanding, loving and forgiving" will get Dan White.[24] Thus does the scene present the city's polarization over the murder trial, with a particular focus on the difference of opinion about the growing gay community in San Francisco. In the Broadway production, Wesley Snipes played the nun in drag and whiteface, thus adding race to the equation.

Both characters represent real people, the Cop a composite of a group of police officers who supported Dan White's release, and Sister Boom Boom a drag queen and local media figure who delivered this speech several times during the trial and its aftermath. But Kleb, writing of the Louisville production, rightly points to these figures' theatricality, claiming that the pair "could be two malignant Euripidean gods, come out for a moment to set the scene."[25] Kleb notes that the impact of the scene, like the previous one, "is primarily emotional, not expository; facts are given, but objectivity seems out of the question."[26] And he goes on to argue that while the Cop may seem "ugly and threatening, he also seems more personal, more real," while the "drag nun, on the other hand, is nothing but a grotesque mask."[27] Thus do we also recognize immediately the antagonism between the two very polarized sides of this legal conflict, and we see these sides represented by two very different agitators: the drag queen emerges from society's margins to confront her audience, costumed so as to accentuate the fluidity of gender and race, representative of what has been or is still considered outside the norms of dress and behavior.

The Cop, whose character suggests a doubling as well as a championing of Dan White, condones and even flaunts his hero's actions by concluding, "Dan White showed you could fight City Hall," and reminding us that the formulaic legal proclamation of the Clerk, "this is the matter of the People versus Daniel James White," becomes something more when transplanted into the performance text: it becomes the play's central conflict as well as the suggestion that yet another agitator figure in the play will be the defendant.[28] The Clerk's line exemplifies the way that legal language becomes literary or dramatic language when it is transferred from one rhetorical situation to another, and yet, as James Boyd White argues, legal texts and literary texts (he speaks particularly of poetry) share at least one function: "to give special and related meanings to sets of words that carry with them in ordinary usage a wide and uncertain range of possible significances and to make these new meanings available to others."[29]

Mann's depiction of the two sides of the Dan White debate provides audiences with a social and political context in which to view the extremity of the ideological polarization that tore the city apart. It is thus a fitting prelude to the trial that follows, and it foreshadows Mann's arrangement of the trial materials, which will highlight the opposition of the viewpoints even as it complicates the "execution of justice." As Mann said in an interview for the *New York Times*, the title of the play "means two things: justice was done, and justice was murdered."[30] Nowhere is this paradox of justice seen more clearly than in the addition of a group of seven that Mann calls the "Chorus of Uncalled Witnesses." While here, as with the Cop, Mann uses composite characters, all the words they speak were actually spoken by real people and thus do these representations remain, at their core, faithful to the "theater of testimony."

Several of these witnesses are specifically named, most significantly Jim Denman, White's jailer immediately following the shooting, and Joseph Freitas Jr., the former district attorney whose career was ruined by the polarizing events of the murders and their aftermath. More important, however, as "uncalled witnesses" they stand apart from even as they participate in Mann's version of the trial, underscoring their absence from the actual legal proceedings as well as their right to be included in it. Their perspectives further animate and complicate the action. Indeed, they are not merely extraneous commentators; their testimony is threaded throughout the trial scenes and therefore adds additional voices and perspectives to the trial as it is dramatized here. As Favorini argues: "the play's intent is not to assign guilt, not to indict society; instead, it attempts to restore to events a fullness that the trial attenuated."[31] With this Chorus, then, Mann adds "fullness," an increase of information and complexity in the actual case, neither of which are needed to determine whether or not White committed the crimes, but which are necessary for the "execution of justice" and for the resolution of trauma.

Moreover, the uncalled witnesses fill in important details of the narrative and help to amplify the prosecution's case, which is muted in comparison with the strident and compelling defense that takes up much of the performance text. The difference between them is striking given all that we hear that was not included in the trial transcript, and it helps to confirm the extent to which the real trial, as well as the one performed onstage, is an interplay of narratives, collaborating or conflicting. In his comparison of the legal opinion and the poem, James Boyd White suggests that the "great merit of reading texts as compositions, made by composers, is that we affirm that we are composers too," thus affirming "our essential equality with the composer whose work we are reading." Furthermore, he says, a consequence of that affirmation is another one, but one that brings with it a question: "We affirm our equality with all composers—that is with all people—and their equality with us. What, then, of the voices we do not hear in the texts that we read, what of the composers to whom we do not attend?"[32] The dramatization of the murder trial that becomes *Execution*, particularly in its inclusion of extralegal narratives, calls attention to the differences between the transcript and the play script: in the way that the legal narrative is reconstructed as a theatrical narrative, and in the way that the reconstruction allows makes space for alternate narratives.

The absence of the prosecution's case is also reflected in the titles of the text's two acts, called, respectively, "Murder" and "In Defense of Murder." While the first act includes material from the prosecution's presentation of its case, it begins with a spot set up as a television report of an actor playing Joanna Lu, a journalist who covered the case, commenting on what appeared to be the prosecution's cavalier approach to jury selection:

"Assistant D.A. Tom Norman exercised only three out of twenty-seven possible preemptory challenges. By all accounts, there are no blacks, no gays and no Asians. One juror is an ex-policeman, another the wife of the county jailer, four of the seven women are old enough to be Dan White's mother. Most of the jurors are working- and middle-class Catholics."[33] It would appear, then, that not only is the prosecution cast as disinterested, but this bit of media news from the archive suggests that the district attorney's lack of commitment produced or at least failed to prevent the composition of a jury inclined to relate to White rather than to the victims. As Lu goes on to conclude, "Dan White will certainly be judged by a jury of his peers"; many people in San Francisco noticed that while Dan White's peers were surely present on the jury and on the witness stand, Moscone's and Milk's were not.

Mann's performance text and its uncalled witnesses do allow, however, for audiences to have a more complete narrative and additional perspectives, even as the inclusion of Lu's report reminds audience members that these witnesses were not able, during the trial, to help sway jury members who might not have been disposed to empathy for the victims. Mel Gussow calls the theatrical chorus "an artful insertion," but the Chorus is also instrumental in providing some evidence that a different ending to the legal proceeding might have been reached if these witnesses had been "called." As an "artful insertion," the Chorus gives power to the dramatic representation of the original event, highlighting the ways that fictional and theatrical forms have certain capacities and a range that legal or other kinds of institutional documentation may not. The playwright is not constrained in the ways that trial participants, even those who write their own "scripts," are constrained by procedure and law. Moments not included or perhaps even not allowed in the real trial or in any trial, as well as opportunities for a larger multitude of voices to be heard, can be accommodated on stage; in the documentary trial play, they can be accommodated as part of a re-creation of a courtroom setting and thereby add to the unofficial record of that fictionalized trial. The volume and range of testimony are multiplied. Although the revision and expansion cannot change the events that led to two dead politicians and the suicide of their murderer several years later, the additional testimony provides a more complex and complete foundation for public opinion and for expanded historical documentation of events, more information on which that same public might base its views and perhaps come to alter its beliefs about the law.

The increased diversification of perspectives also leads to an increased level of contentiousness, apparent when the witnesses' words are inserted into the actual testimony, as the former lines overlap, clash with, and contradict the speeches imported from the legal proceeding. This conflict of words transforms what might otherwise be fact-filled judicial reporting into emotionally heightened, confrontational, and contradictory theatrical and legal moments that express the traumatic elements of this trial and what it revealed about the community of San Francisco and about other contemporary urban American communities. The advances in civil rights that had enabled Harvey Milk to take a government office meant more regular contact for people from different cultural or racial groups, particularly in the workplace. Indeed, it was a workplace interaction, in this case, between a homosexual man and a heterosexual man that had contributed to the murder, for White believed that Milk's presence on the board of supervisors meant that he had undue influence on Moscone and had convinced the mayor not to reappoint White.

A representative example of the linguistic opposition between the legal and the extralegal testimony occurs in act 1, when uncalled witness Gwenn Craig, described in the cast list as a "black lesbian leader," speaks in counterpoint to Richard Pabich, legislative assistant to Harvey Milk. These two figures are not necessarily ideologically opposed, and yet their dialogue juxtaposes a court narrative and an extralegal narrative. Pabich describes White's presence at city hall on the day of the murder, acknowledging the political awkwardness of the situation surrounding White's resignation and Moscone's decision not to reappoint him; Pabich tells the court he was aware "that Harvey was taking the position to the mayor that Mr. White shouldn't be appointed" and that he and Harvey had talked earlier that day about the decision being a significant one. The difference in cast naming in the script is notable as part of the shift from judicial testimony to personal statement, for Milk's assistant is referred to with his last name, while Craig is listed as "Gwenn." Gwenn's lines are focused on the emotional and psychological effects of the murders, not only on the principal people involved but on everyone in the community. She claims that the "assassinations of our friends Harvey and George were a crime against us all . . . I don't mean only gay people . . . I mean all people who are getting less than they deserve." She follows directly on Pabich's assessment that the day in question would, as he and Milk had decided in advance, be a "significant day," important from a political perspective.

Her speech becomes more personal with her confession that she "went into a depression that lasted about a year" after Milk was killed, and "thought about suicide."[34] The testimony of Gwenn and other uncalled witnesses underscores the need to acknowledge the trauma suffered by the citizens of San Francisco as well as the reality that the legal trial did not resolve the issues the assassinations raised, even if only because the ramifications of the deaths had not been thoroughly explored and resolved. Mann's play, by its existence and through its content and style, reveals a city that was dissatisfied by the justice system responsible for settling the case and healing the public wound of the assassinations. The riot that occurred the night the verdict was handed down confirms the unhealed traumatic wound, for the murders as well as the trial that followed exacerbated the social and political divisions already present in the city. The population had grown and evolved in the decades leading up to these events, and the increased diversity meant that a wider range of voices could be heard as part of the political process, but a conflict had been simmering. As Gwenn reminds the audience: "In order to understand the riots, I think you have to understand that the Dan White verdict did not occur in a vacuum."[35] The possibility of community trauma increased rather than decreased as a larger segment of the population felt investment and agency in the city's institutions; when the system failed to protect the mayor and Milk and failed to punish the killer, the violence that White had brought to city hall one morning sparked other acts of violent response by those who, as Gwenn suggests, had felt that a crime had also been committed against them.

The uncalled witnesses enlarge the audience's recognition and under-standing of pain that remains unmanaged or unmitigated, for these narra-tives were gathered several years after the trial by Mann as she prepared the *Execution* script. The insertion of this testimony into the trial's dramatiza-tion extends the communal conflict into the present of the production and lays bare the pain still simmering at the city's psychic core. Mann herself used the language of trauma when describing the events on the eve of the Broadway opening of the play, claiming that when she began her work on *Execution*, she realized that "people who had nothing to do with Harvey Milk, personally or politically or in terms of their sexual preference, were still walking around shell-shocked from the sequence of events. . . . The wounds were really deep, and they hadn't healed."[36] The compulsion to "redo" the trial, combined with the impossibility of doing so, led to the creation of the performance text; its purpose was to achieve some measure of resolution by adhering to the legal language and the legal structure in its composition, but by positioning itself outside the strictures that had hampered the actual case, it has a unique capacity for healing the deep wounds created by the murder and exacerbated by the trial. It holds the accused accountable in the public space of the theater, and it helps to ease the lingering ache of inequity that some citizens had been coping with since the events had taken place.

While the creation and production of *Execution* did not and could not completely close and heal the wounds that Mann became aware of as she researched and wrote the play, her choice of artistic form, the documentary trial play, proved a fitting vehicle for confronting these traumatic events. When speaking of the trials and the art that have attempted to heal the chasmal wound left by the Holocaust, Felman notes that "literature and art do not suffice. And yet, a trial equally is insufficient." But then she goes on to argue that consolidation and cooperation might allow these two forms of narrative to succeed together, for "only the encounter between law and art can adequately testify to the abyssal meaning of the trauma."[37] By creating a theatrical experience from the trial narrative, Mann facilitated the audience's encounter between law and art by enabling her audiences to experience a tentative and temporary resolution to the pain that homophobia, racism, and violence create and cultivate in our culture. Mann's commitment to this kind of theatrical work is not surprising given that some members of her family on her mother's side died in the Holocaust, a family history that offered her early and frequent exposure to unresolved trauma and that led her to explore the links between artistic language and legal language and the ways they might work together toward personal and cultural reconciliation.

Another strand of traumatic narrative included in the performance text is noteworthy for the way that it complicates audience perspective on the events of November 1978 and raises the emotional temperature of the play. It is an enactment of the tape-recorded confession that White made to Frank Falzon, chief homicide inspector, soon after White turned himself over to authorities. Falzon, friends with White from the defendant's time working as a police officer, offers the suspect the opportunity to give his confession "in a narrative form as to what happened that day if you can lead up to the events of the shooting and then backtrack as to why these events took place."[38] We have been acculturated to align ourselves with the police in representations of the law and order system; the officer's incredulousness as he hears of the defendant's actions, and the sympathy he expresses for White, dramatize emotional reactions that audience members might be influenced by when they witness this interview.[39] Indeed, the personal connection between White and Falzon fosters a personal connection between White and the viewer/jurist. Kleb reports on his viewing of the confession segment, maintaining that it "deepens audience involvement with White"; furthermore, Kleb suggests that the scene's staging "turns his confession into one of the most theatrically compelling and emotionally involving scenes in Mann's play."[40] This emotionality is enhanced as a close-up image of the actor playing White is projected on a screen above the stage, thus making in real time yet another kind of "documentary" move, and one that has both legal and artistic components; we are aware, of course, that in this case the video is not from history but from imagination, even though it draws from the original in language and spatial organization.

In an essay detailing her observations of Mann in rehearsal when the playwright directed *Execution* for the Broadway production, Susan Letzler Cole focuses on the emotional impact of this scene for the actors, the director, and the observer. Calling it "the most intense scene in the play," Cole describes watching the actor playing White, John Spencer, cry during rehearsal "so profusely that the actor playing the police inspector leaves the scene and returns momentarily with Kleenex" to wipe Spencer's face. Although Spencer struggles for control as he rehearses the sequence, Cole remarks that "crying is the right physicalization for him; when he turns off the crying he turns off an essential subcurrent of which it is a manifestation."[41] And the published script calls for an outpouring of tears when the defendant finishes his confession: "*Lights change. White sobbing. Mary Ann White sobbing, jurors sobbing. Falzon moved.*" That this weepy tableau occurs just before intermission or "recess" leaves the audience to ponder during the break the intensity of feeling expressed by the actors playing White and his wife.

The gasps and cries for news of Moscone's and Milk's deaths that opened the show have been replaced by tears over White's confession and its implications for his future, even while he has been able to explore and explain the past troubles that have prompted his actions. Just before the house lights go up, the court admonishes members of the jury, which include the audience, "not to discuss the case" or "form or express an opinion until the matter has been submitted to you." Instructed not to think about, discuss, or express opinions about the case after the characters act out this "emotionally involving" and "intense" section of the play, the audience remains in touch with their own feelings and with a heightened sense of the psychological burdens that come with being involved in the assessment of cultural morality.

Act 2, "In Defense of Murder," intensifies the collage structure, and as actors interrupt and talk over each other, we are presented with segments from the psychiatric defense and its barrage of expert witnesses, a moving scene of Mary Ann White discussing her husband's increased moodiness and depression, video clips of the murdered officials, and additional testimony from the uncalled witnesses. Brief video clips of Moscone and Milk begin the segment; in the first Moscone expresses his incredulity at the idea of capital punishment, and in the second Milk conveys his support for the "thousands upon thousands" of minority peoples who can "hope for a better tomorrow" in the election of a gay politician and the promise of a more equitable future. Despite the empathetic representations of the victims that begin the second half of the play, it may prove difficult for audience members to remain focused on the need for justice and the way to justice, caught up as they are in a cacophonous collection of voices conveying conflicting thoughts and feelings. First, however, as the lights come up on the tableau that had ended the first act, with the Whites and several jurors sobbing, the defendant's voice comes across the theater's audio system: "it's just that I never really intended to hurt anybody," he says. Character witnesses begin the formal defense proceeding, all four of them politicians or other government employees. "The Psychiatric Defense" follows, and five psychiatrists in "conservative dress" take the witness stand at once; these costume and staging decisions emphasize the conflict between the conservative community represented by law enforcement and medicine, and the activists and colleagues who spoke out against the murder in the first half of the play.

Just as act 1 had ended with a focus on Dan White rather than on the murdered officials, so goes the play's conclusion. After White committed suicide in 1985, the year following his parole, the play was revised to include news reportage of his death. But in the published version, the actor playing White is alive and onstage at the end, and he has the last word: "I was always just a lonely vote on the board. / I was just trying to do a good job for the city."[42] The fact that Dan White created his own gas chamber inside his ex-wife's garage seems to or may validate what the uncalled witness known only as "Moscone's Friend" testifies to: that "Dan White believed in the death penalty; / he should have gotten the death penalty."[43] For others, his fate may only heighten sympathy for an alienated man troubled by a deep depression that drove him, finally, to end his own life.

As David Richards wrote of the 1985 Arena production, *Execution* is a "deeply disturbing play" not because of the nature of its subject matter but because of its ideological complexity: "it doesn't take one side over another. It takes all the sides and forces you to do as much. Just when you believe you've got your *feelings* in hand and your *thoughts* sorted out, Mann suddenly introduces an angry voice from the streets, a cry from the heart, a plea of utter bewilderment, and all your certainties are swept right out from under you" (emphasis mine).[44] Richards's assessment suggests the overarching purpose and the effect of the documentary trial play: to join emotion and reason so that the assumed opposition between the two is apparent, but so is the extent to which each of the two responses emerges from the dramatic structure and is controlled by it. The recognition that the play "doesn't take one side over another" and requires its audience to manage both "feelings" and "thoughts" at once demonstrates the ways that the two work together in an attempt to make meaning of this form. We cannot understand the facts of history without sorting out our feelings about it; in any case, we may not be able to make peace with the past, but to the extent that we can, it is through struggle, contradiction, and acceptance of multiplicity. Such peace is surely destined to be fleeting.

If Mann's interests in dramatizing the traumatic memories of a community involved in a crisis of justice were realized in *Execution*, it became clear with the creation of a subsequent theater piece that she had not finished that work. A decade after the Broadway production of *Execution* and two years after she began her tenure as the artistic director of the McCarter Theatre in Princeton, New Jersey, Mann composed and directed another trial-based documentary play, *Greensboro (A Requiem)*, which received its world premiere in Princeton on February 6, 1996. The events that inspired *Greensboro* might seem at first glance to tell a familiar story of racially prompted violence. This encounter, between an armed group made up of both Ku Klux Klan and American Nazi Party members against a group of anti-Klan protestors organized by the Communist Workers Party (CWP, also known as the WVO, or Workers Viewpoint Organization), occurred in a predominately black neighborhood in Greensboro, North Carolina, on November 3, 1979, fifteen years after Lyndon Johnson signed the 1964 Civil Rights Act. The group calling itself the CWP, many of them union members by way of their employment at a local textile mill, organized the demonstration in order to protest local Klan union-busting activities and to build solidarity among black and white workers in the struggle for better working conditions. While the conflict had a strong racial component, it was driven by class and ideology differences as well. As in *Execution*, the conflict is driven by a variety of factors; moreover, it comes about in part because of increased contact between agitators seeking to impose their own ideological imperatives on others who do not share their views. That some blacks and whites are working together through the union to combat economic inequities and racial hatred reflects not only the multiplicity of the conflict here but the increased heterogeneity of political confrontations in the contemporary age.

Dubbed the "Greensboro Massacre," the clash ended with five anti-Klan demonstrators dead and eight others injured. One Klansman and a news photographer were also injured.[45] A previous encounter between the two groups had occurred in July of 1979, when members of the CWP disrupted a Klan-sponsored public viewing of *The Birth of a Nation*. Armed with canes and two-by-fours and chanting "Death to the Klan," the CWP had taken Klan members by surprise; Klansmen brandished rifles, and the two groups engaged in a shouting match, but no one was injured. In the aftermath of that conflict, some of the Klan members vowed to take revenge on the CWP. The November march was an event designed to increase the local union's visibility and further its specific causes as well as to promote broader aims of equality and cooperation across racial divides. Two weeks prior to the march, Nelson Johnson, a leader of the CWP, applied for a protest permit, which was granted on the condition that no one could be armed for the event. However, high-ranking members of the police department and other city officials knew through their informant, Eddie Dawson, that the Klan planned to attend the protest and would be carrying guns. Despite this advance notice that violence was likely to occur, the police department directed its officers to steer clear of the designated parade starting point, and so there were no officers present when the two groups came into contact.

Indeed, although the Greensboro Truth and Reconciliation Commission would ultimately find fault with both groups for what happened that day, the commission's final report stated that the "majority of commissioners find the single most important element that contributed to the violent outcome of the confrontation was the absence of police."[46] The commission's findings also indicate that while the police absence may not have been maliciously planned, it certainly resulted from misperceptions and bias:

> The Commission finds strong evidence that members of the police department allowed their negative feelings toward Communists in general, and outspoken black activist and WVO leader Nelson Johnson in particular, to color the perception of the threat posed by these groups. At the same time, we find that the [Greensboro Police Department] also exhibited a clear pattern of underestimating the risks posed by the KKK, which amounted to a careless disregard for the safety of the marchers and the residents of the Morningside neighborhood where the rally took place.[47]

The failure of law enforcement to protect its citizens and, more important, to provide a space in which differences can be aired and explored in a nonviolent way, required recompense for the armed clash that occurred. The community turned to the courts for resolution, and in the aftermath of these proceedings, Mann assembles various kinds of legal and extralegal testimony into a dramatic form that serves as record and "requiem."

Three trials followed the events of November 3. In the first trial, a state-level criminal proceeding, six Klansmen were indicted on charges of murder and felony riot. In the performance text, there is no dramatization of this trial; rather, an interview with the lawyer for the plaintiffs in the civil case that follows, and with one of the plaintiffs, narrate the highlights of that first trial in an interview with Mann. The lawyer, Lewis Pitts, calls the first trial "an example of good old-fashioned southern justice," as "most of those folks let on the jury weren't against the Klan." Plaintiff Marty Nathan, widow of one of the victims, reports that "when the first trial opened, we already knew that we were not going to get any kind of justice—it was just gonna be aimed at us and not at the Klan and Nazis who had killed us." Her narration of the trial continues with a description of events that recalls the binding and gagging of Bobby Seale in *Chicago Conspiracy*: she says that "Floris Cauce and I stood up in that courtroom that first day and said: 'This trial is a farce. This trial is a sham. The police killed our husbands.' Our mouths were taped. We were hauled out of court and thrown into jail for contempt of court for thirty days."

According to this testimony of the events of the first trial, the ideological differences that had fueled the conflict entered the space of justice and impacted impartial resolution; moreover, injustice is the fault not only of the state, but of citizen-participants who supported Klan efforts, one of the jury members allegedly saying that the Klan was like "the NAACP for white folks."[48] An all-white jury acquitted the Klansmen, despite videotape of the events that was submitted into evidence and that provided what might be considered incontrovertible evidence of guilt. Attorneys for the defendants argued that their clients had acted in self-defense, and key CWP members refused to testify for the prosecution. In May 1980, before the murder trial had concluded, several CWP members were indicted for incitement to riot, interfering with a police officer, and disorderly conduct. Although all these charges were eventually dropped, the charges seemed to justify the fear and suspicion that many members of the CWP felt toward the local police, which in turn kept them from cooperating with local and state authorities in the first trial against the Klansmen.

In January 1984, four years after the state trial, federal officials indicted nine of the Klansmen on charges that the shooters were motivated by racial hostility and had violated the victims' civil rights. Once again the defendants were acquitted on all charges by an all-white jury. The third trial was a complicated civil suit brought against the Klansmen and members of the Greensboro Police Department. This jury awarded substantial compensatory damages for wrongful death to the widow of one of the five victims killed but awarded no damages for the other four deaths. Minor monetary compensation was also eventually awarded to two CWP members who had been assaulted; one of them had sustained permanent injuries. In November 1985, six years after the killings took place, the city of Greensboro agreed to settle the case and pay the judgment but did not admit to any responsibility for the wrongdoing. No Klansman was ever forced to pay damages.

The formation in 2004 of the Greensboro Truth and Reconciliation Commission—charged with investigating the Greensboro incident twenty-five years after the fact in an attempt to "get at the full truth of what happened that day in order to create an environment for healing those wounds in that city"—suggests the continued negative effect that the events and their aftermath had on the community of Greensboro.[49] The documentary trial play is created with similar intentions: to fill a space that judicial resolution failed to fill. Indeed, the justice system's failure or inadequacy in resolving the issues at hand, and in some cases, its further exacerbation of them, can often lead to additional acts of violence or to increased alienation of the groups involved and can require additional interventions to break the cycle of resentment. As the Truth and Reconciliation Commission stated about the Greensboro tragedy: "We find one of the most unsettling legacies of the shootings to be the disconnect between what seems to be a common-sense assessment of wrongdoing and the verdicts in the two criminal trials. When people see the shootings with their own eyes in the video footage, then the trials lead to verdicts finding that no crimes were committed, it undermines their confidence in the legal system."[50] The commission's report goes on to say that, according to many people in the Greensboro community, "the murder acquittal was its own form of trauma, creating its own confusion, fear and distrust over whether our system of law enforcement and justice will protect them."[51] Emily Mann's interest in staging this story is thus not surprising, given her interest in the traumatic trial as a crux in her playwriting. In violent events and in the legal proceedings that follow, first in *Execution* and then in *Greensboro*, she traces patterns of social and political agitation, doing so through theatrical emotion and spectacle, and focuses community attention on ongoing cultural conflicts while introducing revised narratives of law that support resolution.

So too, like *Execution*, *Greensboro* is constructed entirely from found and gathered materials: as a screen displayed at the opening of the show attests, the play *"consists entirely of verbatim interview material, courtroom transcripts, public record and personal testimony. All of the play's characters are real people."*[52] Mann's performance text, in this instance, originated as a courtroom television drama script for which she had been commissioned by NBC; when the network decided not to go ahead with production of the show, they allowed the rights to remain with the playwright. She was prompted to proceed with what she had begun to create and to develop the work as a stage play, she said, after the 1995 Oklahoma City bombing "underlined the continued and alarming presence of a minority of Americans bent on expressing their views through acts of terrorism."[53] Although *Greensboro* has not received as many productions or as much critical attention as *Execution*, it was performed as part of the twenty-fifth anniversary commemoration of the massacre, a memorial held in Greensboro on November 13, 2004. The commemorative ceremonies included a march in support of the Greensboro Truth and Reconciliation Commission, which had been founded in June of that year. The march and the performance of Mann's play, taken together, echoed the rally during which the shootings took place, but they also represent a move forward from the stasis of a community's pain to the action through representation.

The intersection of *Greensboro* with the Truth and Reconciliation Commission activities demonstrates that attempts to resolve community trauma often emerge through multiple, intersecting formats, and that the documentary theater, and specifically the documentary trial play, occupies a role not only in the cultural assessment of history but in its political assessment as well. Indeed, in this case the Truth and Reconciliation Commission, which was formed eight years after Mann's play premiered, provides a useful lens through which to view the theatrical effort, particularly since both focus on trauma and reconciliation. The similarities are striking, as revealed in the language used by the commission to define its intentions: both efforts worked to "examine the 'context, causes, sequence, and consequences'" of the event in order to move participants "some distance away from the half-truths, misunderstandings, myths and hurtful interpretations" that had marked this story. Neither the play nor the Commission sought to "create a monolithic understanding within the community, but rather to amplify the community's multiple voices, perspectives and experiences of these events and their lasting impact. One end goal is thus a collective memory that incorporates these diverse points of view and a depth of historical understanding within the community that relies on contextual analysis and self-examination."[54] Similarly, in his *New York Times* review of *Greensboro*, Vincent Canby noted that the work "uses characters to evoke, analyze and set into context a terrible event that itself must be remarked upon."[55] Both the commission and the production do what the law cannot or does not do: indict both sides; complicate the conflict, by exploring the multiplicity of character and incorporating diverse points of view into new understandings of what happened on the streets of Greensboro. The legal proceedings are finite, whereas reconciliation through dramatization is ongoing and can even resist a direct move to resolution, serving its communities not by concluding an event but by keeping it in a kind of perpetual present. Each time the play is performed the issues are raised again and examined again.

At the time of the original production of *Greensboro* at Princeton, Dudley Clendinen reported that the goal Mann and her company had set for themselves was "to select the words, the characters and events, and give life to them in a way that is honest, that makes a compelling story from an apparently incoherent episode." In an interview just days before the play's premiere, Mann told Clendinen, "No one's getting off easy here."[56] In keeping with that intention, Mann changed the play's working title from "To Know a Monster," which "focused on the fascination and banality of evil," to "Greensboro (A Requiem)," which suggests that the survivors, at least in representation, might now have, as Johnson says in the play, the opportunity to make peace for themselves "on the other side of sorrow."[57] Rather than being concerned with knowing a monster, the play shifted its goal during development to the recognition of feeling and its healing power; by attending the "requiem" and by seeing characters emerge peaceful on the "other side of sorrow," we are exposed to a fuller version of the story, a version that includes context and complexity, evocation and emotion. *Greensboro*'s strategy is to witness suffering so as to heal it, to testify to what happened, to gradually put to rest feelings of injustice and revenge.

In considering the political implications of Mann's work in the genre, Claycomb calls her plays "staged oral history" that "do not primarily attempt to re-vision what happened in the past," but by "reframing the past not as a series of individually held views, but rather as the kind of dialogue that can prevent future misunderstanding, these plays are revising the discourse around the past." This discourse creates dialogue "around violent events where none existed" and serves as a remedy for the moment of violence itself.[58] The trial version of what Claycomb defines as staged history is both tied to and distinct from the court proceeding it reimagines, for the work of "revising the discourse" and "creating dialogue" are part of the documentary trial play's unique approach to the facts of the legal case. The performance text goes beyond referencing those facts to incorporating them in its body as theatrical dialogue, and the facts become part of the substance of this cultural performance in a very direct and therefore recognizable way.

At the same time, this re-creation of the trial adds information not gathered earlier, adding a backward-looking perspective to what has already become history rather than reality, and resisting a legal decision which, with the *Greensboro* events, had been multiple decisions defined by dissat-isfaction and lack of closure. Mann creates a version of the event that had not before occurred and yet seems to offer a rough, inconclusive truth as a salve for the traumatic wounds of the massacre specifically and race ha-tred generally. Rather than merely dwelling on the striking imperfections of justice, however, the play concludes with a focus on education and cultural progress. In the play, Reverend Nelson, an African American minister and survivor of the massacre, discloses his decision to ask members of the Klan to meet with him in a "faith venture," reporting that he was able to "actually [get] them to kneel down and pray with me." He thus narrates a vision of peace and harmony, for in kneeling and praying together the minister and his former enemies enact the submissiveness of kneeling and the acknowl-edgement of their common link to a higher power.

Nelson's words are followed in the play by a reconciliation ceremony performed by the White Minister and the Black Minister, to dedicate the ground where the blood was spilled and thus further ritualize the play: this final "action" within the play's action creates a memorial in honor of the victims, a ceremony performed and a site established for a lasting reminder: "so our city—all the people of our city—will never forget."[59] The ministers make this proclamation as one, the Black Minister speaking the middle words of the sentence, the White Minister's words framing them, their words embracing and echoing each other's. The conclusion thus stages the movement toward reconciliation that has been in progress since the incident. The play closes on a legal note, with a message projected onto the screen titled "First Step": "In 1985, for the first time in American legal history, local police and the Ku Klux Klan were found jointly liable in a wrongful death. The city of Greensboro paid the judgment for the police. No Klan or Nazi member has paid the judgment."[60] Resolutions and other movements to justice are multiple and sometimes makeshift, not fully af-firming equality and not fully delivering complete resolution. But first steps may lead to second and third steps in the journey toward the prevention of further acts of racially motivated violence.

A *New York Times* article written by Alvin Klein about the postplay symposium that followed one of the matinee performances of *Greensboro* suggests that the play did succeed in covering an expansive range of inter-connected subjects: "racial injustice, children's rights, mental health, social apathy, economic inequities and corporate power—then and now—as well as the possibilities of hope among the cynical and helpless." It was all, Klein concludes, "a testament to the playwright's role as provocateur."[61] In her role as provocateur, as yet another kind of agitator in the form of interviewer, playwright, and director, Mann pushed the dialogue on these subjects into difficult territory and exposed some of the underlying causes that contribute to acts of group conflict and violence. She went even further in this role of expansive provocateur by inserting "herself" into the text, incorporating many of the interviews she conducted into the script as such, so that they were presented not as solo testimony but with an actor playing her as "Interviewer." Mann herself does not actually appear, but we see her, or at least the interviewer persona she puts on and that an actor adopts, interacting with her subjects and providing some direction for audience reaction. This allegiance becomes most significant during scenes when Mann interviews Klansman Edward Dawson. Mann spoke of the challenge it was to interview Dawson, which she said "was like sitting in a room with the devil"; it was her contact with Dawson that initially prompted the "To Know a Monster" working title. Her interview with him took place on the fifteenth anniversary of the massacre, and as Dawson was filling out the release form she required of him, he noted the date and laughed. When Mann was interviewed about her work on the play, she told reporters that she had just been diagnosed with multiple sclerosis when she sat down with Dawson, and that she had had to spend the morning before she met with him doing breath work to prepare herself; that preparation was necessary before she was able to "walk into that interview and sit there." Although she struggled to complete the session, she said, "I didn't walk out of there. That's an obvious example of, emotionally and physically, how much it can cost."[62]

Besides speaking openly about the challenge it was to face Dawson, she talked at the time about her perception that all persons believe they occupy a legitimate position in the world, and that the sincerity of their beliefs makes them deserving of a chance to tell their stories. In a March 1996 radio interview during which Mann spoke of her experience as an interviewer, she expands on this idea: "people who have really committed heinous acts in their lives have found a way to live with themselves, and they give their own version of the story as themselves as hero or victim, never at fault. And what was my challenge was to make sure, as I do with all of my pieces, that I'm not writing in a biased manner. I'm trying to let each person advocate themselves. And what I said to him was, I want to hear your side of the story."[63] It is significant to note that besides the Interviewer's appearance with Nelson Johnson at times throughout the play, she is only present during the testimony of Dawson, with whom she interacts the most, and during a phone interview with David Duke. Her questioning of Dawson is the most pointed example of the mediation role of the Interviewer, which indicates the extent to which Mann felt the need to explain Dawson and contextualize his words. In the interview itself, she heard his "side of the story"; in the performance, the presence of the Interviewer helps to mediate the effect that the story might have on an audience.

Dawson, as an FBI informant, certainly had some part in bringing these groups together on that day in November but considers himself an "Escape Goat" (Mann maintains his malapropism) who was discarded by the police. As he puts it, "Police, FBI / let me go down the drain / like a rotten piece'a meat."[64] He acknowledges having feelings about what happened, "a terrible ordeal . . . regardless what they were, what you were, Ku Klux Klan, Nazi, communist . . . it bothered, it has to, if you're a human being."[65] But he goes on to narrate, by way of comparison, the story of David Matthews, the longtime Klan member who shot four of the five people killed that day at Greensboro: Matthews said about his actions, according to Dawson, "I am not a criminal." Dawson assesses Matthews as different from himself, one of those types of people who "just don't have no feeling, I guess."[66] When the Interviewer asks what has happened to Matthews, who Dawson also calls "a little whacky," the response is as casual as can be: "Nothing. He lives here. Up the road."[67] Dawson goes on to claim that he himself tried unsuccessfully to get an injunction from the city attorney to abort the protest as a way to avoid violence, then laughingly recalls accepting a personal invitation to attend the rally from Nelson Johnson and answering, "Oh, I'll be there."[68] Even though the Interviewer circles around him in what seems to be an attempt at containment, we end up with an inconsistent picture of this Klansman informant, another agitator figure who pushes the racial tension of the town toward violence but also, indirectly, toward the reconciliation that follows or emerges from the violence.

Claycomb argues that by inserting the Interviewer into the performance text, Mann works to expose her biases by helping to "overtly contextualize the subjectivity of the interviewer onstage." He adds that the interviewer's status as just another character in the play (and not played by Mann herself) "helps to further diminish the univocal quality of the interviewer's rhetoric."[69] This interview structure, interspersed with moments acted out from the time of the events, dominate the first act of the play, and the juxtaposition reminds us of the time that has passed between the events discussed and the play's present in recalled testimony. This sense of time that has passed in pain and mourning heightens the emotional level of the work and emphasizes that, as the subtitle suggests, it is a commemorative act calling to mind not only those who died on November 3, 1979, but also the mourning of those who spent years imprisoned by the trauma of that day.

Interviews with Nelson also dominate the text, and he provides narration of the events in question during the early sequences. Johnson and the others members of the CWP present that day are listed in the cast as "survivors," while the spouses of the dead are designated as "widows," thus explicitly writing into both of these identities the trauma and loss the characters have endured. The need to have this trauma shared with others is significant from the first line of the play, which follows immediately on the company's a cappella rendition of "It's So Hard to Get Along." In the first line Johnson announces that "something happened in Greensboro, North Carolina I think you should know about."[70] Thus does he proclaim the purpose of the play: that the survivors and others will tell and we will listen to what we "should know about." The survivors and the widows share their story in individual spots with their names projected on screens. They are not questioned by either the Interviewer or Lewis Pitts, the lawyer for the plaintiffs in the civil trial, whose examination and cross-examinations of law enforcement and Klan members constitute the trial segments of *Greensboro*.

The two criminal trials that resulted in acquittals are not dramatized here, although the Klan's use of self-defense in those trials is evident in their speeches and dialogue. David Matthews is heard in the enactment of a taped interrogation with two officers on the night of the shootings; after having claimed self-defense in that the CWP members fired first, he admits to having made the statement, "I got three of them."[71] He also acknowledges that there were "some innocent people shot," or so he is told. But his defense for himself is as follows: "I was shooting at the niggers. . . . I was shooting at them niggers that had riot guns."[72] The survivor testimony makes it clear that their group may have incurred increased wrath by changing its name, just two weeks before the shootings, from Workers' Viewpoint Organization to Communist Workers Party. The conflict here is between white men and white men, at least in part. The Klan sees Communism as dangerous to their way of life as is race equality, and the Jewish intellectuals who brought Communist ideas to the union tables in Greensboro pose a threat seen by some as just as dangerous to the existing social and economic orders as are the African American activists and the civil rights leaders.

While it is clear from Matthews's interrogation and from other moments in the play that the Greensboro incident had at its heart a strong racial component, the standoff also resulted from the clash between the Klan and the Communists. Many of the latter were white and Jewish, and, indeed, three of the five killed were white men, Communist activists. It seems that the police department's reticence to provide protection for the CWP was prompted by political difference as much as by racial difference. It seems that the deaths of white men, along with the deaths of an African American woman and a Cuban American man during a prounion rally are not enough to convince a jury, even with videotape evidence to view, to punish those responsible for the deaths. Gary Fisher Dawson claims that *Greensboro* suits "the healing definition of fin de siècle drama of the new epic theatre."[73] It and *Execution* demonstrate a trend in documentary theater creation that continues into the present: the impetus for these plays comes in part from the community involved in the traumatic events, as theaters take it upon themselves to stage the trials in order to help the various communities reconcile their feelings about the events.

<u>4</u>

Individual Interrogation, Communal Resolution: *Unquestioned Integrity: The Hill/Thomas Hearings, Gross Indecency: The Three Trials of Oscar Wilde,* and *The Laramie Project*

When Los Angeles police officers stopped Rodney Glen King for speeding on March 3, 1991, the incident, captured on videotape by a bystander, quickly became one of the most famous police/civilian encounters in American history. Roughly one minute in length, the tape recorded by George Halliday showed four officers standing over King and striking him repeatedly while other officers looked on; it received extensive airplay in the press and fueled debates about law and order, police brutality, and race. The incident's arguable resolution played out over several years and in several trials, criminal and civil. When the first of those trials, a criminal proceeding that tried four officers charged with excessive force, was decided in a Simi Valley courtroom, three officers were acquitted, and a single charge against the fourth officer came to a deadlock. The verdicts, delivered live on television, sparked four bloody and destructive days of riots in South

Central Los Angeles and surrounding neighborhoods, resulting in fifty-eight deaths and over $1 billion in damages. As a city and a nation witnessed these events, many Americans recognized them as the eruption of a race hatred that continued to simmer below the surface of contemporary life.

Three years later, another newsworthy and publically recorded encounter between police and an African American man confirmed the presence of ongoing racial tensions in Los Angeles; however, the man being pursued in this automobile chase had little in common with Rodney King other than skin color. On June 17, 1994, live aerial footage of a white Bronco traveling south on Interstate 405 in Los Angeles kept ninety-five million Americans glued to their television sets as football sports legend O. J. Simpson, the passenger, with his friend Al Cowlings behind the wheel, led the LAPD in a low-speed pursuit that ended at Simpson's Brentwood home. There he turned himself over to police officers for questioning in connection with the murders of his ex-wife, Nicole Brown Simpson, and her friend Ronald Goldman. Sixteen months later, on October 3, 1995, the longest jury trial in California history ended with a not-guilty verdict for Simpson on all charges.

One hundred fifty million people watched the outcome and witnessed the look of relief that registered on the defendant's face as he was released from custody. Polls throughout the trial and afterward indicated that although a majority of all Americans believed him guilty, the racial divide was sharp: 50 percent more white Americans than black Americans surveyed thought he should be convicted. The much-publicized split in popular opinion and the high-profile nature of the case prompted many citizens to fear that violence would follow the verdict no matter how it was decided, for the trial had brought issues of race tension (the victims were both white) and class tensions back into the spotlight of public debate as well as back into the courtroom. Simpson's economic privilege and his celebrity were considered by many experts and lay persons the reason for the acquittal; certainly, they contributed to the quantity and quality of his legal representation.[1]

As the 1990s began then, it seemed that if high-profile trials were destined to find their way onto the stage during this period as documentary theater, they would most likely be focused on race. Indeed, the two incidents briefly described above underscore the volatility of race relations in Los Angeles and, perhaps, the nation, as the 1990s began, complicated significantly by economic factors. Developments in market forces and changes in social policy during the 1980s had eroded the capacity of lower-class Americans to improve their economic standing, and the destruction of property during the riots that erupted after the Simi Valley verdict in the Rodney King case hinted that the disparity of class and income was as significant to the conflicts as was racial difference. Erosions to affirmative action policies had begun in the late 1970s and continued through the 1980s, leading to limitations in graduate school and in employment opportunities for women and Americans of color. By 1997, Proposition 209 in California would pass a ban on all forms of affirmative action in the state. Washington, Florida, Michigan, and other states have since followed suit. Wilson Gilmore argues that the year of the riots, 1992, is "the year of the rehabilitation of white, male heterosexuality: its return to sites of centeredness, beauty, prosperity, power."[2] While women and minorities had continued to enter the workforce in record numbers, they remained undervalued and underpaid.

Meanwhile, urban gentrification pushed poor minority groups into smaller, less prosperous areas of the city, and in Los Angeles the area known as South Central was a powder keg of a neighborhood that was ripe for the looting and burning that ensued after the police officers were acquitted of unlawfully attacking King. The riots, which set black against white but which also revealed that tensions existed among members of other minority groups, evoked a broad range of sociological and political response and commentary and did in fact provide the inspiration and material for a documentary play, albeit not a documentary trial play.[3] When the riots occurred, playwright and performer Anna Deavere Smith was in the process of staging her one-person show about another recent example of racially motivated urban violence: *Fires in the Mirror: Crown Heights, Brooklyn and Other Identities* (1992). Part of an ongoing series Smith calls "On the Road: A Search for American Character," *Fires in the Mirror* had been constructed with excerpts from a series of interviews she conducted after an uprising that had occurred in Brooklyn during August 1991, when two black children had been hit, one of them killed, by a passing motorist in a Hasidic Jewish motorcade. Several hours later and within blocks of the accident, a Hasidic Jew, a visiting history professor from Melbourne, was stabbed by a young Trinidadian American and subsequently died in the hospital. Destruction of property, arson, and looting plagued the area for several days, and it would take years of reconciliation to heal the wounds between the immigrant groups who had each claimed part of the same troubled neighborhood but needed to learn to live side by side.

Smith's attraction to sites of racial conflict would take her next to Los Angeles, where a commission by Gordon Davidson of the Center Theatre Group in Los Angeles prompted her to compose a documentary performance text in the immediate aftermath of the 1992 Los Angeles riots. Smith conducted two hundred interviews and spoke to people from every corner of the metropolis about the King beating, the violence that followed, racial and economic divisions in the city, and attitudes toward law enforcement. She attended the subsequent federal trial of the officers charged with violating King's civil rights, thus having what Richard Stayton called "the most coveted theater ticket in Los Angeles."[4] Stayton's comment underscores the theatricality of these legal events and the interest they gathered in this diverse community. However, Smith's remarks about the trial indicate that diversity was visible but regulated: "The only groups of people of color who came in were from the public. . . . I didn't expect it [social segregation] there because the trial was so much about race." Not only was she in the courtroom when the verdicts were read, but she also told Stayton that her time in the field "was under the shadow of the trial. So when they began to read the verdicts, I felt like I was waiting for personal news, afraid to open the letter and see if it was going to be yes or no."[5] In the meantime, Smith had gathered evidence of her own that she used to create a polyphonic narrative of the riots and their aftermath, and she said that the verdicts in the federal trial gave the show a focus as she worked on it right up to its premiere.[6] The trial was on the minds and in the words of those interviewed, but she did not use its transcripts as dialogue or its courtroom as setting.

Another even more deadly assault, possibly racially motivated, had occurred close to the time of King beating, and was considered by some Los Angeles residents to be an added catalyst in the violence that followed the first jury trial in the King case. A fifteen-year-old African American girl was shot by the Korean American proprietor of a convenience store for allegedly stealing a container of orange juice; a store security camera recorded the shooting, which took place just two weeks after the King incident, on tape. In October, a jury found the female defendant, Soon Ja Du, guilty of voluntary manslaughter. She served no jail time for the crime. Smith includes interviews about this trial and verdict in *Twilight*, but none of the trial transcripts are used in her script. While it seemed possible or even likely that Smith would have created a documentary trial play about the riots, especially since *Twilight* was commissioned by a theater company known for the gestation and production of several other contemporary documentary trial plays, she did not. Rather, she stuck to the format that she had established for her ongoing series about American character, which was to interview a variety of Americans and then dramatize them in a solo performance.

Arguably, her decision not to stage these trials reflects a similar void of documentary theater created about the O. J. Simpson case. His story was never used as source material for a documentary trial play, although it did serve as the basis of several television documentaries or dramatizations focused on Simpson's rise to fame, his marriage to Nicole Brown, the murder trial and aftermath, or all three.[7] Considering that the trial itself was televised and the verdict viewed by over half the US population, the media saturation so complete, expert analysis and water cooler discussion so interminable, such coverage may have precluded the need for the kind of performative verbatim recreation that had motivated playwrights to dramatize the details of other, similarly notorious high-profile trials. As representatives of moments in time and contrasting snapshots of urban California life, the King case and the Simpson case suggest that although issues of race continue to provide contested narratives for legal proceedings, confounding and inflaming citizens at all levels of society, they did not serve as the raw material for documentary trial plays in the contemporary period. The absence of these cases from the theatrical docket does not mean that the need for documentary theater had subsided, however: three American documentary trial plays staged several years apart over the 1990s (the third premiering in the early months of 2000) all investigate another subset of issues that define the age, best described as those at the intersection of gender, sexuality, and power. The politics of gender are put on trial and cross-examined in three plays, equally spaced over the course of the decade: *Unquestioned Integrity: The Hill/Thomas Hearings* (1993) (*Unquestioned Integrity*), *Gross Indecency: The Three Trials of Oscar Wilde* (1997) (*Gross Indecency*), and *The Laramie Project* (*Laramie*) (2000).

The first of the three plays, *Unquestioned Integrity*, dramatizes an event that occurred during the period between Rodney King's beating by members of the LAPD and the initial acquittal that sparked the 1992 riots. It was an event that, like the beating and its aftermath, brought a debate about race and power to the forefront and, like both the King and the Simpson sagas, was broadcast for and viewed by a national audience. It was the controversial Senate confirmation hearing for Supreme Court justice Clarence Thomas, nominated by President George H. W. Bush in July, 1991 to replace retiring justice Thurgood Marshall. Marshall was the only African American to have ever served on the Court; Thomas, also African American, had little prior experience as a judge and promised to bring a conservative perspective to the bench. The objections raised by his candidacy about race were, ironically, raised by representatives of the NAACP and NOW, who opposed the appointment because of Thomas's criticism of affirmative-action policies. However, during the final days of the confirmation hearing, an FBI report that was leaked to the press raised sexual-harassment accusations against Thomas. Anita Hill, who had worked with Thomas at the Department of Education and at the Equal Opportunity Employment Commission during the 1980s, alleged that he had spoken and acted inappropriately toward her on more than one occasion. Hill was called to testify before the Senate confirmation committee, and the specific allegations that Hill made, some of them claiming that Thomas had used sexually graphic language in the workplace, were widely publicized when the hearings were televised over three days in October 1991.

The images of an all-white confirmation committee interviewing an African American man and woman about possible sexual impropriety brought attention to the complicated racial climate of the decade, as Thomas famously called the proceedings a "high-tech lynching for uppity blacks."[8] However, the lasting legacy of the hearings, and the trend that emerged from it in the documentary theater, would ultimately highlight sexual harassment, gender discrimination, and gender-based violence as the standout legal issues of the decade. *Unquestioned Integrity* was conceived by Larry Eilenberg and composed by Mamie Hunt; the play premiered at the Magic Theatre in San Francisco in the early months of 1993 and has subsequently been produced in Seattle, Atlanta, Washington, DC, Los Angeles, and Chicago. At the time of the work's composition, Hunt was serving as artistic director at the Magic, having succeeded Eilenberg in the job.

Hunt does not consider herself a playwright, but her previous experience on new play development and dramaturgy convinced her that she could rework the hearings into a dramatic piece. Hunt documents her process in an author's note, admitting to having "condensed and re-choreographed portions of the transcript for this dramatic presentation of the event," but also explaining that every word is "taken directly from the transcripts of the hearings."[9] In paring down the three hundred pages of the hearings transcript, specifically the sections that contained interviews of Hill and Thomas on the subject of Hill's allegations, Hunt realized how guarded much of the testimony was. In order to direct the play toward revelation, she "collected those moments when the mask dropped . . . to try to get some soliloquy so we could see a personal side of her, and of him."[10] As is the tradition of the documentary style, true words are rearranged in order that their truth (or some new truth) might emerge from them.

Because the hearings were televised—seen and heard by millions as they occurred—and Hill's testimony recorded and repeated, Hunt grappled with whether or not there was need for or interest in a theatrical rendering of the proceedings. Critics shared that concern when the play appeared. As reviewer Heather Mackey suggested, the play is a questionable endeavor: "part post-modern commentary on a media spectacle and part dramatic recreation, with a little group therapy thrown in. For many Americans, the confirmation hearings were a collective trauma—a process of disillusionment, betrayal and anger experienced en masse. Why sit through that again?"[11] Ultimately, however, Mackey's query provides hints about why Hunt went ahead with the project, for it is the "anger experienced en masse" that arguably creates the need for a play allowing audiences to work through the emotions stirred up by the legal proceeding.

In a 1994 telephone interview, Hunt explained that when a friend told her that she had listened to the hearings on her car radio and felt isolated by the experience, Hunt remembered "feeling similarly isolated at the time of the hearings and [thinking] that this was probably the experience 'of many others.'"[12] Hunt also argued, in an interview at the time of the original production, that the three days of hearings were, in her opinion, "an unfinished thing, an open sore."[13] Furthermore, Mackey herself acknowledges that in light of the increased appearance of real trials and hearings aired on television, it's not surprising "to start seeing theatre tackle the unresolved issues left in television's wake."[14] But the trend did not arise from the increase in television airings of trials that became common in the 1990s; rather, the impetus for this kind of ambiguous trial play emerges, in Hunt's opinion, more directly from the "unresolved issues" that some such trials leave behind.

Unquestioned Integrity underscores the contentious and often traumatic relationships that connect race, gender, and power in American culture, just as the Thomas confirmation hearings reminded Americans of the racism and sexism that continue to plague our nation. The hearings and the play that followed quickly on them called attention to workplace inequities and harassment and confirmed something other than the Clarence Thomas nomination: they confirmed, for many, the advances and the setbacks of the women's movement while serving as a reminder that cultural power, in Washington and elsewhere, remained the purview of the white male. The extent to which power is sexualized was evident at the hearings, as a table full of white male senators questioned Hill about pubic hair and pornography in the context of Thomas's bid for a lifetime appointment to the highest court in the land.

Hunt took the title of the play from the original transcripts, from a speech in which Senator Strom Thurmond argued that the most important quality of a Supreme Court appointee is "unquestioned integrity." The title proves ironic, of course, since what emerged in the hearings, among other things, was the Senate's determination to question Thomas's integrity; Hill's testimony did this as well, and in response to her testimony, both Thomas and the committee called Hill's integrity into question. An issue that Hunt claims was not revealed in this dramatization as much as she had expected it would be: the issue of race, which she claims, remained, "as underspoken in the play as [the issue was] in the hearings themselves." Hunt's faithfulness to the words of the transcript, then, meant that her adherence to the documentary record set limits on what *Unquestioned Integrity* could accomplish, and, moreover, on what issues would emerge as central to the play and of foremost importance to this decade of documentary theater.

If the hearings and the play did, to some extent, diffuse the topic of race, the actual proceedings and their recreation exposed, explored, and helped to define the parameters of another significant manifestation of power inequity in American culture and society: sexual harassment. In her author's note, Hunt provides some historical context that calls attention to this topic and to the role of the hearings in narrating a change in public perception and level of awareness: "In the year following the highly publicized, thoroughly televised hearings, tide of public opinion about the Senate, sexual harassment in the workplace, and the incredibly complex issues of race and gender that were brought to the surface during those three days shifted dramatically."[15] What followed was dubbed by media the "Year of the Woman," as women went to Washington in record numbers: in 1992, four women were elected to the US Senate and twenty-four were elected for the first time to the House of Representatives.[16] Claims of the arrival of long-overdue gender equality filled the airwaves, and the promise of women's rights, finally honored, did indeed make for a union of good will and good policy. But the advances then seemed to stall, as a backlash period followed the winning election year, and traditional roles for women were reasserted or newly configured.

A glance back at the Hill/Thomas hearings during the subsequent year of advances made the appointment controversy look like the last gasp of the oppressive work environments of the past, and Hunt's rapid move to distill and immortalize the events might suggest an attempt to capture for the record the waning misogyny in its recession and as recorded in the official context of a government hearing. The committee of senators who questioned Hill was all male, so the unprecedented election of women the following year, more than had been elected in any *decade* prior, certainly seems to suggest that voters believed in the candidates they chose but that they also may have recognized the need for increased gender equity on Capitol Hill. Surely, many Americans believed, more women in leadership positions, beginning at the top with an increase of elected officials, would insure that women in the Senate room and in the workplace might now expect equal treatment rather than harassment and discrimination.

The play also reinforces the rarity of the public airing in harassment complaints; in Hill's explicit description of what she alleged that Thomas said to her during the time they worked together, we hear the repetition of things that she would have preferred not talking about or reliving, and we experience the discomfort level such truth telling evokes in all concerned. We witness her attempt to answer the questions as directly as possible, a strategy that judicially makes her a good witness but that, in this kind of case, actually undermines her integrity by associating her with the untoward behavior she claims she was subjected to. For example, the committee asks that she explain why Thomas continued to barrage her with inappropriate discussions of pornography and other topics after she had refused to date him; her assertion that he "did continually pressure me to go out with him, continually" and that "he would not accept my explanation [that it was not good for an employee to date a supervisor] as being valid" implicitly implicate her in the offenses she claims, especially since she had worked for him at not one, but two government agencies.[17] If she had been able to prevent or terminate his inappropriate advances, this line of questioning seems to suggest, she would be a more credible witness; paradoxically, however, it is the difficulty of avoiding this kind of behavior that helps to define sexual harassment and determine if it is taking place. Thus do claims of gender discrimination or attack present a circular and confounding legal dilemma or shortcoming; the powerlessness of the victims is often recreated in the courtroom, as witnesses are called on to describe and sometimes defend the powerlessness that created the circumstances of victimization.

Unquestioned Integrity has a cast of just three characters: Hill, Thomas, and the Senator, the latter a "compilation of several members of the Senate Judiciary Committee."As such, then, there is a streamlined and focused quality to this work, as well as a triangular relationship among the three characters quite distinct from the dynamic of the actual proceedings. According to the script's character description, actors who play the Senator should seek to avoid impersonations of "individual Senators" and to eschew the use of accents; rather, the goal is to distinguish "facets of the personality and strategic shifts of this one very powerful white man."[18] The Senator tells Hill during the questioning that while he does not "regard this as an adversary proceeding," his "duties run to the people who have elected" him, and "in the broader sense as a United States Senator, to constitutional government and the Constitution."[19] Despite speeches that denote impartiality, the visual impact of two men, one in an elected legislative office and the other vying for a powerful judicial office to which he will be appointed for life, and one woman, a university professor called to witness to he said/she said closed-door encounters, conveys a gender and power imbalance that fuels the play's dramatic tension and reflects societal inequities.

For the first half of the performance, however, Hill and the Senator occupy the stage without Thomas, who does not appear until the end of scene 2, after Hill has provided the bulk of her testimony. In the hearings that Americans viewed on television, Hill and Thomas never appeared together, but when Hunt has Thomas make his entrance at the end of scene 2, there is a dramatic moment of visual confrontation: as the stage directions note succinctly, *"Judge Thomas enters. They see each other."*[20] The triangular nature of this setting, a result of Hunt's decision to keep the cast list limited and to have Hill and Thomas briefly confront each other, focuses audience attention on identity and representation. It also minimizes the communal nature of this legal proceeding: no lawyers, no press, no spectators are present to remind us that the events we are watching are public, or that they are being transcribed for posterity, or that they replay events from the historical record. Thomas's first speech, on the other hand, focuses on the public nature of the proceeding, accusing the Senator of being involved in a "travesty" in which "this sleaze, this dirt" was leaked to the media and aired "at prime time over our entire nation." He notes that this is not a "closed room," not an "opportunity to talk about difficult matters privately or in a closed environment"; rather, it is, he proclaims, "a circus" and a "national disgrace."[21] The juxtaposition of private and public, highlighted by the contrast between staging and dialogue, thus becomes central to the interrogation of gender and law, for the question of how personal choices and personal behavior, what is done behind closed doors, is an issue of public concern when those choices or behavior violate civil or criminal codes. Furthermore, documenting and proving that the private behavior is a public violation, and deciding what ought to be aired publicly, are dilemmas that create questions, not provide answers.

At the opening of scene 3, Thomas is standing on the stage at lights up with Hill and the Senator, and from that point on the three characters share the performance space until the play's conclusion. Thomas blames the Senator for spending the entire day "destroying what has taken me 43 years to build, and providing a forum for that." The "hearing," the public proceeding that has the legislative power of confirmation, in this case also has judicial power both individual and communal. The testimony might have next gone on to a courtroom, for Hill could have decided to file a formal complaint against Thomas: ironically, such a complaint would have been managed by the EEOC, one of two agencies where Hill and Thomas worked together. The Senator responds to Thomas's charge of personal destruction in a public sphere by reminding him that "Judge Thomas, you know, we have a responsibility" to "get to the bottom of this"; he attempts to reassure the Judge that "if she is lying, I think you can help us prove that she was lying," a statement that to some extent shifts Hill's position from witness to defendant. Thomas believes that "others put it together and developed this" (the narrative of harassment) thus claiming that the story was concocted and may have even been some kind of measured plot against him.[22] In scene 5, he reminds the committee that "in this country when it comes to sexual conduct we still have underlying racial attitudes about black men and their views of sex," and his counterclaim to the charges is that the atmosphere he created in the workplace was the opposite of any such stereotype.[23] By continuing to maintain his innocence throughout, Thomas managed to withstand the scrutiny and secure an appointment to the nation's highest court; however, he was seated by the narrowest margin in one hundred years.

Hill, Thomas, and the Senator share some commonalities in background and training, specifically legal education, and therefore are they all equipped with skills in reasoning and persuasion. Furthermore, their job histories indicate that all have significant experience with governmental operations. But certain elements of the play are designed to delineate gender differences, and in several instances implied accusations are leveled at the accuser. As the Senator tells Thomas, "just because we take harassment seriously doesn't mean we take the charges at face value," and "one of the aspects of this is that she could be living in a fantasy world."[24] The hearings expose and challenge Hill when she agrees to bring forth information that she alleges is important to the confirmation decision as it inflicts again on her the harassment that she reports. The gendered elements of what Hill is asked to describe, in detail, and therefore experience again, have no doubt been at some level experienced by the actor who plays Hill and by every woman in the theater audience, thus evoking a uniquely gendered experience of the law.

As Robin West argues, women sustain injuries in life (and, she claims, in law) "which have no or little counterpart in men's lives." West's further delineation of the kinds of harm women are exposed to are not only physical and therefore invasive, or emotional and therefore isolating; women also, she suggests, suffer "distinctive harms to their subjectivity, or sense and reality of *selfhood* and politically, they suffer "distinctive harms of patriarchal *subjection* that again have no correlate in men's lives" (emphasis in the original).[25] Although Thomas is the one being investigated, the hearings have a certain similarity to rape trials in that the witness becomes a kind of defendant whose witnessing often comes with the need to defend herself and her position. The Senator asks Hill toward the end of her solo testimony, "if you wouldn't mind repeating to me what went through your mind, why . . . you would stay there after this happened several times" and "why you would proceed on to another job with someone" who had "gotten into the explanations and—expletives and the anatomy and what have you that you pointed out to us today."[26] While the Senator's question is not unreasonable, it fails to account for the feelings of entrapment that many women experience when they are being harassed, and it fails to account for a decision that may keep a woman in a position of subservience to maintain job security and the possibility for advancement.

The inherent drama as well as the cultural and political impact of these hearings was clearly evident to theater critics who remarked on both the hearings and on the play that followed closely behind. Speaking of the real events in her review of the original production, Sue Adolphson calls the hearings "at times more titillating than a soap opera, and more intriguing than a Hitchcock whodunit," a "very real drama, and one that would affect" ["the millions of Americans who watched"].[27] Similarly, Steven Winn describes the hearings as "part courtroom mystery, part televised titillation and part warning siren about sexual harassment, entrenched white male attitudes and power in the American workplace and halls of elected officials," suggesting that the risk of taking on such recent and well-known history paid off, and that the play provided a clear focus on the hearings without using editorial direction that might have distorted audience perspective.[28] Mackey calls the transcripts "the raw material for a meditation on race, class and gender in America."[29] Although Joe Adcock of the *Seattle Post* says of that city's production that the play is as "frustrating and irritating" as the hearings they are based on, he concludes that as a "container for political enthusiasms, aversions and perplexities," *Unquestioned Integrity* is "as full of goodies as a piñata."[30]

The penultimate scene establishes a compelling dramatic link between Hill and Thomas, as the two, in alternating monologues, offer brief narratives of their personal backgrounds and training. The two speeches are delivered in a parallel structure, emphasizing the similarities and the differences in the two witnesses, particularly in their upbringings. Hill describes her early life on a farm in a large family and Thomas's memories recall him catching fiddler crabs and skipping shells in Georgia, but Hill's large and loving family contrasts sharply with Thomas's description of living with his mother in a tenement before he and his brother are taken to live with grandparents, "two little boys with all their belongings in two grocery bags."[31] Hill describes the religious atmosphere in which she was raised and her current membership in a Baptist congregation as a "very warm part of my life at the present time"; Thomas speaks similarly of his education at Yale, which had "opened its doors, its hearts, its conscience" to him as a minority student, and, as he says simply, "I benefitted from this effort."[32] While Hill names the warmth of family and spirituality as the main contributions to her success and Thomas singles out his Ivy League education, both narratives suggest the importance and impact of community, of finding a like-minded group to provide allegiance and support.

Although Hunt claims that her decision to use only transcript material resulted in what she considered the continued obscuration of race issues while "the gender issues of the hearings rise to the emotional and intellectual surface of the play rather easily," this scene provides some context for which to compare the backgrounds of Hill and Thomas and thus consider issues of race and class.[33] It is difficult to read this scene, let alone see it performed by actors of color, without being reminded that the career successes the two of them have enjoyed, law school, prestigious university and government positions, have come about against the odds and, for Thomas, came about because Yale determined to "recruit and admit minority students," an effort he acknowledged worked to his benefit.[34] It is significant, in fact, in light of the play's overarching focus on gender, that their advancements are most striking when each mentions her or his mother: Hill's, described by her as a "farmer and a housewife," and Thomas's as a domestic who "only earned $20 every two weeks."[35] Thus are race, class, and gender issues encapsulated in these simple and very personal testimonials about the past, the defendants using not the language of the law but the language of emotion in order to express their innermost selves.

While they are not, legally speaking or strictly speaking, defendants here, the extent to which both are asked to defend their actions as well as their identities is central to the script's energy. Earlier in the play, before Thomas takes the stage, this theme of defending identity is underscored as the Senator questions Hill about her motivations, claiming that to do so is to help him determine who is telling the truth. As he tells her, his experience as a "lawyer, judge, is that you listen to all the testimony and then you try to determine the motivation for the one that is not telling the truth."[36] That said, he proceeds to ask speculating questions about why she has come forward with these charges against Thomas. "Are you a scorned woman? . . . Do you have a militant attitude relative to the area of civil rights? . . . Do you have a martyr complex? . . . Are you interested in writing a book?"[37] The adjectives in the first several examples stress the inevitably negative elements in her possible motivation: if she is not "scorned," then perhaps she is "militant." In either case she must be angry. On the other hand, she may choose to inflict herself with the suffering of a "martyr." If, however, she is not suffering from an emotional condition that colors her judgment, then her motive might be mercenary, to promote herself and her story as bankable. Hunt's compression of the Senator's dialogue heightens the comic elements of this testimony, the questions and their speaker conveying the humor of this interrogative process as Hunt has collected this line of questioning and strung it together.

This segment of the performance text reflects the Senator's attempt to control the interview as well as its outcome. As Peter Brooks says of the process of interrogation: "The interrogator thus seeks to pattern the unfolding narrative according to a preconceived story. . . . Above all, the good interrogator maintains control of the storytelling, so that the suspect is put in a position of denying or affirming—often, affirming through denials that lead to entrapment—the unfolding narrative that, one notes, is largely of the interrogator's own making, his 'monologue.'"[38] The goal that the Senator has stipulated, that is, truth gathering, is being pursued in a way that makes it plain that the "unfolding narrative" is controlled by the interrogator, and as such this goal exerts control over the formation of Hill's identity in the testimony prompt the Senator to ask about jealous love, strident political views, and a persecution complex. The questions label her actions and her identity as unreasonable or unbalanced: the "scorned woman" who seeks revenge for having her romantic advances or feelings spurned; the "zealot" who has a "militant" attitude toward civil rights; a person with a "martyr complex" or an immersion in fantasy, which might indicate psychological imbalance and emotional extremism. The final question suggests that Hill might have fame or money or both in mind when she came forward with her allegations. All the possibilities offered in this version of the questioning sully the confirmation process, marking Hill for bringing the sordid and the mercenary to bear on what ought to be a patriotic process.

In contrast to the establishment of Hill's identity in the play emerging from a personal interrogation signaled through specific questions from the investigator, Thomas's character is defined during his first appearance and in a long statement he makes without any questioning or prompting. This speech contains, among other things, his famous accusation that the proceeding is "a high-tech lynching" for African Americans who "in any way deign to think for themselves, to do for themselves, to have different ideas."[39] While this assertion in reality has always been seen as outrage expressed in defense of himself, in the context of Hunt's construction of the hearings it follows immediately upon the Senator's interrogation of Hill and might therefore be interpreted in the performance piece as an accusation made on her behalf as well. After all, both witnesses appear to be at the mercy of the investigation. Thomas's use of the word "lynching" has powerful racial implications, and it references an act of revenge that takes place outside of the rule of law, significantly distinct as it is from government-sanctioned hanging as a form of execution. Lynching, however, is a fate that historically befell many more men than women, and it is a punishment that was often meted out for a sexual crime. Hunt's selections and arrangement thus expose tensions that mingle, cross, and even contradict each other: old prejudices that depict blacks as overtly sexual, as untrustworthy and even dangerous, particularly if they are smart and ambitious; newer frustrations in the face of inclusive ideas about class and position, about gender and professionalism, about race and justice. The individual, particularly one from an underrepresented group, seeks out a place from among the often conflicting identities offered by the dominant culture, in this case quite persuasively represented by the Senator.

Thomas calls the proceeding "a circus" and "a national disgrace" that African Americans must heed, for it sends "a message that unless you kowtow to an old order, this is what will happen to you. You will be lynched, destroyed, caricatured by a Committee of the U.S. Senate rather than hung from a tree."[40] The repetition of the lynching metaphor is telling even as his words conversely demonstrate some increased level of equality in contemporary times, an indication of a newer order in which the African American is allowed to exercise freedom of expression and register strong public (televised) protest without the fear of physical violence. The rights that African Americans exert by challenging the system are in evidence, and they are coupled with the very fact of this confirmation hearing. Both African American witnesses, verbally and visually, testify to or imply the advances of race, with the contrast between them more strikingly indicative of gender inequality than of racial inequality. Hill and Thomas offer two views of Americans striving for and achieving success through the combination of individual talent and effort, community faith and assistance, political development and advancement; while it is Thomas whose public persona is ostensibly under scrutiny, *Unquestioned Integrity* performs a version of the hearings that highlights the attack on Hill, leaving viewers with an overwhelming sense of turned tables. The accuser becomes the accused; the alleged victim becomes the guilty party. It is a reversal that was in evidence during the actual hearings but that becomes more strikingly dramatic and more unsettling in Hunt's arrangement of the transcript material.

Thomas's attacks on the committee, the press, the FBI, and the nation's sad tradition of institutional racism are soon followed by Hill's attempt to make her own case two scenes later. Her speech, not delivered to the committee but as she sits alone onstage *"speaking from her bewilderment and the bittersweetness of her appearance here,"* is not an attack on the system that produced such a situation, but a defense of her own attempts to avoid it. She says repeatedly in one way or another, "I made a great effort to make sure that it did not come to this."[41] She hearkens back to the Senator's earlier accusations that she might be testifying for her own benefit when she asserts," I'm not interested in writing a book / I have nothing to gain. / No one has promised me anything. / I have nothing to gain here." While the content of Thomas's speech surely reminds us of the pain and trauma of racism, his character projects that trauma outward onto a society that would seek to prevent him from what he considers to be his desire to think for himself and do for himself. He speaks plainly and deliberately, in the reasoned language of legal testimony. Hill's language, on the other hand, is punctuated by frequent "I"s, by hesitations, and by pauses. She testifies to the disruption of her life: the personal risk, the threats against her, the negative impact on her professional career.

During her only opportunity to take the stage alone, Hill further emphasizes the personal ramifications of her appearance before the committee and decries the publicity of the case, insisting that she was "making every effort to make sure this public thing did not happen" for she thought that if she were "cautious enough" that she could "control it so that . . . it would not get to this point."[42] As we see, then, the opportunity that Hunt provides us with in the reconstruction of these hearings is the chance to revisit them at some distance from the original events, but also to contemplate what was said in that hearing room in contrast to the sensationalism of the actual events, for in the performance text the latter is considerably underplayed. Having excised, for the most part, the "titillating" details that were the focus of so much interest and commentary at the time of the proceeding, the playwright allows other topics, including interpersonal and legal dynamics, to take the stage. She also offers a look into the complicated nature of sexual harassment claims; the he said/she said nature of them, but also the fact that gender politics play an important role not only in the creation of this kind of power dynamic, but also in the adjudication of the complaints that follow.

The final moments of the play focus on a chilling exchange between the Senator and Hill, with Thomas remaining onstage but silent. It suggests that ultimately, it was the questioning of Hill, not of Thomas, that was the lasting legacy of this hearing. Indeed, Thomas's two decades on the Supreme Court have helped to obscure the controversy of his appointment. Hill's final words in the play, however, provide both an echo of the gender issues raised at the time of the hearings and a refrain that is still heard. When asked by the Senator "why in God's name, when he left his position of power or status or authority over you, and you left it in 1983, why in God's name would you ever speak to a man like that the rest of your life?"[43] Hill responds, "I believe you have to understand that this response—and that's one of the things that I have come to understand about harassment—this response, this kind of response, is not atypical." Finally, she emphasizes, "it can happen, because it happened to me."[44] Robin West argues that the "experience of morality most common to women—that of nurturing *even fully wanted and celebrated* fetal and newborn life—is diametrically at odds with the willed, principled, universalized rationality which for the Kantian is the necessary foundation of the moral act" (emphasis in the original).[45] West's model behavior references motherhood, but she is using it as an example in order to demonstrate that women have been taught "to act deferentially so as to please others" rather than to act on the basis of their own desires. This difference leads to very different personal and professional expectations and—even in an age during which most Americans experienced some level of increased access to politics, law, academia, and other arenas of social and cultural influence—it becomes clear that the challenges that emerge from diversity require institutional policies and procedures that equalize the opportunities for all the nation's people.

Sexual harassment policies, training, and adjudication procedures are now standard in the workplace, in part because of the national attention these hearings brought to the issue. But the challenges that Hill faced in confronting Thomas and the trauma involved in making her story public continue to prevent women from speaking out against similar abuses of authority. In another documentary play several years later, a solo piece by Anna Deavere Smith, Anita Hill is once again performed, her character recalling her life after the hearings. In this play, *House Arrest*, the figure of Hill aptly explains that her space now is "very limited" and "really limited to [her] physical home," and she describes an encounter with a stranger who acts "as though she was interrogating me! / As though I was some kind of an imposter." For as she goes on to say, "I still have to / deal with the question of who I am and what I'm doing here."[46] The complicated if not impossible-to-navigate identity politics produced by centuries of oppression followed by several short decades when restrictions loosened is as much the subject of *Unquestioned Integrity* as are the racial issues and issues of law.

Gender identity and politics would continue to be the focus of American documentary trial plays created and produced during the 1990s, and a major source of this kind of dramatic interrogation was a New York City–based theater group, the Tectonic Theater Project. The group was founded in 1991 by Moisés Kaufman and Jeffrey LaHoste; the word "tectonic" in the title "refers to the art and science of structure and was chosen to emphasize the company's interest in construction—how things are made, and how they might be made differently."[47] Although in its early years the company produced works by other playwrights, Kaufman soon realized that in order to be "rigorous about exploring theatrical form, the company had to deal with the issue of text."[48] He went on from this recognition to make two original contributions to the contemporary documentary theater within several years of each other, and in both cases he would, as did other playwrights interested in this genre before him, look to the law and to the availability of trial documentation to find fitting subjects for dramatization.

The two plays that Tectonic produced, with premieres in 1997 and 2000 respectively, might appear to be quite different from each other in method of construction, setting, and the extent to which each deals with American identity politics. They are very different, but examined from within a common framework of gender and legal issues, they suggest significantly similar perspectives. The first one, *Gross Indecency: The Three Trials of Oscar Wilde* (*Gross Indecency*), was composed by Kaufman after he received from a friend a book of selected writings of Oscar Wilde. In that volume were included excerpts from the transcripts of three trials in which Wilde was involved that took place in London in 1895: in the first, as the plaintiff, and, in the second and third, as defendant against the charge of gross indecency. His conviction in the third trial, which brought with it a sentence of two years of imprisonment and hard labor, ended with his death, not long after his release from jail, in November of 1900.

Kaufman claims to have been fascinated by what he found when he read the legal transcripts: the situation of "an artist being asked to justify his art in a court of law!" As he goes on to explain in his introduction of the published play script that he composed about Wilde's legal travails, he set out to "tell the story—*a story* of these trials" (emphasis in the original) as a way of exploring the reconstructions of history through the theater text and performance. Noting that "there were as many versions of what had occurred at the trials as there were people involved," he decided to stage "the diversity of accounts" he had uncovered in his research.[49] Kaufman's attempt to engage in this reconstruction of history and to wrestle with the complexities of doing so is reflected by the epigram he chose for the printed performance text, an aphorism by Wilde himself: "The truth is rarely pure and never simple."[50] The dramatic narrative that follows the epigram, ironically, demonstrates the "truth" of Wilde's assertion, and in both content and structure *Gross Indecency* exemplifies the conflicts of narrative and of perspective that are consistent with the generic markers and the components of the documentary trial play. While Kaufman recognizes the impossibility of reconstructing history, especially from a pile of old books and newspaper clippings, *Gross Indecency* nonetheless does provide historical details, neither pure nor simple but certainly compelling, about three trials that called into question the artistic and sexual identities of a man who prefigured the modern both personally and professionally. Despite the notoriety of the trials at the time they occurred, many contemporary theatergoers may not know this story in advance, even though Wilde's life has been taken up by several films.[51]

Beyond its explanation of the performance text's construction, Kaufman's commentary about his discovery and dramatization of Wilde's trials raises questions about the inclusion of *Gross Indecency* in this critical study: the play does not draw on recent or near-recent events for its raw material but looks backward an entire century; geographically, it departs from American shores and seems to abandon the focus on American culture that links the other performance texts examined here; it does not concern itself with either contemporary or American subject matter. The law practiced in Wilde's England is different from the law practiced in the United States, and the laws themselves that come to be at issue in these trials, particularly the offense of "gross indecency" of which Wilde is convicted, is of another time and place. The act itself, however, of sodomy, is one that is being singled out as a transgressive act in this historical moment, and Wilde and his trials are instrumental as a kind of text case for the legislation prohibiting homosexual activity that would become prevalent in the twentieth century.

Gross Indecency situates Kaufman's work and his dramatic concerns squarely within the issues under consideration here, and although it is not based on an American story, it is an American documentary play about law and gender. James Nicola, artistic director of the New York Theater Workshop during the period when *Gross Indecency* had several development readings there, compared the play to *Angels in America* and *Rent*, all three "'expressions of fin-de-siècle anxiety in America.'" The anxiety expressed in century's-end American theater, Nicola suggests, is "'no longer about socialism or democracy,'" according to Nicola. "'It's about more personal issues like sexuality.'"[52] Because of the centrality of the issues it raises, *Gross Indecency* quickly became a critical success for an unknown playwright and a spare Off-Broadway production with a single set that received attention in a New York season crowded with "megabudget productions"; although the documentary trial play was well established by 1997, Kaufman's play surprised critics with the dramatic success of its form, drawn as it was "entirely from contemporary court documents, books, and newspaper accounts" with "no scenery and set in a courtroom, where emotional highs derive from heated cross-examination."[53] In addition to moving the American documentary play and very American issue of gender forward with a subject that was not American, *Gross Indecency* enabled Kaufman to finance a subsequent documentary play, *The Laramie Project*, which would debut at the century's close and continue the exploration of gender, sexuality, and the law that drove the decade's documentary impulse.

Another element that sets this documentary play apart from its predecessors on the American stage is the apparent focus on a single central character. Wilde's name is in the title, and it is possible to consider this performance text an exploration of one's carefully constructed identity under fire in a culture that does not accept or understand him. As Ben Brantley wrote in the influential review that promoted the play and contributed to its success, Wilde as subject is presented as a man "struggling to define something" that was "never before the topic of such widespread public discourse."[54] The title of Brantley's review, "Oscar Wilde, Stung by His Own Tongue," suggests that *Gross Indecency* dramatizes the experience of a writer at the height of his creative powers ultimately caught up and harmed by his own words. Wilde "loses control of his rarefied language," which, as Brantley points out, had turned "carnal appetites into Apollonian art"; he is then open to losing "not only a legal battle but his sense of identity as well."[55] The documentary form rarely pins its drama and trauma on a single character's life or circumstances, so it is striking that this play is so invested in the individual life. Its investment in the individual is ultimately shared with and sharable by the community, however, particularly with the contemporary community that became the audience for this version of Oscar Wilde's story.

This dramatized experience of Wilde as an early and very public example of the homosexual subject, self-constructed, a self situated in relation to his cultural moment and to ours, connects the individual and the community, and Wilde is rendered as a kind of ultimate representation of the political, cultural, and legal model of resistance. Reviewer Margo Jefferson explains that Wilde is "still the supreme genius of self-invention" and that although he went to prison for being a homosexual, he was also condemned, "it is now clear, for being a radical esthete who believed that art could help us seek (and find) liberty, justice and equality, with beauty and pleasure for all." Her supposition about the play was that a viewer's first thought would probably be, "'how timely; how contemporary Wilde and his struggles were,'" before quickly revising that thought as follows: "'No, it isn't that he's caught up with us, it's that we're still catching up with him.'"[56] Jefferson's commentary on *Gross Indecency* helps us to recognize the play's contemporary nature and its trials as the enactment of the quest for very American virtues: "liberty, justice and equality." And this documentary play, chronologically situated between *Unquestioned Integrity* and *The Laramie Project*, contributes to our understanding of the connections between the American documentary theater and the law.

By April 1895, when the first of the three trials began, Wilde had attained popular and critical success as a writer and celebrity: he was a well-to-do Londoner with a wife, two children, and two acclaimed plays simultaneously on the boards of West End stages. When the trials began, it was not widely known that Wilde sought out men for sex; his relationship with Lord Alfred Douglas was not, in Wilde's view, a homosexual one, but rather a male love relationship with an intellectual component. Douglas's father, the Marquess of Queensbury, was nonetheless incensed by the influence that he thought Wilde exerted over his son, from whom the Marquess was estranged, and the young man's father left a calling card at Wilde's club with its infamous misspelling, "Oscar Wilde: posing somdomite [*sic*]." Wilde sued Queensbury for criminal libel, and the situation gathered public attention when the case went to court. As S. I. Salamensky reminds us, "posing" is a crucial part of Queensbury's charge against Wilde; the initial issue "did not, technically, concern sexual practices or identity," but that Wilde "performing as—rather than actually being—a 'sodomite' was Queensbury's sole complaint."[57] Queensbury tells Wilde, "I do not say that you are it, but you look it. . . . You look it, and you pose as it, which is just as bad."[58] Both history and this theatrical performance of history, then, put the "posing" on trial, so to speak; the Marquess tempers his own case by leaving the act of sodomy out of his condemnation of Wilde, and this omission rendered the making of his case against his opponent more difficult for Wilde. The Marquess need only prove that Wilde is a poser, but Wilde, it turned out, was forced to defend himself against a charge of flagrant self-construction.

Salamensky argues that the "notion of charging Wilde with posing as anything, of course, carries with it an ironic twist, as Wilde's artistry and intellectual project were based on playful experimentation with appearance" and on his interest in "exploring the spaces between sign and signified." Therefore, "a court bent on discovering the truth about Wilde faced, in this pursuit, a formidable challenge."[59] As Wilde himself says, "I do not pose as being ordinary, great heavens," which seems to confirm that he does in fact, pose. Thus do we see, even in the very origin of this legal proceeding, that representations of identity have to them a postmodern sensibility; the flux of self-creation is intrinsic not only to Kaufman's play and its 1990s themes, but to Wilde's own conception of himself and even to the "charge" that the Marquess makes on his calling card, the originating document in what becomes a contest of written words. What *Gross Indecency* seems to suggest, however, is that Wilde is guilty of having constructed an identity in a very self-conscious way that is about one hundred years ahead of its time.

With the staging of *Gross Indecency*, Kaufman places the documentary self-construction front and center with a playing area at audience level, below and in front of the main level of action. The long table at stage front is covered with books, and the play's narrators quote from them throughout the action. As Robert Myers explains, with this "kind of chorus" reading selections from printed materials, Kaufman has developed a "new kind of wordplay, a polyphonic pastiche that requires the actors and members of the audience to almost repeat the process of research, interpretation and evaluation he engaged in to construct the play."[60] The performance text, as structured by the trials, is performed with nine actors, and Wilde's part is played by an actor who has no other roles, while the other eight actors, who all serve as narrators, play all the other parts. Narrators 1 through 4 sit at the table, which gives the impression of a library's reading room or, as Ben Brantley put it, of "investigators in a Senate hearing."[61] Brantley's comments are particularly striking in the context of this study, for the investigators face the audience and thus suggest that the spectators (in their self-constructions?) may be under investigation too. The proximity of the table to the crowd also emphasizes to the latter that the play "simultaneously puts the actors and audience in the action of uncovering evidence in an attempt to discern the truth(s) of Wilde's trials."[62] The performance area above and behind the table is sparely furnished with tables, chair, and a podium. This staging, as Kaufman stipulates in his script, allows for a Brechtian approach to inform the acting style: that the performers "should portray the characters in the play without 'disappearing' into the parts,'" and that it should be an "actor-driven event," with actors making all the set and costume changes.

The first trial is punctuated by brief scenes of Wilde consulting his lawyer or his friends, with the other actors, as narrators or other characters, reading from a wide variety of documents: Wilde's writings, many of which expound on his artistic theories; Douglas's memoirs; other first person accounts of the events; newspaper reports of the trial; and so on. A textually investigative atmosphere dominates, enhanced both by actors reading from texts and by narrators announcing the author and name of the book or newspaper from which the text comes. As Brown remarks, "the textual form not only supports the direct content of the quoted material, but also visually encompasses the play's theme of questioning and investigating."[63] While this dramaturgical technique underscores the importance of documents to the construction of the play text, Brown points out that it also reflects a "kind of Brechtian dramaturgy in which the actor constantly shifts between demonstrator and character."[64] The disjunction thus created keeps the audience from losing itself in the action and from losing sight of the presentational nature of the documentary form. An author's note by Kaufman also suggests that these "readings" are intended to convey orderliness and stability: "As the play progresses and Oscar Wilde's world collapses, so does this formal device. Therefore, in the second act not all sources are stated."[65] Finally, viewers are made aware that many of the actors' lines did not originate in speech but in writing, and these lines contrast sharply with the spontaneous (and ultimately dangerous) spoken wit and verbal banter that Wilde brings to his judicial testimony.

The structure of *Gross Indecency* demonstrates as much, for the questioning of Wilde, by his own lawyer and then by defense counsel Sir Edward Carson, dominates the first act, and the addition of excerpts from his writings and lectures contributes to the effect that his voice resonates above all else even as his views are being slowly but consistently challenged, critiqued, and ultimately, condemned. Just as the documentary trial play uniquely dramatizes the intersections of fact and fiction, reason and emotion, legal evidence and more ephemeral kinds of knowledge, in his time on the witness stand, Wilde consistently points to those collisions and blurs the lines between them. As he tells Carson, "I cannot answer apart from art."[66] Wilde's shrewd and pithy responses undermine and mock the legal world and its values.

The trial sections of *Gross Indecency* do not come from the original courtroom transcript (lost to history), but from a book by H. Montgomery Hyde: what Stephen Bottoms calls "not a word-for-word transcription" of the trial testimony "but a book compiled decades later from various shorthand records, with all the slips, omissions, and inaccuracies they are likely to entail."[67] Bottoms argues that this dependence on secondary sources is not a shortcoming, however; the unreliability of the texts Kaufman noted as he prepared to construct the piece, and on which it was necessary to rely, serves to strengthen the dramatic conflict woven into the play, with the playwright using the textual contradictions to heighten the work's self-referentiality. The play takes up residence on multiple planes of history and reality, a situation made visible by the piles of books and the diversity of voices that read or speak the words the playwright has collected in his research. Because some large part of these stacks of words present law's stories, the various narratives driving the legal cases forward, the table and its contents serve to challenge the notion that law or history can ever truly go uncontested.

From a theatrical standpoint, in Bottoms's opinion, a strain of self-referentiality is "precisely what is required of documentary plays if they are to acknowledge their dual and thus ambiguous status as both 'document' and 'play.'" For, Bottoms continues, without a "self-conscious emphasis on the vicissitudes of textuality and discourse, such plays can too easily become disingenuous exercises in the presentation of 'truth,' failing (or refusing?) to acknowledge their own highly selective manipulation of opinion and rhetoric."[68] With *Gross Indecency*, according to Bottoms, Kaufman presents an essentially linear dramatic narrative about actual events, "relying for its appeal and accessibility on such time-honored devices as the courtroom cross-examination."[69] At the same time, Bottoms insists, the play "carefully demonstrates the way the texts of the trials, and the many citations with them, stage a disorientating, performative collision between the discourses of art and literary criticism and those of accusatory legal questioning."[70] This collision also makes plain the disjunction between the performance of law and the achievement of justice, a disjunction that is the subject matter of the documentary trial play; despite the regular failing of the legal system, however, the genre presents dueling narratives and renders their telling a necessary if not urgent cultural activity that occupies the courtroom and the theater. As is the case in *Unquestioned Integrity*, ideological and political conflicts are interwoven with questions of identity in *Gross Indecency*. With Queensberry's accusation of Wilde, the legal case that begins the matter compels Wilde to defend himself, for the Marquess has made public, with his calling card, the extent to which Wilde's self-presentation is an affront to Victorian mores. Behind this moral accusation is a legal consideration that will eventually prove damaging to Wilde: Salamensky reminds us, that under British law, "the object of a libel suit bears the burden of proving that the words in question are not in fact libelous because true."[71] Even before the court officially turns to a prosecution of Wilde, his appearance as a witness in the first case puts him in the position of defending himself; not disproving an accusation of "being" a homosexual, or engaging in acts of sodomy, but defending the accusation that he poses as a sodomite. Although Queensbury's libelous remark does lead to questions about Wilde's sexuality, the initial challenge from the Marquess indicts the *performance* of identity, not identity itself. As the questioning in the first trial unfolds, the defense's attempt to meet its burden of proof transforms the plaintiff into defendant, a pattern that bears a striking similarity between this case as presented on the documentary stage and the Hill/Thomas hearings as staged by Hunt.

In *Unquestioned Integrity*, the character of Anita Hill is questioned by the Senator about her motivations, the latter implying more than once that her testimony may be false and that she may have ulterior motives; this line of questioning puts her on the defensive, even though she is not the defendant in the case and she has appeared voluntarily to give her statement. *Gross Indecency* similarly places Wilde under scrutiny, beginning with the very opening of the initial trial, when the defense counsel puts forward a "plea of justification" for his client that asserts the truth of Queensbury's accusation: Wilde published or caused to have published (1) a magazine "relating to the practices of persons of unnatural habit" and (2) "a certain immoral and indecent book with the title *The Picture of Dorian Gray*."[72] Because Queensbury was required by law to establish to the court that his accusation of Wilde's posing was "not in fact libelous because true," the English legal system subsequently requires that the plaintiff prove otherwise. Prosecutor Sir Edward Clarke goes so far as to request that Wilde assure him, "on your honor that there is not and never has been any foundation for the charges that are made against you," which Wilde does.[73] The word "charges" underscores Wilde's legal vulnerability well before he is in fact charged with any crime; judicial tactics and the legal structure of the criminal charge against the Marquess turn accuser into accused.

Furthermore, *Gross Indecency* poses questions about one's self-identity as part of a group; while the initial attack is against Queensberry's behavior, his peers ultimately find him without fault. Once the state (Victoria's monarchy) focuses its prosecutorial attention on Wilde, however, the community unites against the former plaintiff and finds him guilty of unlawful behavior. During the first trial, Queensbury's position is strengthened when the defense counsel threatens to call witnesses who would testify that Wilde had in fact committed acts of "gross indecency" with them; the libel charge instigated by Wilde presents a greater threat to the plaintiff's reputation than Queensbury's accusation did, and it will lead to the indictment of he who served as plaintiff in the first case.

On his lawyer's advice, Wilde drops the suit against his enemy; the defense, however, unsatisfied with this outcome, urged the court to take an additional step to resolve the case before closing it: "as far as Lord Queensbury is concerned, that if there is a plea of not guilty, this plea must include that his plea of justification has been proved." The court grants this request, the clerk confirms that Queensbury's initial accusation "was published for the public benefit," the Marquess is discharged, and with "three strikes of the gavel," the court is adjourned.[74] With these gavel strikes, the defendant's legal closure is attained, while the plaintiff's legal vulnerability is exposed. Particularly, his gender identity will come under heightened scrutiny and condemnation. Although Wilde was ultimately persuaded by

Clarke to forego his legal pursuit of Queensbury, he did not take his attorney's other piece of advice, which was to flee the country in order to avoid having charges of gross indecency brought against him. The second and third trials did just that, the third necessary when the jury of the second trial could not reach a verdict. Wilde was found guilty in the third trial.

In *Gross Indecency*, prior to intermission and before the second trial has begun, however, we witness the court of public opinion turning against Wilde with a newspaper account of the first trial decision announcing a "most miserable case ended" and the Marquess "triumphant," followed by the prediction that his accuser "may now change places with the Marquess and go into the dock himself."[75] Several other journalistic comments follow, along with the information that Wilde has been charged with a violation of the "Criminal Law Amendment Act signed the 1st of January 1885 by Queen Victoria," notably a fairly new law on the books. The legal battle between two citizens in opposition is thus reconfigured before our eyes, as the collection of historical fragments that Kaufman has arranged in this scene shift the law's focus from two gentlemen's warring perspectives to society's pursuit of a criminal. That gross indecency had only recently become a violation of the penal code adds irony to Wilde's situation even as it underscores the constructed nature of the regulation of sexual mores in his period as well as in our own. Finally, this segment of the performance text establishes the parameters of Wilde's new legal contest: he must defend himself against the specific charge of gross indecency while battling a Victorian culture that has succeeded in legislating morality. From script and performance standpoints, this reversal as positioned just prior to intermission adds potency to the theme of identity performance, for we can expect to encounter (and we do) another version of the character Oscar Wilde during the second half of the play.

An interview between an actor playing Moisés Kaufman and an actor playing Wilde scholar Marvin Taylor serves as the opening segment of the play's second half and as an interlude between the first trial and the two that follow. The character of Taylor argues here that the trials eventually go badly for Wilde as he "comes head on up against legal discourse" and "legal-medical discourse," losing as he does to "this sort of patriarchal medical discourse that makes him appear to be a homosexual, as opposed to . . . hum . . . someone who has desire for other men."[76] Taylor goes on to claim that "there is this real nexus of issues that are on trial with Oscar Wilde and they have to do with the role of art, with effeminacy, with homosexuality, with the Irish in England, with class."[77] Although the appearance of Taylor and his postmodern sensibility between the play's two acts function as an academic parody, Brantley suggests that Taylor "fumblingly deconstructs Wilde's performance in court with insights that are none the less valid for being presented satirically."[78] Brantley's critique of this section of the show underscores the idea that *Gross Indecency*'s main subject of legal debate (in this case, did Wilde commit acts of gross indecency or not) can bring to the surface a host of other social and political issues that charge and complicate the legal proceeding, whether or not they are discussed openly. As Frank Harris, Wilde's literary editor and friend, tells Wilde in the play: "An English law court is all very well for two average men who are fighting an ordinary business dispute. That is what it is made for, but to judge the morality or immorality of an artist is to ask the court to do what it is wholly unfit to do."[79] Unfit as a court in any land may be to do such legislating, the law is sometimes forced to grapple with matters that resist adjudication.

Wilde's trials, and Kaufman's reenactment of them, dramatize situations in which a court becomes entangled in the legislation of art and morality. The opportunity that the trials provided for the media was similarly significant: as Morris B. Kaplan argues, the case "fully occupied newspapers across the political spectrum offering a confrontation between two of Victorian Britain's most conspicuous figures. It provided the spectacle of courtroom drama while allowing the press to moralize about life and art, family and friendship, aristocracy and celebrity."[80] So too, as we saw in *Unquestioned Integrity*, the questions of identity are raised when one or more minority groups are, as Ferguson suggested is common for the high profile trial, "endangered or alarmed by majoritarian assumptions at play." In both the plays that Kaufman wrote (he has directed many others), he staged trials, but the trials that ultimately defined the works were not necessarily or entirely the legal trials that are explicit in the texts; they are the cultural trials that pit differing ideologically bound groups against each other in defining or determining some cultural shift or impasse.

As Margo Jefferson wrote in her review of the New York production, speaking of both Wilde and of Michael Emerson's portrayal of him in the play: "It is as if he were ravishingly naked and ravishingly clothed all at once."[81] By exposing himself in all his finery of style and thought, the Wilde of Kaufman's play intoxicates the audience at the outset, only to gradually emerge from behind his own words and become increasingly vulnerable to the legal machinations of the interrogation. As practiced observers of law's due process, American audiences of the play might be seduced by plaintiff Wilde's verbal power and his apparent talent for confounding the opposition's attorney; the contemporary documentary trial play is prone to dramatizations that expose the shortcomings of the judicial system.

When Wilde succumbs to a slip that legally implicates him in behavior that would seem to confirm not only the libelous charge of posing as a sodomite, but his identity as one, his confidence wanes and he falters in his position as the most powerful speaker on stage. In a court proceeding based on words, which have up to this point been Wilde's most valuable cultural currency, the error proves fatal.

The moment that foreshadows his downfall then, not surprisingly, occurs during Carson's cross-examination in the first trial and the first act. The exchange also provides an example of the collision between Wilde's attitudes and his examiner's. Asked if he had ever kissed a certain young man employed as a servant, Wilde responds, "oh, dear no. He was a peculiarly plain boy. He was, unfortunately, extremely ugly. I pitied him for it."[82] What is surely intended as a bit of sarcasm on Wilde's part has a chilling and foreboding effect, and Kaufman's play highlights the shift, for the stage directions stipulate that the *"court falls silent. Pause."*[83] Action briefly ceases and suddenly, the fluidity with which Wilde uses words turns against him, for a simpler answer not only would have sufficed, it would have been to his advantage.

As Wilde's emotions swell to the surface, the barrister's interrogative strength increases, and he repeatedly questions Wilde as to "why did you mention his ugliness?"[84] We see the crack in Wilde's façade. First he *"can't find the words to continue,"* and then he recovers briefly only to berate his questioner and expose himself further: "You sting me and insult me and try to unnerve me; and at times one says things flippantly when one ought to speak more seriously. I admit that."[85] This emotional turn signals Wilde's transformation from the confident plaintiff to the fearful and weak defendant who says, in the middle of the third trial, "I feel that public disgrace is in store for me, I feel certain of it. I never knew what terror was before. I know it now. It is as if a hand of ice were laid upon one's heart. It's as if one's heart were beating itself to death in some empty hollow."[86] His society's insistence on outlawing homosexuality; their exposure and punishment of difference, of ambiguity, are exposed as dangerous and even fatal, not just to the individual but to the larger community.

Wilde's imprisonment hastened his death and made for a premature withdrawal from the world of a creative mind and personality. At the end of the play, just after Wilde is sentenced but before he is led from the courtroom, he says to the judge, "And I? May I say nothing, my lord?" and "his lordship made no reply beyond a wave of the hand to the wardens, who hurried the prisoner out of sight."[87] The epilogue mitigates the darkness of this conclusion somewhat, by reminding the audience that "by the year

1920, Oscar Wilde was, after Shakespeare, the most widely read English author in Europe."[88] While Wilde is silenced by a judicial process that finds him guilty of social reprehension, his artistic influence survived the attack. The condemnation of the courts cannot control public opinion, at least not permanently. A reputation ruined by the legislation of morality can be redeemed by the audience, the critics, the playwrights, the filmmakers who, one hundred years later, tell a new version of the story, however imperfect and contradictory. But the loss remains.

Indeed, *Gross Indecency* dramatizes the loss that comes when a society seeks to legislate culture; it also dramatizes fears about what might happen if we open ourselves to endless possibilities, be they in the performance of identity or lifestyle choices. Kaplan suggests the significance that the trial had for literature specifically and for the culture at large, when he says that "Wilde's conviction had set back more than just his own personal fortunes or the social status of same-sex desires; it marked a containment and moralization of the critical force of literature as such."[89] In *Gross Indecency*, then, the contemporary documentary trial play once again demonstrates its facility for crossover: its use of found objects and original invention; its foundation and structure in legal proceedings that never fail to bleed outside the boundaries of the courtroom; its determination to examine identity, ideology, and their intersections.

In the late autumn of 1998, Kaufman and ten members of his Tectonic Theater Project traveled together to Laramie, Wyoming, to work on a new documentary theater text. Just one month after the murder of Laramie resident Matthew Shepard, a gay student from the University of Wyoming, the Tectonic group spent a week interviewing Laramie residents about the murder, the town, and the people of Laramie, and they would return to Wyoming five additional times over the next fifteen months. The group's work interviewing the people of Laramie in the immediate aftermath of the crime recorded and contributed to the national attention that was focused on this small, isolated city of the intermountain West; in a moment of collective crisis, the townspeople struggled to understand the change in community identity, particularly as determined by outsiders, that accompanied the event. As one resident told the members of the acting company, "If you would have asked me before, I would have told you Laramie is a beautiful town. . . . After Matthew, I would say that Laramie is a town defined by an accident, a crime."[90] One of the Tectonic group members claims that he has "no real interest in prying into a town's unraveling."[91]

What is at issue here, it would seem, is how this performance text, based largely on interviews with individuals directly involved in or witness to the aftermath of Shepard's death, not only draws attention to the ways that a group can come to see itself differently after a high-profile crime and the trial that follows, but also to the possibility that the town could take advantage of the unraveling in order to reconfigure itself as a different kind of community, one that will forge ahead into a new century with a new conception of tolerance and equality. After the successful run of a documentary trial play about Oscar Wilde, and the attention it brought to gender politics and law in another time and place, Kaufman and his company used the stage to shape a current-day legal case into a symbolic debate about homosexuality in the public sphere, in the present moment.

The assault on Matthew Shepard, on the outskirts of Laramie, Wyoming, took place the evening of October 6, 1998, and he was pronounced dead of severe head injuries at a hospital in Fort Collins, Colorado, six days later. He had met his assailants, Russell Henderson and Aaron McKinney, at a bar on the night of the attack and had accepted a ride from them. The two drove Shepard to a remote rural area, robbed him, beat him, tied him to a fence, and left him for dead. He was found, unconscious but still alive, by a cyclist, eighteen hours later. Henderson and McKinney were arrested and arraigned; Henderson pleaded guilty and thus avoided the death penalty but received two consecutive life sentences. McKinney was found guilty of felony murder by a jury and could have received the death sentence; Matthew Shepard's father spoke in favor of allowing McKinney to live in prison, and the speech he made to the court is included in the play. McKinney is serving consecutive life sentences without the possibility of parole.

The murder case received national attention primarily because Shepard, a twenty-two-year-old University of Wyoming student, was openly gay; although the police initially suspected that the motive was robbery, court papers filed several days after the attack, when the two defendants had been charged with the assault, suggested that the victim's sexual orientation may have been a factor as well. As Shepard lay dying, then, what happened to him quickly became an "issue" event, sparking reports and editorials about homophobia in small towns and the absence of hate-crime legislation, particularly in western states that have resisted its enactment, and especially in cases of crimes directed against people because of their gender or sexual orientation.[92] Indeed, local and national discussions of the murder and its aftermath echoed with the question, "Could it happen here?" reflecting, as does the title of the play, that place and community quickly became key pieces of these national debates. The death of African American James Byrd, who was dragged to his death behind a pickup truck in Jasper, Texas, just four months earlier, had all too recently reminded Americans that bigotry and hatred continued to promote violence in our culture. The Rodney King beating and the public discussions that it prompted as well as the changes it brought to the police department in Los Angeles made us aware that citizens of certain races and genders continue to be endangered when their visible identity markers are wrongly perceived as reasons for violence.

The attack on Shepard challenged the myth of a tolerance that we often presume (despite much evidence to the contrary) has replaced the homophobia and hate of earlier ages. Considered together, then, both of Tectonic's performance texts explore the dangers, past and present, of being homosexual, and they investigate the damage that discrimination and fear pose to the social, political, and cultural fabric of a nation. Kaufman described the Shepard murder as a "'watershed moment,'" one that produces an environment in which "'ideas float around in our culture, and an event like this becomes a lightning rod as the ideas come together, parallel subjects like gay issues, community issues, violence, class.'"[93] That Wyoming, a state exemplifying a strict code of western masculinity while touting space, literal and figurative, is the setting for this crime brings into sharp relief the tension between the rigidity of social mores and the flexibility required to enact individual rights and equality. Furthermore, the New York theater group's descent on a small rural town in the intermountain West, having arrived with the express purpose of interviewing people about Matthew Shepard, his death, and the community's attitudes toward homosexuality, exemplifies a red-state/blue-state confrontation guaranteed to raise various and contentious issues of values and lifestyle.

Laramie premiered at the Denver Center Theatre in February of 2000 before going on to a successful production at New York's Off-Broadway Union Square Theatre, where it opened on May 18 and ran for five months. The second most produced play of the 2001–2 theater season, it was subsequently made into an original movie for HBO, and—with scores of stage productions in regional and local theaters, universities, and high schools across the country—it became the most widely produced new play of the century's first decade. When he conceived the project, Kaufman did so in part because he had noticed that national debates about homosexuality and violence had sprung up in the wake of the Shepard assault, and he wanted to foster this open discussion, using theater to do so. He went to his company and posed the questions: "What can we as theater artists do as a response to this incident?" And, more concretely, "is theater a medium that can contribute to the national dialogue on current events?"[94] He also wondered, before the incident, "did anyone in Laramie ever have to talk publicly about these questions? I wanted to hear what they were saying among themselves."[95]

Laramie dramatizes the aftermath of a violent crime, a crime sparked by the perceived danger of a difference in sexual orientation, at a time when citizens and lawmakers, nationwide, were debating (and have continued to debate) the need for hate-crime legislation that would demand a priority response to violent bigotry. Although the real events depicted in Laramie and in *Gross Indecency* occurred one hundred years apart, they similarly explore the law's role in legislating morality: in the case of Oscar Wilde, he was considered a criminal because of his sexual preference, although the play goes on to theorize that his aesthetic approach to art is dangerous to the state as well. In the case of Matthew Shepard, murder is the actual crime, but its occurrence raises issues about whether and how a society ought to provide protective legislation that discourages prejudice by enforcing extraordinary punishments as deterrence.

While the Tectonic's theatrical strategies have much in common with other examples from the documentary theater, *Laramie* offers the most transparent example of how form, content, and theme can come together in this genre. Claycomb calls the play "an exemplar of the staged oral history," most particularly because of the way "that the community of performers integrates with the community represented in the piece."[96] This community integration is relevant to the presentation of law and justice, as well, rendering *Laramie* another kind of "exemplar," one that proposes the investigation of murder, particularly in its exploration of the collateral damage that accompanies the act, as an artistic responsibility. At the same time, the blending of the legal case with the cultural exploration of a community's identity underscores the extent to which the judicial decision is complicated by a multiplicity of voices and perspectives even as it serves as a necessary anecdote to violence and injustice.

In its temporal urgency and its emergence in the moment of its origins, this play hearkens back to its documentary predecessor *Catonsville*. Like the earlier play, *Laramie* recorded an event and its aftermath as events occurred, staging them as legal and cultural developments to the story were ongoing. The completed performance text was produced on the stage less than eighteen months after the murder served as the work's inspiration and reason for being, and during the Tectonic company's final visit to Laramie in November 2000, the group staged the show for the individuals and the community featured in it. The proximity of event and representation was further expounded on in the multiple roles that the Tectonic company members played in the process: initially participating as interviewers, they went on to act as writers shaping and editing the script; in production, they acted all the parts, playing themselves as well as their interviewees when delivering the finished product to audiences. The complexity of relationships in this text, of interviewers/subjects and writers/actors/participants, to name but a few, places the focus on how individuals interact during a tragedy; both the murder and the play that emerges from it bring the people of Laramie together as a community to identify themselves, not singularly or univocally, but as a diverse group of characters adding layering and various kinds of intricacy to the town's past and present.

As in *Catonsville*, the writer figures are involved in creating the dramatic action and appear within it as characters; in performance, Kaufman and his colleagues appear not only as themselves but as various townspeople, these interconnections calling attention to the role that various communities, local, national, and cultural, play in producing a trial text, recording the crime while conveying the impact of the high-profile trial that follows. One significant difference, however: Berrigan was a defendant in the case he dramatized, whereas the Tectonic Project collaborators are included in the narrative because of their decision to document and dramatize the incident. The play makers in this case are also the players and the participants: they solicit, script, and soliloquize the testimony we receive through the performance text.

Interviews with Laramie residents make up the bulk of the text; these dynamic documents, created in part by those who would perform them, cast a different theatrical light than many of the other documentary trial plays, whose contents were culled primarily or solely from archival materials, legal and journalistic.

By creating the play with the community who lived the events, the members of the Tectonic Project created yet another community made up of all those involved in the theatrical production. As such, then, its comparison to *Catonsville* and its similarly timed production in the immediate wake of the crime and the trial that follows indicates the increased cultural visibility and power of the documentary trial play, for *Laramie* came to be a more widely disseminated documentary trial play than any of its predecessors. Furthermore, it pressed on the relative objectivity of the documentary theater form by inserting the playwright(s) into the action. Reviewer Ben Brantley notes the similarity between *Laramie* and the performance texts created by Anna Deavere Smith but suggests that this more recent play "feels less clinical than Ms. Smith's works in presenting its subjects, and the lack of distance is not always an asset."[97] For while the "cast is more than capable in its creation of an affecting emotional climate," Brantley continues, "only a few of its members have anything like Ms. Smith's ear for revelatory speech patterns and are able to summon portraits that feel correspondingly authentic."[98] He does acknowledge, however, that Kaufman finds the "implicit music in repeated phrases and themes . . . and those echoes conjure the feelings of horrified astonishment that certain acts of brutality can still elicit," calling to mind a candlelight vigil, "a stately procession through which swims a stirring medley of emotions: anger, sorrow, bewilderment, and, most poignantly, a defiant glimmer of hope."[99] While Brantley's assessment may call attention to the less seasoned talents of the Tectonic Project's interviewers, it also reflects a general critical agreement about the show: that it packed an emotional punch, one that might have the capacity to employ emotion in the service of judgment.

The final script contains reflections of the intense and personal interplay that marked the interactions between members of the New York theater group and the residents of Laramie. Because *Laramie* is not only about Shepard's murder (indeed, Shepard does not appear as a character and his attack is not represented in the play) but also about the local reaction to the incident and about how a community can survive and thrive under such circumstances, it was significant that the research for the show involved these two very different communities coming together to share their feelings about what had happened. At the time, Kaufman explained what a unique dynamic this situation created when it came time to decide which interviews would be included in the final script; he recalled a "collaboration that led to intense arguments and emotional pleas by company members, campaigning to have their subjects included."[100] Laramie resident and University of Wyoming professor Rebecca Hilliker later reported that the interview period was an extremely important cathartic experience for all concerned.[101] Although Mann's *Greensboro* had used a character named the Interviewer to represent her, that character never speaks outside of the frame of the interview and reveals little of her own feelings. In *Laramie*, the group that visited Laramie shares with audiences the experience of having been involved in such a project, and the extent to which this "field work" informed their attitudes about Shepard's murder, the West, and the impact of tragedy on a community.

The dramaturgy of this show only enhances these connective elements. Don Shewey discusses how it is that *Laramie* reaches audiences and draws them in, suggesting that the actors sustain a "compelling tension through a narrative whose outline is surely known to almost everyone in the audience" by establishing a connection to the audience as themselves, since we are always aware of them as actors, and by "representing the people of Laramie in ways that allowed the residents to recognize themselves."[102] Kaufman's notes on staging reinforce these qualities even as they reflect the playwright's Brechtian roots, when he stipulates, as he did for *Gross Indecency*, that the show should be actor-driven and, furthermore, that "costumes and props are always visible."[103] Michael Janofsky, the chief of the Denver bureau of the *New York Times* who covered the Shepard case and then went on to review *Laramie*'s premiere in his city, noted its similarity to *Gross Indecency* in attempting "to answer similar questions about similar issues," but argued that the "presentation is more personal [in the later play], even though the play focuses less directly on the murder than on its impact on the town."[104] The bare set, containing only a few tables and chairs; the simplicity of the costumes and props; the intimacy of the dramatized interviews: all these features allow for or create space for an informal theatrical experience that reflects and recreates the small town environment of Laramie.

Moisés Kaufman claims to be interested in what happens on stage, at "the intersection of language and form."[105] In a text note for *Laramie*, Kaufman describes his "moment work," a technique he developed to "create and analyze theater from a structuralist (or tectonic) perspective."[106] A theatrical moment in this case is a "unit of theatrical time," says Kaufman, "that is then juxtaposed with other units to convey meaning."[107] Influenced by Mary Overlie and her theory of a "horizontal" dramatic structure that levels the text, so to speak, by putting it on par with other theatrical elements, such as acting, blocking, lighting, and so on, Kaufman developed his "moment work" strategy in order to theatricalize his interview materials. Short sequences of action are created "based on raw interview text . . . that have been isolated and developed in rehearsal so as to foreground theatrical imagery as a complimentary means of storytelling, on par with verbal content."[108] As Rich Brown reports, "Kaufman is the first person to acknowledge that he could not have written *The Laramie Project* alone. . . . The combination of collaborators, technique, and content in *Laramie* formed an ideal situation for the use of Moment Work."[109]

The structure of the action emphasizes the inclusion of the interviewers in this narrative about Laramie, particularly in the "moments" entitled "Journal Entries." They convey the company's hesitations about participating in this project, as in Andy Paris's confession that he has "no real interest in prying into a town's unraveling," and their first impressions of Laramie upon arrival: "we could be on any main drag in America," although "the buildings still look like a turn-of-the-century western town."[110] Several members of the group are gay, including Kaufman, who expresses his concern about "taking ten people on a trip of this nature" and the need for safety rules (travel in pairs with cell phones).[111] Quickly, however, the focus on the company shifts to an introduction of some of the townspeople through a variety of interviews, although the Tectonic Project members provide a brief description to each local who takes the stage and thus we are aware that we are meeting the Laramie residents through the company member. This strategy serves to remind us that while what we hear has actually happened, it is being mediated through the artistic experience of the piece and that which we come to know is what Kaufman and his group have chosen to share with us.

We also come to know both Matthew Shepard and Laramie through these interviews, their good qualities and their quirks, their strengths and their shortcomings, their uniqueness and their sameness. In the case of Laramie, what people say confirms the company's first impression of a town that could be anywhere and a town that is specific to the western tradition. In the case of Shepard, we learn of a shyness combined with a "beaming smile"; "manners," "politeness," and "intelligence" are words that describe him, as well as "little rich bitch."[112] Finally, we hear various local attitudes toward gays, and like everything else we've seen so far in Laramie, they reveal a range of conflicting opinions: the Baptist minister's wife, for example, explains that her husband "doesn't condone that kind of violence" but also "doesn't condone that kind of lifestyle."[113] A "moment" called "Live and Let Live" reveals anything but: lesbian Zackie Salmon confirms that she "would be afraid to walk down the street and display any sort of physical affection for my partner." And Jonas Slonaker "translates the 'live and let live' philosophy as, "if I don't tell you I'm a fag, you won't beat the crap out of me."[114] The documentary theater style, with its method of combining disparate voices, insures that no easy answers, no pat conclusions will ease an audience's way through the web of details and ideological viewpoints. Laramie and Matthew Shepard both are revealed as having complex and contradictory identities.

Unlike *Gross Indecency*, the personal interview, not the written text, dominates the action, and courtroom procedure does not provide the main structural framework. But there is one "moment" in act 2 and a handful of sequences in act 3 that are set in the courtroom where McKinney and Henderson stand trial. The first one, entitled "The Essential Facts," on the surface might seem to be just that, for half of it consists of the judge presiding over the arraignment of the two defendants, reading the charge against them. But before and after the judge relates the facts of the case, we hear from Catherine Connelly, a lesbian professor from the university who says she found out that the arraignment was to take place and decided, "I'm just going."[115] She describes the scene: "probably about a hundred people from town and probably as many news media," with everyone "waiting on pins and needles for what would happen when the perpetrators walked in." When that moment came, she reports, it was "incredibly solemn," and "lots of people were teary."[116] The judge reads his statement, but toward the end of his speech, the stage directions stipulate that he go sotto voce, and as he does, Connolly talks over him, saying, "I don't think there was any person who was left in that courtroom who wasn't crying at the end of it."[117] This description of the arraignment does serve to highlight a community's involvement in the legal process, even if it is primarily as spectators.

The contrast between the system of law and its community is quite striking, the former concerned with facts, the latter with feelings. And because of the overlap between the courtroom activity and Connolly's narrative, we can see beyond the legal situation to its effect on people: the attendees, of course, but also the defendants, who Connolly describes "in their complete orange jumpsuits and their shackles." Although this proceeding is only an arraignment, we have a foreshadowing of McKinney's and Henderson's fate as prisoners. And it is significant that Connolly reports the presence of tears before the details of the assault are read, this suggesting that the people are teary for the defendants who, after all, are "kids themselves, local kids," as she reminds us.[118]

Furthermore, in performance we do not see McKinney and Henderson in this scene, which serves not to separate them out as monsters, but to perhaps suggest that they are still part of the community. At the same time, any sympathy for them that is hinted at here is mitigated by the description of what they did to Shepard, and the final line of the scene is from the judge, ending his statement by saying that the "defendants left the victim begging for his life."[119] This brief "moment" sparely but effectively conveys the emotional impact that the attack has had on the community, while at the same time it suggests that justice will have its own disturbing and lasting effects. Both the murder and the punishment of that murder confront the community with unimaginable trauma, and although the performance text does not limit itself to a court setting, the defendants' arraignment and trials serve to determine the theater company's visits to Laramie and thus become an intrinsic part of the text's structure.

Act 3 contains several more legal "moments" that dominate the final section of the play: "Jury Selection," "Russell Henderson," "A Death Penalty Case," "Aaron McKinney," "The Verdict," and "Dennis Shepard's Statement." The scene titles make clear that the focus of these scenes is not on the victim, Shepard, but on what will happen to the defendants; quite specifically, on whether they themselves will live or die because of what they've done. In "Jury Selection," Trish Steger relates what she has heard about the process;

particularly that the death penalty is being considered and that Russell Henderson is in the courtroom as each potential juror is asked, "Would you be willing to put this person to death?"[120] Henderson pleads out and is sentenced to two life sentences, to run consecutively, despite an impassioned entreaty from his grandmother not to "take Russell completely out of our lives forever."[121] But McKinney proceeds to trial, and it is during this section of the play that we finally see and hear from one of the defendants. Described by the narrator as a tape recording of McKinney's confession, this section is acted out as a two-part interview conducted by Rob Debree that is uninterrupted by a narrator or any other speakers. Indeed, it is perhaps the most extended conversation between two characters in the play, and, like the "Essential Facts" sequence, it provides specific details about the attack: not, as the former was, from a representative of the justice system, but by the individual whose life hangs in the balance for what he has done. Significantly, it is placed immediately before "The Verdict" and "Daniel Shepard's Statement."

Beyond the actual trial scenes, many of the interviews with townspeople have the ring of courtroom testimony, and both prosecution and defense witnesses are represented. While Shepard's friends defend him, for the most part—against the kind of victim blame common to rape trials that leads local Murdock Cooper to claim that the assault was "partially Matthew Shepard's fault and partially the guys who did it . . . you know, maybe it's fifty-fifty"—the assailants also have their share of character witnesses.[122] An anonymous friend of Aaron McKinney describes him as "a good kid," who "just wanted to fit in," who "acted tough," but "you could get in his face about it and he would back down, like he was some kinda scared kid."[123] Another local resident speaks out hesitantly, not in defense of McKinney and Henderson but in order to question the attention that the case is getting and to criticize the media for "portraying Matthew Shepard as a saint." Laramie resident Sherry Johnson admits that she didn't know the victim but is resentful that his murder has gotten such focus when another recent death, in a traffic accident, of a highway patrolman, a colleague of her husband, earned "just a little piece in the paper."[124] She ends with an argument against hate-crime legislation when she wonders, "What's the difference if you're gay? A hate crime is a hate crime. If you murder somebody you hate 'em."[125] She also questions Shepard's morality, calling him a barfly and suggesting that he was "spreading AIDS and a few other things, you know, being the kind of person that he was."[126] Johnson's speech underscores the kinds of judgment that take place throughout the play, much of it based on morality rather than legality, and much of it directed at Shepard rather than at the young men who killed him.

Not surprisingly, organized religion plays a major role in these judgments. Its representatives debate the morality of homosexuality and the morality of murder, and this discussion serves as another kind of trial and another kind of judicial system that examines both the victim and his attackers to decide guilt and innocence. The verdicts in this realm are quite mixed. An early scene called "The Word" gives us a sense of the religious spectrum in regards to the murder and to homosexuality by including testimony from a Baptist minister, a Mormon ecclesiastical leader, a Unitarian minister, and a Catholic priest. In the wake of murder, they speak of the morality of homosexuality, and the priest expresses amazement that some of the ministers in town chose not to participate in the vigil that took place as Shepard lay dying. Stephen Mead Johnson, the Unitarian minister only recently arrived in Laramie, tells his interviewer that, on the religious spectrum, he (Johnson) is so far left that he is sitting by himself.

Two other more intense debates take place when Baptist minister Fred Phelps from Kansas, well known for his public condemnations of homosexuality, comes to town to attend Shepard's funeral and the first trial. As Phelps preaches his message of condemnation and intolerance, he is challenged by two groups of Laramie youth. At the funeral, Kerry Drake tells us that as some high school kids starting yelling at the Fred Phelps group, the kids were joined by a "skinhead" dressed in "leather and spikes everywhere." Drake, expecting trouble from the boy, is surprised when the young man instead leads the group in singing "Amazing Grace." That "moment" is linked to another public confrontation that takes place outside the courthouse between Phelps and one of Shepard's friend, Romaine Patterson. The young woman has convinced her friends to participate in a plan she calls "Angel Action," which has them dressing up in angel costumes with "big-ass wings" and using them to obscure Phelps and his group. As she tells her interviewer, "this big-ass band of angels comes in, we don't say a fuckin' word, we just turn our backs to him and we stand there."[127] So while these ideological confrontations say much about the potential polarization that the murder has brought to the forefront, the challenges to the condemning voices of organized religion succeed without argument or reasoning or biblical debate: they come in the forms of song and silence.

While in *Gross Indecency* we saw morality legislated in the courtroom, here such legislation takes place in the homes, in the streets, in the churches of Laramie. And its appearance does not originate with the crimes of Henderson and McKinney, but with the identity and lifestyle of the victim (Sherry Johnson objected to the fact that Shepard was what she called "a barfly" as well as a homosexual). But moral judgments are, in the end, also levied against the defendants: one from an institution, and one from an individual. The first comes with the report that as a result of his crime, Henderson has been excommunicated from the Mormon church. As the Mormon Home Teacher tells us, "what that means is that your name is taken off the records of the church, so you just disappear."[128] Conveyed to us just after he is sentenced to two consecutive life sentences, meaning that he is physically about to disappear from Laramie and the outside world, it represents a kind of death that, religiously speaking, is more consequential than anything the court could have imposed on him. The other moral judgment, of a sort, is levied against McKinney after he has been found guilty on all counts; it comes in the statement that Dennis Shepard, Matthew's father, makes to the court to persuade the jury not to impose the death penalty on his son's killer. He advocates for McKinney's life, but he acknowledges that despite his decision to "show mercy to someone who refused to show any mercy," he does not forgive him and does not expect to, and "gives" McKinney his life "in the memory of one who no longer lives" primarily so that McKinney can live to remember Matthew and to remember his crime. It is, therefore, a condemnation wrapped in a reprieve.

Dennis Shepard also reminds the audience that Matt's suffering and death "focused world-wide attention on hate. Good is coming out of evil." The image of Matthew tied to the fence, even if it is a mental one for us, reinforces the sense of Matthew's martyrdom. The idea that good is coming out of evil provides some hope and reminds the audience how these events and the play that emerged from them did ripple out from Laramie and charge a nation to face issues that continue to divide us. As Don Shewey wrote in 2002, when hundreds of productions of the play were being staged in every kind of theater: "Clearly, 'The Laramie Project' has entered the mainstream of American culture in a way few plays do. More than a docu-drama fleshing out a news story, it has become a catalyst for communities to discuss something of urgent importance: in this case, hate crimes, homophobia and the treatment of difference in American society."[129]

While legislative strides on these issues have been stalled or defeated, the discussions continue, as do the strides for equality and understanding. Shewey's remarks remind us that theater, in this case documentary theater, can indeed play an important part in promoting such discussions. And as *The Laramie Project* in particular makes plain, the theater's place, unlike the courtroom's place, is to provoke but not necessarily resolve; to not avoid or evade contradiction and difference of opinion; and to provide a space in which emotion can govern us without negative consequence. Trials in a theater need not offer a definitive and satisfactory verdict. While doing so may provide a particular kind of aesthetic pleasure, we are willing to forfeit that for a more complex and ambiguous theatrical experience and perhaps a more profound political experience. When we exit the theater we are, hopefully, energized and newly committed to finding answers, seeking consensus, working toward a more equitable and peaceful society. But the theater has allowed us to consider many facets of experience and opinion, and that variety will be to our advantage as we transform the artistic experience into a guide for the lived experience.

Robert Ferguson speaks of the surprise factor that marks the high profile trial, noting that there is an unsettling element to all of them: often enough, he claims, "this uneasiness involves a minority grouping that feels endangered or alarmed by majoritarian assumptions at play." However, the "threatening factor can also be more general: an entire community can be forced to reflect on behavior that is unprecedented, particularly horrifying, or invasive."[130] The 1990s witnessed a handful of high-profile trials and three documentary trial plays: in each of the latter, one or more minority groups are "endangered or alarmed by majoritarian assumptions at play" and present cases in which conflicts are "unprecedented," "horrifying," and "invasive." Another trend connects the high-profile legal proceedings of the 1990s, and we can see it developing in history as well as in theater.

Beginning with the Rodney King case and the O. J. Simpson trial and then moving to the trials or hearings documented by this decade's theater of fact, a disturbing trend emerges. In all cases except for the Simpson murder trial, a man of color, a woman, or a gay man was, at least initially, on the plaintiff's or the government's side of the aisle. King was the victim in a police brutality case; Hill was called as a witness for the state. Wilde was initially the plaintiff in his libel case against Queensbury, and although Matthew Shepard was deceased at the time his killers were tried, his sexuality and the threat it posed, at least according to the defendants, factored into the violent act that ended his life. The emphasis on law has, we have seen, shifted from the central power of the judge and the government to the individuals who will either attempt to make a difference or attempt to squelch difference. But in the last decade of the twentieth century, another dramatic paradigm is enacted through the rediscovery and reinvention of traumatic trials—a shift in focus to the community and its values in its judgment of itself, its perspective on how its members contribute to or contaminate the whole of the society, and particularly its various cultural communities. In each case put before us by way of the documentary theater, we see that the ultimate tension between private and public is presented in issues of sexual activity or gender identity. It remains to be seen which way majority opinions will go during the new century, for these works do not provide definitive direction for us, shifting their views as they attempt to tell a full if not fully integrated version of historical events dramatized.

For *Unquestioned Integrity* and *Laramie*, recent postscripts have been added to the historical narratives captured by the performance texts that demonstrate a continuation of the debates about identity and law that each trial or hearing and its representation brings into view. A personal rather than a theatrical addendum to the Hill/Thomas controversy, the following newsworthy item demonstrates Hill's role, almost two decades after her testimony, as a still-troubling if not dangerous cultural presence. On October 19, 2010, the *New York Times* reported that Virginia Thomas, the justice's wife since 1987, had recently called Anita Hill at the latter's Brandeis University office to ask for an apology from Hill for testifying against the judge during his confirmation hearings. Hill played the voicemail she received for the *Times* reporter, Charlie Savage, who quoted it in full: "'Good morning Anita Hill, it's Ginni Thomas,' it said. 'I just wanted to reach across the airwaves and the years and ask you to consider something. I would love you to consider an apology sometime and some full explanation of why you did what you did with my husband.'" Ms. Hill responded to the call by turning over the tapes to university police; the FBI subsequently verified that the voice belonged to Ms. Thomas (and the latter confirmed that she had made the call). Hill's response, also quoted in the *Times*, was to state that she had testified truthfully about her experiences with the future Justice Thomas and that "she had nothing to apologize for," also noting that Ms. Thomas "can't ask for an apology without suggesting that I did something wrong, and that is offensive."[131] The incident represents yet another assault on Hill, another effort to contain the unmarried accuser who had spoken out against her male supervisor; this time the attack on her character came from another woman.

The time that has passed since Matthew Shepard's murder and the staging of *The Laramie Project* prompted an actual epilogue, theatrical and widely shared, witnessed by more than fifty thousand people in all fifty states and fourteen countries simultaneously. On October 12, 2009, the Tectonic Theater Company presented a new eighty-minute documentary play titled *The Laramie Project: Ten Years Later*, a collection of interviews that had been gathered in the decade following the attack on Matthew Shepard. The play was performed at Alice Tully Hall in New York City on the eleventh anniversary of Shepard's death. It was staged by more than 150 theater companies, professional and amateur alike, all of them connected via webcast to the Lincoln Center production. Moisés Kaufman and his company introduced the play via the simulcast and then used online tools to facilitate a question-and-answer session following the performances.

Having returned to Laramie in 2008 to examine how the community had come to terms with its tragedy, the Tectonic company used the new piece to explore changing attitudes about Shepard's death and about homosexuality more generally. Among those interviewed for the epilogue were a handful of Laramie residents who had appeared as characters in the first play, reflecting on what had and what had not changed since Shepard's death a decade earlier. Also included in interviews in the epilogue were Matthew's mother, Judy Shepard, who with her husband, through the Matthew Shepard Foundation that they founded after their son's death, fights tirelessly for hate-crime legislation. A lack of resolution marks the new piece and demonstrates the continued ambiguity about the crime and its aftermath, as well as about larger issues of gay rights. The imprisonment of Shepard's attackers had not entirely quelled questions about the motivations for the murder, and *The Laramie Project: Ten Years Later* attempted to mitigate the belief by some, encouraged by a 2006 report on *20/20*, that the murder had been a robbery gone wrong, not a hate crime.

While the discussions sparked by this collaborative theater production testified to the relevance of the original play's continued and expanded life, news from Capitol Hill just two weeks later served to remind all Americans that the legal ramifications of Shepard's murder were ongoing: on October 28, 2009, the Matthew Shepard Act, an expansion of the 1969 federal hate-crime law, was signed by President Barack Obama. It had originally been introduced in 2001 and had died several times in committee during the intervening years. Challenges to and revisions of the laws that govern us continue to unfold: on stage, in court, in the legislature. The defining documentary trial plays of the last decade of the twentieth century shined a spotlight on equality and identity, and the conflicts and debates that these performance texts dramatized remain relevant and current as both theatrical and political markers of a national landscape dotted with legal cases that define American life, that document discrimination and hate among the nation's citizens, that persecute the innocent for speaking out against oppression, that punish the guilty for acts they commit against fellow citizens.

Conclusion: Cultural Legislation

Differences of opinion about the Vietnam War sent citizens into the streets during the 1960s and the 1970s in protest of national policies, and the protests put pressure on law enforcement and the federal government to control and punish citizens whose demonstrations turned violent or destructive. The war took many Americans beyond our borderlands, as they were drafted to fight on unfamiliar terrain with an enemy that existed across a great cultural and political divide. Other pressing issues of the period underscored the domestic differences that contributed to public strife in the contemporary age, beginning but not ending with opposing attitudes toward the defense of country and the defense of rights. These differences exacerbated a generational divide that was then acted out on the street and in the courtroom. Civil disputes that emerged from race, gender, and class inequities generated crimes that began or ended in legal proceedings. Government hearings challenged individuals on their politics and their mores; legal debates ensued on freedom of speech and expression, diversity rights, and the tension between private and public values and behavior. While none of these issues were new, they were renewed in representation through the development of their documentary theater recreations.

Legal issues in the last three decades of the twentieth century, particularly as they found their way into the public sphere through dramatic documentary representations, proved, both politically and theatrically, varied in perspective and in their methods of examination. Overwhelmingly, the high-profile cases that migrated from the courtroom to the theater focused on national debates, encouraging American audiences to examine their identities, define their social roles, and reassert their allegiances. Although a new century and millennium has not meant the end of these debates, the events of September 11, 2001, have forced Americans to finally, perhaps permanently, and more fully acknowledge its membership in a global world, and to devote increased attention to its relationships with peoples and nations beyond its shores. National security issues have become increasingly focused on global terrorism; the shock and the aftershocks of the September 11, 2001, attacks, as well as subsequent terrorist acts around the globe, have prompted an unprecedented engagement with world politics for Americans, many of whom had little prior knowledge of the geography of the Middle East, let alone its religious, political, and economic complexities before the attacks on the World Trade Center and the Pentagon. For these reasons and others, the documentary theater of the twenty-first century has been focused primarily on international terror, prosecutorial torture, contested territorial boundaries, and other transnational topics.

Anna Deavere Smith's dramatic meditation on illness, suffering, resilience, and the human body, performed in her signature solo style, was an important exception to this trend. Her performance text on death and dying, with its critique of an inadequate American medical system and an unsupportive community structure, ascended the boards during the fall 2009 theater season; *Let Me Down Easy*, in its New York production, was staged by the Public Theater just as the national debate on health care legislation hit Congress and the press. International themes, on the other hand, provided the genesis for a handful of other documentary works: the British play *Guantanamo: Honour Bound to Defend Freedom* (2004) by Victoria Brittain and Gillian Slovo, which premiered at London's Tricycle Theater, examines the life of detainees held at Guantanamo Bay. The London stage has also been the site of origin for other new plays using verbatim materials drawing from the political and, in the first two cases, international arenas: *Stuff Happens* (2004) chronicles the political positions displayed and the debates ensuing over the months leading up to the beginning, in 2003, of the Iraqi war, using real speeches and re-created conversations as well as fictionalized exchanges. *My Name Is Rachel Corrie* (2005) was edited by Alan Rickman and Katharine Viner from journal entries and e-mail messages composed by the title character, an American killed by an Israeli Army bulldozer in Gaza during a protest over a house razing. The show was produced in London before moving to New York amidst a blaze of angry objections to its perceivably pro-Palestinian politics. *Frost/Nixon* (2006) was assembled by British film director and dramatist Peter Morgan with materials from the videotaped interviews with Richard Nixon that David Frost negotiated and orchestrated, and that aired on US television in 1977.

Smith's solo performance is the only one of these post-9/11 plays composed by an American and originating on an American stage; all of them, however, focus on events from American political history, particularly as that history connects national agendas to global identities and conflicts. And as British playwrights revise and recount US involvement in the Middle East or our nation's attempts to control the spread of global terrorism, the documentary theater has experienced a shift in perspective: no longer the self-narrative of a nation's internal conflicts, this style of theater has developed, in the new century, as part of a transnational dialogue whose multiplicity of meaning is aimed outward to the world. And as the events of 9/11 and its aftermath have cast a bright and often critical spotlight on the United States and its foreign policies, the documentary theater has developed an increasingly global identity and proliferation that has, to some extent, significantly developed the theater of fact and testimony in new directions. As this increasingly international content has developed, so has the documentary form, argue Alison Forsyth and Chris Megson in the introduction to their 2009 volume of essays, *Get Real: Documentary Theatre Past and Present*: "Although the documentary form has always been, and remains, a powerful tool for polemic and advocacy, the ways in which these are instantiated have evolved to include means other than a central controlling narrative voice or dominant point of view, based on a material and invariably textual notion of the document." The chronological approach that I have used to organize this book helps to make visible this evolution, for even though the plays I have focused on are linked by law's structures and themes, it is possible to discern in the documentary trial play the kind of "ongoing diversification" that Forsyth and Megson attribute to the form as a whole, "its inclusion of a more varied range of 'evidence' (including testimony, orature, and anecdote), and its annexation of a batter of reflexive performance techniques" to indicate a "self-conscious acknowledgement of the complexity of 'reality.'"[1]

Legislative debates, judicial inquiries, and political power struggles continue to fuel the genre, even if not all the above examples are, strictly, speaking, "trial plays." Two other additions to contemporary documentary theater, both created on native soil by American playwrights, also reflect an ongoing interest in using this theatrical form to interrogate the legal system and delineate its shortcomings. Although the first one is not a trial play, it bears mention here, for it documents and dramatizes a collection of personal narratives drawn from citizens treated criminally by the criminal justice system. In 2002, a theatrical effort to promote social justice through performance was staged in New York by the Culture Project: *The Exonerated*, by Jessica Blank and Erik Jensen, which emerged from their interviews with former death-row prisoners who'd been falsely convicted of capital crimes and had served years or even decades in prison before exoneration and release. *The Exonerated* played to sold-out houses in New York City for eighteen months before touring the country; its success in New York and other major cities was due in part to the rotating cast of well-known actors who contributed their names and their talents for the cause of justice. Performances of the show have helped groups such as the Innocence Project attract more than $800,000 in donations to provide legal and economic assistance to individuals depicted in the play and to other falsely convicted death-row inmates, In December 2002, members of the cast staged a private performance of the play for Governor George Ryan of Illinois as part of an effort to influence the governor's position on capital punishment. Before he left office less than one month later, Ryan had commuted the sentences of the state's 167 death row inmates. That same year, the Court TV network honored the creators and actors of *The Exonerated* with its fourth annual Scales of Justice award, established to acknowledge "individuals and organizations that show extraordinary efforts and courage in the fight for justice."[2] A ten-year anniversary production of the show was staged at the Culture Project in New York City in the fall of 2012.

The immense success of *The Exonerated* in performance, particularly its star-studded incarnations, was followed in 2007 by a revival of the first American documentary trial play discussed in this study. Originating as a benefit reading by Tim Robbins's Los Angeles theater company, the Actors' Gang, and directed, as the original production had been, by Gordon Davidson, the revival of *The Trial of the Catonsville Nine* featured Hollywood actors, many of them "prominent antiwar thesps" who "combined offstage passion with onstage skill to create persuasive sketches of the nine Catholic clergy and laity in the dock."[3] Tim Robbins and Martin Sheen read the parts of the Berrigan brothers. Reviewer Bob Vernini noted the connection between past and present, calling the play "a trenchant document that deserves to be back on the boards as often as possible, especially now that the issues it addresses are so relevant and pressing."[4] The positive reception of this revival helped to reinforce the continued currency of the documentary theater from the past, as new subject matter and the influence of technology determine the form's future.

Catonsville and its early foray into fact-based theater recorded the exploits of a group of Catholic dissidents destroying government documents in order to protest a civil authority intent on pursuing what these priests and nuns considered an immoral and violent national agenda. Daniel Berrigan concludes *Catonsville* with his own statement of thanks to the court and to the prosecution for what he considers "the greatest day of our lives," for they had successfully relocated their objections to the war from a Maryland parking lot to a federal court, their attempts to protect draftees from having to serve as "cannon fodder" for what they considered to be an unjust war thus transferred to a national stage.[5] Their court case and its documentary representation were also notable for the particular kind of legal contest that they presented: The question of guilt or innocence did not depend in this case on whether or not the defendants had committed the acts in question. They did not deny doing so. Rather, the defendants claimed that their actions put them above the law, answerable as they were to morality rather than law; if the legal system was supporting immorality, they asserted, it could be and should be violated by moral people. The challenge, then, is to the rule of law itself.

Thirty-five years after *Catonsville*, another conflict that unfolded in the public sphere between religious and secular law would enter the legal sphere before being transformed into documentary theater. The events were transferred to the stage even as the real crisis continued to develop: a criminal, legal, and religious scandal unparalleled in the contemporary age for its scope and for its shocking revelations. Although complaints about the sexual abuse of children by Catholic priests had been registered in parishes and dioceses for decades, it was during the 1990s that increased public scrutiny and the initiation of multiple high-profile lawsuits brought such cases to light. In one of the earliest publicized cases, sixty-eight men and women agreed in December 1992 to a collective financial settlement of more than $5 million as a result of their lawsuit against former Roman Catholic priest James R. Porter, who they alleged had sexually molested them in the 1960s while he served in parishes near Boston. One year later, twenty-two additional victims testified against Porter in a sentencing hearing after he had been found guilty in a Massachusetts criminal court of dozens of sexual offense charges. He was sentenced to eighteen to twenty years in prison, was consistently denied parole, and died of cancer in a Massachusetts prison in 2005. That the abuse spanned thirty years, during which he traumatized dozens of children, indicates that his behavior was not only tolerated but shielded from censure for decades, as he and priests like him were shuffled in and out of parishes with brief stints at counseling centers or other hospitals where they were "cared for" and "cured."[6]

Indeed, many of the civil and criminal cases ultimately brought against the offending priests listed dozens of plaintiffs or witnesses for the prosecution. Moreover, investigative journalism of the highest order, primarily undertaken by the *Boston Globe* and the *New York Times*, contributed extensively to the fact-finding mission involved in the indictment of priests who had committed hundreds of offenses over decades. As a result of domestic and international investigations, some of which continue to today, these abuse cases have been documented in thousands of pages of court transcripts, newspaper articles, and websites.[7] There have been extended legal debates about accessibility to church records, and for the most part these documents have been released into the public sphere. Many of the cases have been argued in open forums as a result of this freedom of information; names, dates, locations of abuse, the string of parishes, all easily charted out by anyone interested in doing so. The church's excellent record keeping proved to be at odds with the amnesia that many priests and bishops claimed when they found themselves involved in the scandal when their names came up in letters or reports. The existence of extensive documentation, however, also nods to *Catonsville*, in its reminder that the Berrigans and their codefendants chose to "attack" documentation in protest, an act they also seemed to believe would delay the employment of the innocent young men whose draft records had disappeared in the parking lot fire. The nine involved, many of them with or formerly with the Catholic Church, understood the power of documents in determining the fates of accusers and accused, the individuals and the institution.

When the allegations of Porter's actions went public, the bishop of the Boston archdiocese, Cardinal Bernard Law, who became the public face of the scandal, was called on to defend or explain the church's response. Cardinal Law would go on to become emblematic of the church's reaction to the case. The cardinal initially declared Porter's behavior an aberration, speaking on the record about what he considered to be the media's overplay of the topic; as the *Boston Globe* and other coverage would reveal, however, Porter was only one of the priests about whom accusations went public and only among the first to be convicted in criminal court. Hundreds were exposed as the victim toll rose into the thousands worldwide, but many accused priests escaped prosecution, some dying before they could be brought to justice, some acquitted or not brought to trial for lack of evidence beyond the personal testimony of the plaintiffs decades after the abuse took place. Throughout the height of the scandal, Cardinal Law continued to downplay the hundreds of other accusations made against Catholic priests, even as the Porter case proved to be anything but aberration.

Cardinal Law himself would face increased pressure as the years of scrutiny and controversy incensed citizens and legal officials alike and prompted insistent investigation into the past. Evidence came to light that implicated Law in the cover-up of cases involving repeat offenders, including Father John Geoghan, whose case eventually involved some 150 people who put forth allegations of abuse against the priest. Finally, in 2002, Law was compelled by the state court of Massachusetts to undergo direct questioning by the plaintiff lawyers in two civil cases, and the transcripts from these depositions, along with thousands of pages of internal court documents, became public information. The details of the involvement that forced Law into a deposition room eventually led to his resignation in December 2002. According to the *Boston Globe* coverage at the time, Law's resignation came in the wake of a superior court judge's decision to release eleven hundred pages of church documents, including many from the archdiocese's records going back several decades, contradicting Law's sworn testimony that he and his aides were not complicit in returning abusive priests to parish work without first determining that they posed no risk to children.[8]

The cardinal was ordered to be deposed prior to several civil cases going to trial, in part because the judge feared that Law could be transferred to a church position outside the United States (as he eventually was), leaving the country before the cases went to court. Sections from Law's 2002 deposition testimony, as well as selections from the church documents in the public domain, were used by Michael Murphy in the construction of his documentary play *Sin (A Cardinal Deposed)* (*Sin*), which had its New York City premiere in September 2004.[9] The conflict here originates with the separation of church and state, for the Catholic Church abides by its own rule of law, established centuries prior to the formation of the United States and many other nations. Recent measures now require church officials to report child abuse to law enforcement, but prior to these changes in religious legislation, the Catholic clergy and its administration regularly chose not to share information about priestly infractions with secular law enforcement, preferring to handle the cases internally.[10] The church's right to deal with its own offenders had been a mostly uncontested reality that has now been challenged; the silence of the past has given way to the statements and revelations, through very substantial paper documentation, that journalistic and legal forces have brought to public attention. The documents that came of discussions with victims and the careful reporting done, assembled, and archived by leading newspapers and specific watchdog sites have led to the dissemination of information about the accused and their current status. More victims and citizens have come forward to corroborate one another's stories. More pressure on law enforcement to do its part in pursuing cases has contributed to the amount of testimony available.

Sin enacts the church's journey of confronting its own documentation without guilt, and so does the genre of verbatim theater allow for the reinforcement of the ways that history regularly unfolds in the confrontation between memories and documents. Murphy reveals in his introduction that he developed his play by relying on the online availability of unprecedented documentation about the case. BishopAccountability.org contains letters, court documents, church archival texts, and so on, on the scandal as it unfolded worldwide, its many links to the archival texts revealing a facsimile of the original document that increases its usefulness with this additional contextualization. The word "accountability" in the site's title explains the purpose of what is called "a comprehensive archive of the evidence"; it is only in the open revelation of facts that justice can be had for crimes committed, and so the site proposes to publish "every conceivable perspective on the crisis," "every relevant diocesan and Vatican document." The website explains its existence by noting that for true "'bishop accountability' to occur, two things must happen: 1) there must be a full 'account' of the bishops' responsibility for the sexual abuse crisis, both individually and collectively, and 2) bishops who have caused the abuse of children and vulnerable adults must be 'held accountable.'"[11] The "account" of the bishops' responsibility for the crisis has so far come through the witness of survivors, through documents unearthed by law enforcement and the legal system, through depositions taken by lawyers, and through media reports. BishopAccountability.org is dedicated to consolidating and preserving that record, and *Sin* provides a way of performing some of those documents in a procedural documentary drama.

David Cote calls the play an "artful distillation of the public record" through "more than 15,000 church correspondence, witness testimony, and depositions" given by Law.[12] Reviewer Tim Unsworth, reporting on the Chicago production, describes the "bubbling anger" that creates a "compelling two-hour drama that left the small cast exhausted and in tears."[13] The frustration that emerges from Law's "frazzled and obfuscating" persona, with no good answers for the questions he faces, creates some of the exhaustion, no doubt, the tears generated by the recognition of the dozens of victims who will suffer every day of their lives in response to what has been done to them. The setting is a deposition room rather than a court-room, but it features elements familiar from the contemporary American documentary trial plays that have preceded *Sin*: a static set, long table and chairs, a water cooler and file cabinets, some of the latter piled with boxes or documents, an American flag in a downstage corner, papers in front of and taken up by the two lawyers throughout the proceeding. Christopher Isherwood called the play "first and foremost a straightforward depiction of a dry legal proceeding," noting that it was "not a case of documentary material transformed into a work of art by theatrical wizardry, as in Moisés Kaufman's 'Gross Indecency: The Three Trials of Oscar Wilde,' a play similarly derived mostly from verbatim testimony."[14]

Law, his attorney, and a composite plaintiff attorney are each played by a single actor, and a single plaintiff, Patrick McSorley, is seated behind the deposition table throughout most of the action. Two other actors play twenty additional characters, primarily other victims or members of victims' families, who appear in a spot set apart from the deposition room. The first, designated Anonymous Mother, reads a letter preserved in the archdiocese's files and dated 1964, reporting her son's allegation that a diocesan priest has molested him. There are other letters by plaintiff witnesses that punctuate the action, but *Sin* is composed primarily of the plaintiff's attorney's questions for the cardinal and of his defensive testimony as he attempts to justify his actions, or, more accurately, his inactions, rationalizing the decisions made to postpone or completely avoid prosecuting priests accused of multiple counts of sexual abuse against children. As is revealed throughout the dramatized proceeding, however, the cardinal is implicated as a coconspirator in the abuse, having facilitated continued contact with children for priests who were accused of or suspected of abuse but whose actions were not reported to secular authorities.

What *Sin*'s evidence and the testimony reveal is that unfortunately, in most cases, investigation into an accusation may have resulted in no more than some church-sponsored therapy that would facilitate the production of what Law calls a "medical attestation" that was it safe for the accused priest to reassume a parish assignment. Although the offender was often assigned to a different parish, the new assignment usually placed no re-strictions on the accused clergy member's interaction with children.[15] Law acknowledges that child molestation is a mortal sin, but not an unforgivable one, and his attempts to separate himself from the fault and guilt exist primarily of denying knowledge of the abuse cases, claiming that a lack of awareness of the details of the accusations kept him from calling for more strident measures to prevent further criminal activity. A sworn affidavit from a witness named Jackie Gauvreau reports a confrontation with Law, "face-to-face," over an accusation against Father Paul Shanley, another priest accused of multiple offenses but whose case floundered in appeals court for years in part because the testimony against Shanley had emerged from therapy designed to draw out repressed memories.[16] The documents available on Shanley are so multiple and so specific that it is hard to imagine any challenge to the case against him; yet the uncertainty surrounding the best way to handle accusations that had been hidden in the past and only come to the surface with therapy reflects a challenge to the judicial power and the resistance that such a plan might work.

The character of Law begins the play with a disavowal of his pending resignation, explaining that the relationship of a priest to the church is a marriage of sorts, and one would not therefore "walk away" from the responsibility to stay and help fix the problems. The deposition begins with the announcement that the action against Law involves "failing to protect the plaintiffs [eighty-seven of them] from sexual abuse by Roman Catholic priests of the Archdiocese of Boston."[17] The question of Law's culpability is, in part, a matter of chronology, for he points out that many of the abuse incidents preceded his tenure as archbishop; it is a matter of hierarchy as well, for he explains that his aides were responsible for making some of the decisions, and he denies always being informed about the cases. Another strategy for justifying the church's methods of dealing with the abuse was to stress that a cardinal has a responsibility to pasture his own flock, and in his testimony about Father John Geoghan, he argues his responsibility to be "pastorally present to a priest who, in his life, did minister well to a number of people," although he ends that sentence by acknowledging that Geoghan "at the same time, terribly abused children."[18] In a *New York Times* interview at the time of the production, playwright Murphy notes that Law's decisions, even bad ones, "were based on precepts that we might all agree with, such as people deserve a second chance, or no one is a hundred percent evil."[19] The commitment Law claims to his clergy is not wrong in itself, but as attorney for the plaintiff Orson Krieger conducts his questioning, the audience comes to understand that faithfulness to his priests took precedence over ministry to the victims: indeed, he left the latter to his aides. When Law reads aloud, at the plaintiff's request, from a letter he wrote to Father Geoghan expressing support, McSorley *"will storm out,"* to be retrieved soon after by Krieger.

In *Sin*, the seating arrangement of the deposition room puts all official figures of the proceeding on the same level in that informal space; although civil cases pending compel the cardinal to testify, he is not under arrest and is never charged with any crimes. There is a reflection of the old in this new picture, as the cardinal's black suit and holy pendant recall the ritual-heavy judicial robes donned in other, earlier documentary trial plays. A member of the clergy is once again in the defensive position, just as the Berrigans and their colleagues had been in *Catonsville*. That other collection of priests, nuns, and former religious were examples of the church establishment fringe, however, some of them dismissed from their duties because of their political activism. The priestly figure being questioned in *Sin*, on the other hand, presides over the most powerful Catholic archdiocese in the United States, and he is being called to explain why he did not actively bring the accused molesters to justice. He is finally being accused of inaction by the victims who have come forward to testify; and those victims have been aided in their pursuit of the guilty priests by investigative journalism and by the therapeutic community. Murphy's performance text notes that Cardinal Law resigned in 2002, but by 2004 the cardinal had been assigned a post at the Vatican with dual citizenship. At the conclusion of *Sin*, the announcement of this new and prestigious position is made just after Law and his attorney depart the stage, having never provided explanation, apology, regret, or anything other than a show of innocence and a mask of confusion about the accused priests and about the indictment of the cardinal and his archdiocese administration.

What follows Law's departure from the stage reminds audience members about the tragedy of such denial, as plaintiff McSorley narrates his version of the events that have brought him to this day of questioning, beginning with the suicide of his father, a loss that left him vulnerable to the priest's advances of friendship. An invitation out for ice cream represented luxury and piety both, the full measure of a priestly relationship. However, the abuse follows and before "I knew it," McSorley claims, "his hands were up my shorts and he was grabbing at me."[20] One line then interjected by Krieger informs us that McSorley died of a drug overdose one year after the proceedings, at age 29. But we hear from the plaintiff once more, as he repeats the words his abuser spoke to him: "'let's just—just you and me. No one else has to know about this.' (*Curtain*)." The conclusion is marked by its lack of resolution, even though the report of McSorley's suicide suggests the end of worldly pain for him. Although the priest had instructed his victim to keep their activities confidential, insisting on the need for secrecy about the events that had left the boy "shocked, petrified," the legal proceeding, while hardly definitive or satisfying, does provide an opportunity for the victim to release his long-standing shame.[21] *Sin* offers audiences a complex situation for its consideration: a church official not charged with any crime

179

despite his complicity in denying decades of child abuse cases. He may disavow knowledge of his priests' behavior, but the play suggests the extent to which Law was tried and found guilty in the court of public opinion, thereby offering some measure of community resolution.

The contemporary documentary theater continues to remind its audiences of the political component in drama, and one possible way to develop that component is as it regularly intersects with law. Be it an attempt to heal the scars of civil protest through artistic representation, or to provide solace to a community in the wake of shocking criminal cases, the documentary trial play helps to explicate and demonstrate the legal and the emotional components of each event and the complexities of its situation. The trial, the tribunal, and the government hearing have become one of the most significant public venues and symbols of a group's need for the release of trauma; since World War II ended, they have become increasingly visible as some of the primary political structures that either individuals or groups can employ to bring their own histories forward, particularly those histories that are riddled with injustice and oppression. A unique manifestation of a centuries-old tradition of dramatizing history, documentary theater has adapted many twentieth-century and now twenty-first-century trials, demonstrating the significance of the law in the decisions and revisions of American life and culture.

As courtroom proceedings or rhetorical forms, judicial models in the theater emphasize the important role the trial serves in contemporary art and experience. The trend toward documentation, toward representations of truth, however complex and contested, has developed in film, theater, television, and photography, unabated, to the present day; it has proven influential in shaping commercial and noncommercial world theater in its time. But Peter Weiss also called the documentary theater "an element of public life."[22] The comingling of the real and the representative is necessary, Weiss insists, and the documentary form must always achieve a creative purpose as well: "documentary theatre [that is] intent on being primarily a political platform, and which gives up being an artistic achievement, calls its own validity into question."[23] Martin writes that what makes documentary theater provocative "is the way in which it strategically deploys the appearance of truth, while inventing its own particular truth through elaborate aesthetic devices."[24]

Beginning in 1970, American playwrights and theater companies have built a body of work in the field, as a variety of subject matter has raised and staged the major topics of our age: civil rights and civil disobedience; urban unrest and violence; sexual orientation and sexual harassment. The frequency with which the resolution for these issues has been attempted in a courtroom, and the facility with which judicial documents can be transformed into theatrical dialogue, has contributed to the development of a significant and coherent subset of the form: the documentary trial play. It provides audiences both information and critical distance through which to view landmark legal cases from contradictory or ambiguous perspectives; if viewers remain unresolved in their feelings, they are nonetheless educated about the case and its complexities. The static meets the course of change as we move from dramatic texts drawn within the space of the criminal court and ruled strictly by the judge, a powerful figure of the law, to an increased emphasis on cultural and civil representatives and institutions affecting if not transforming the rule of law. In 1970, the patriarchal emblem who sits above all and wears a black robe, a costume of authority, reflects the central power of the court, the system, in guiding us as we seek to determine our values, particularly our attitudes about law enforcement, violence, freedom, and peace. The experience of the early contemporary American documentary theater reinforces the post–World War II hierarchy in which white, male, fatherly figures dominate (even visually on stage) and all action and reaction comes about to and through that judge who presides over all.

We see too, that even in dramatizing events from the period that encapsulated the intense rebellion against the hierarchy, it is the dominant and very visible representative of that hierarchy who emerges most powerfully as the theatrical interest point in each work, albeit for very different reasons: the Judge of *Catonsville* strikes just the right balance of reason and empathy, while the portrayal of Judge Hoffman in *Chicago Conspiracy* all too chillingly portrays the judicial force gone wild in a narcissistic frenzy, the suppression of individual personality nowhere in evidence. Despite the outrageousness of the latter, however, the overall visual and structural movement of each play is to recapture the frustration of a world gone mad with war and death, young American men threatened with extinction. Although the priests and the Yippies have their day in court and the opportunity to proclaim their positions, both legal and ideological in some cases, the defendants are found guilty, and each play ends with the declaration of verdict and/or sentence. In reality, few of the latter were borne out, as appeals and other factors mitigated these renderings. More importantly, however, we are left with an impression of the judicial system as one empowered by a linear authority that is comfortable enforcing domestic uprisings through legal means.

In reality and in representation, it seems, the earliest plays of the contemporary documentary theater influence us to take our cues from the man on the bench. Cultural perceptions about the law, specifically those we carry around with us each day, arise from images of a legal system that allows little space for difference, for multiplicity, for the level of unrest that might naturally arise in a diverse nation. Quickly contained by laws that prohibit or discourage acts of protest, even, in the case of Bobby Seale, the only defendant of color in either play, physically bound and gagged, the citizens are held accountable in criminal court and are found guilty. The changes their actions have wrought are debatable; what is more significant to this discussion, however, is the picture of power we are left with when the documents of the age are put together in theatrical renderings of a system of law. Not yet toppled or at least discomfited, by other wars, the culture wars, to come, the image and voice of the government comes down to us from the height of judicial authority.

Contemporary law and life come together and thus underscore the connections between the individual, the judicial, and the political. This link destabilizes the assumptions of individual identity even while offering audiences an alternative. As Claycomb argues, documentary plays "take the discourse of history- and life-writing, and shift their discursive conceptions of the subject from the single protagonist to the greater community. This radical approach to subject formation not only disrupts the empowered status of the subject's authority, but also encourages the integration of the audience into the tenuous sense of community created by the theatrical event itself."[25] The documentary trial play also allows for the predominance of emotion in a situation that mirrors the law but is not the law. It does not have to solve the problems of a legal dispute. Theater plays out the roles that empathy and emotion should and do play in such contested situations, and thereby it contributes to our understanding of the complexities of law even while declining to meet its more rigid demands of keeping society safe and deciding outcomes in the face of danger/death/delinquency.

Dual strains of the documentary trial text set it apart from itself at times: its emphasis on the rationality of law but within the psychological framework of dramatic structure and language. The "stereopsis" of German documentary theater, its "in-depth image of reality," and what Paget calls "two, distinct, but interlinked, structures of feeling," one positivist and one skeptical, in his definition of the "documentariness" of a cultural product, are in the contemporary American documentary theater two contradictory representations of fact and feeling, of faith and doubt; they prove crucial in formulating statements and questions about the American legal system.[26] And the legal system proves crucial for examining, if not settling, the major issues of the age.

Elayne Rapping indicts television for supporting and advancing what she argues is the "drift of criminal justice policy" that has occurred since the 1990s and which has shifted "the pendulum toward the public's major concern with the punishment of 'wrongdoers.'" Her major theme is, she says, to expose the "criminalization of American life."[27] She rightly relies on both fictional depictions and on documentary developments of the small screen to show that despite the failure of such enforcement plans as the "war on drugs," the "popularity of harsh criminal law policy continues to hold sway among American voters and poll participants."[28] While her theory about the connection between culture and policy is one that suggests the increased rigidity of attitudes about justice and an embrace of a "law-and-order" system, something of the opposite might be suggested if the documentary trial play is also considered as a less pervasive but nonetheless accurate barometer of another direction of cultural perceptions about the law.

Ultimately, the multiple perspectives teach a new series of truths, to be believed or denied. They are often one and the same, as suggested by the conflicting viewpoints that emerge from theater works that reimagine reality. These dramatic pieces further complicate our perceptions of a system that awards unearned privilege for randomly assigned designations such as race, class, and gender. Courtroom narratives that mock, evade, or embrace equality become performance texts that prompt us to think rationally and feel emotionally about the systems that produce them. We thus experience conflicting reactions to a type of theater that recreates history even as it unhinges itself from history, honoring a system of truth telling while calling the truth a provisional circumstance.

The law is the Law. Not so, says the documentary trial play. Law shifts from constant to changing as it attempts to achieve justice for all. In their ubiquity, their uniformity, and their uniqueness, contemporary documentary trial plays pose challenges to the law even as they uphold its authority, in many cases, by recreating the court case details with astonishing faithfulness. Nonetheless unlimited by the historical texts produced in the original proceeding, they are also free to invoke artistic license to uncover additional themes and issues that may unfold when the real events are treated by stage artists, visual or verbal. Spurred on by the drama of the legal arena, the trial transcripts and interviews that have been preserved by government or gathered in dramaturgy can take on additional weight when coupled with theatrical spectacle and enhanced with additional personal testimony, newspaper sensationalism, or technological wizardry.

In "The Judicial Opinion and the Poem," James Boyd White compares those two kinds of texts in order to establish their similarity and to explore what we might gain by the comparison. His essay dwells extensively on the significance of composition to our understanding and appreciation for texts. To read a legal text as a composition "made by one mind speaking to another" and as a "text whose author decided what belongs within it, and what will be left out" is to read, he says, "not merely as a reader, but as a writer or composer." And he goes on to say that as "composers of texts that are addressed to those who will read what we write not as commands or declarations but as composition, and as readers who insist upon reading that way, we create for the moment a world together in which our common circumstances, and with them our common humanity, are confirmed."[29] The trial play offers audience members and readers this kind of composition, and the documents allow for the creation of such a world, a world of common humanity.

The potential for the development of the documentary theater in general and the trial play in particular is far from exhausted. The search for truth and justice through documentary theater continues into the twenty-first century, complicated by issues of globalization and the impact of international law along with an increased awareness of world politics. Indeed, the playbills of current theater both nationally and internationally suggest that the form has and will continue to develop and continue to present us with ever-changing perceptions of reality. As inequity continues to mark individual and cultural encounters on the world stage, the legal system appears in guises that are at once documentarian and dramatic. Truth edges into the stage spotlight, takes a bow and shows its face briefly before stepping back into the shadow of the past or the present. History and theatricality merge and the contemporary age is remembered and recognized in its transformation into a style of art that revises the very system it replicates and leaves behind a collection of stage symbols that recall the institutions and the crises of the age: books, a gavel, a church's stained-glass window. The rule of law is challenged when one part of the system sees the incident as a legal point of difference, or when the rule itself is not the best one for resolving the issue of conflict. The legal case is made, but it does not satisfy its constituency; either additional litigation or a more public form of resistance in the form of community violence or representative violence may follow. What also follows is a performance text restricted in its language and therefore in its action, but expansive enough to explore the big issues by taking on the events of history: performance texts that make us think about the legal events that shape our world, but texts that will also make us feel about the events. In a dramatic form that downplays realism and its emotional richness, the community of viewers nonetheless faces searing moments of confrontation with the words of the past; such confrontation can demonstrate that the documents of history allow us to feel their truths, however incomplete or fragmented these truths may be. As transformed into a very stylized form of theater, their observations about the world reach us in a structured and artistic manner that has retained enough pure reality to remind us to think while we are feeling, to judge while we are suffering, to believe while we are mourning.

NOTES · SELECT BIBLIOGRAPHY · INDEX

Notes

Introduction: Legal Representation

1. Robert Ferguson, *The Trial in American Life*, 1.

2. Ferguson, 2.

3. Attilio Favorini credits Brecht with using the word "documentary" in a theatrical context for the first time in 1926, commenting on Erwin Piscator's early experiments with the form in postwar Berlin. Although historical drama has long had a place in the theater, Piscator capitalized on technological developments and used photographs, sound, and early moving pictures to construct theater based exclusively on existing documents. See Attilio Favorini, *Voicings: Ten Plays from the Documentary Theater*, xvii. In the 1960s and 1970s, reviewers used the term "theater of fact" to describe this developing genre. Emily Mann, a major force in documentary theater during the 1980s and 1990s refers to her documentary plays as "theater of testimony," and the current wave of this style of theater in Britain is referred to as "verbatim theater."

4. Derek Paget, *True Stories? Documentary Drama on Radio, Screen and Stage*, 1.

5. Paget, 42.

6. Eric Bentley, *Are You Now or Have You Ever Been, Rallying Cries: Three Plays*, 3.

7. Carol Martin, "Bodies of Evidence," *Documentary Theater*, 9.

8. Constructing a play directly from the public record reflects the twentieth-century preoccupation with the real, and thus do the inclusion of verbatim testimony, interviews, and language lifted directly from various kinds of public records prove rich source material for the talented documentary playwright or company. This style also embraces the use of other modes of visual art central to documentation

and its principles, such as film and photography. In the drive for "cultural leverage," Piscator and many subsequent documentary playwrights have thus incorporated multimedia sources; film clips, slides, music, and sound recordings serve to help convince audiences of this theatrical style's unique perspective on world history. While the use of multimedia formats marks the genre as distinctly modern, the trial as a dramatic structural device is an ancient development, dating as it does in Western drama all the way back to Aeschylus.

9. Ferguson, 30.

10. Martin, "Bodies of Evidence," 11.

11. Ferguson, 25.

12. Ferguson, 27.

13. Bruce Weber, "On Stage and Off."

14. Barbara Lewis, "The Circle of Confusion: A Conversation with Anna Deavere Smith," 56.

15. Will Hammond and Dan Steward, eds., *Verbatim Verbatim: Contemporary Documentary Theatre*, 10.

16. Carol Martin, "Anna Deavere Smith: The Word Becomes You," 52.

17. Peter Weiss, "Fourteen Propositions for a Documentary Theater," 375.

18. Laureen Nussbaum, "The German Documentary Theater of the Sixties: A Stereopsis of Contemporary History," 239.

19. Martin, Carol, "Bodies of Evidence," 9.

20. Nussbaum, 239.

21. Nussbaum, 240.

22. Weiss, 376.

23. Shoshana Felman, *The Juridical Unconscious: Trials and Trauma in the Twentieth Century*, 1.

24. Felman, *The Juridical Unconscious*, 1.

25. Felman, *The Juridical Unconscious*, 5–6.

26. Felman *The Juridical Unconscious*, 6.

27. Felman, *The Juridical Unconscious*, 107.

28. Felman, *The Juridical Unconscious*, 107. Two documentary plays of German origin, both first produced in the early 1960s and both focused on the Holocaust, helped to create interest in this theatrical style among American playwrights and theater producers. *The Deputy* (1963), by Rolf Hochhuth and directed in its German premiere by Piscator, indicted Pope Pius XII for his failure to speak out against the Holocaust; it was staged in a shortened version the following year in New York City and was subsequently produced by Gordon Davidson at UCLA. Davidson went on to become a major creative force in the development of the American documentary trial play. *The Investigation* (1965), by Peter Weiss, drew on documents gathered at the Frankfurt Auschwitz trials, and the subsequent publication of his theoretical manifesto "Fourteen Propositions for a Documentary Theater" proved to be a significant influence on the form.

29. Nussbaum, 240.

30. Clas Zilliacus, "Documentary Drama: Form and Content," 230.

31. Pnina Lahav, "Theater in the Courtroom: The Chicago Conspiracy Trial," 7.

32. Robert M. Cover, "Violence and the Word," 212.

33. Cover, 212.

34. Cover, 214.

35. James Boyd White, *Acts of Hope: Creating Authority in Literature, Law, and Politics*, xi, 40.

36. White, *Acts of Hope*, 42.

37. White, *Acts of Hope*, 42.

38. Lahav, 10.

39. Lucy Winner, "Democratic Acts: Theater of Public Trials," 151.

40. Peter Brooks, "The Law as Narrative and Rhetoric," *Law's Stories*, ed. by Brooks and Paul Gewirtz (New Haven, CT: Yale University Press, 1996), 16.

41. Brooks, "The Law as Narrative and Rhetoric," 16.

42. Susan A. Bandes, *The Passions of Law*, 1–15; 1–2.

43. Shoshana Felman and Dori Laub, *Testimony: Crises of Witnessing in Literature, Psychoanalysis, and History*, 57.

44. Felman and Laub, 57.

45. Felman and Laub, 59.

1. Judicial Identification: *The Trial of the Catonsville Nine* and *The Chicago Conspiracy Trial*

1. "A Survey of ROTC's Status in the Ivies," *Harvard Crimson* 28 September 1973. http://www.thecrimson.com/article/1973/9/28/a-survey-of-rotcs-status-in/. Accessed 18 January 2010.

2. D. Graham Burnett, *A Trial by Jury*, 161–62.

3. Samuel H. Pillsbury, "Harlan, Holmes, and the Passions of Justice," 330. It is important to note that Pillsbury sets up the norm of legal culture and its attitude about the judge, however, in order to compare the extent to which the "passions of justice" were manifested in the subjects of his essay, John Marshall Harlan and Oliver Wendell Holmes, and the effect of either passion or its absence on the judicial legacy of each.

4. Paul Kahn, *The Reign of Law: Marbury v. Madison and the Construction of America*, 105.

5. Kahn, 107.

6. Kahn, 107.

7. Ferguson, 36.

8. Dan Isaac, "Theater of Fact," 109. Isaac's essay is a useful examination of the staging of two 1971 productions: the first New York production of *The Trial of the Catonsville Nine*, and the Washington, DC, production of *Pueblo*.

9. Daniel Berrigan, *The Trial of the Catonsville Nine* (Fordham ed.), 34. This version of the script is the original one and was the script used for the first production in the New Theater for Now series in Los Angeles. The acting version of the text, roughly half the length of the original script, was published by Samuel French. The Fordham edition is the only one currently in print, but the Samuel French edition has been and remains the one most commonly performed. Unless otherwise noted, the reviews quoted in my discussion are of the Samuel French version. My textual analysis will include some comparison of the two scripts, especially as pertains to representations of law and justice.

10. Berrigan, 38.

11. See "Fire and Faith: The Catonsville Nine File," vers. 1.0, November 2005, Enoch Pratt Free Library, 20 November 2007, http://c9.mdch.org/index.cfm. Accessed 25 June 2010.

12. This video was also included in the documentary film "Investigation of a Flame," dir. Lynne Sachs, 2001, which is available on DVD.

13. United States of America v. Philip Berrigan, et al., United States District Court for the District of Maryland, Criminal Trial #28111, 225.

14. United States of America v. Mary Moylan, Appellant, et al., United States Court of Appeals for the Fourth Circuit, Nos. 12988–12996, 417 F.2d 1002, 1969, 2.

15. Berrigan, 40.

16. Berrigan, 41.

17. Berrigan, 41–42.

18. Berrigan, 42–43.

19. John Simon, "Theater Chronicle," 291.

20. Daniel Berrigan (Fordham ed.), xvii–xxi.

21. Berrigan (Fordham ed.), xvii.

22. Berrigan (Fordham ed.), xviii.

23. Berrigan (French ed.), 42.

24. Berrigan (Fordham ed.), xviii.

25. The initial run of *Catonsville* served as the second offering in the 1970 season of the Center Theater Group's New Theater for Now, a series developed by artistic director Gordon Davidson to introduce new playwrights and new plays to Los Angeles audiences. This early version of *Catonsville* ran for six performances beginning on Thursday, 6 August 1970, with Davidson directing. The script as revised by Saul Levitt then opened Off Broadway on 31 January 1971, produced by the Phoenix Theater at the Good Shepherd Church, just off Lincoln Center and held over several times. From there it moved to Broadway, where it played at the Lyceum Theater for twenty-nine performances, from June 2 to 26, 1971. This version was then produced as a main stage production at the Mark Taper Forum and ran from June 17 to August 1, 1971. A film version, faithful to the stage play as it had been revised by Saul Levitt, was released in 1972. It was directed by Davidson and produced by Gregory Peck. A most recent one-night performance of *Catonsville Nine* occurred on 18 August 2007, a star-studded reading of the play whose $250 price tag benefited the Actors' Gang and the Office of the Americas, an international justice organization that provides educational programs. A short video of an interview with the actors and Tim Robbins talking about the Actors' Gang is available for viewing at http://www.playbill.com/news/article/110390.html. Reviewer Bob Verini welcomed the play's comeback, calling it a "trenchant document that deserves to be back on the boards as often as possible, especially now that the issues it addresses are so relevant and pressing." "The Trial of the Catonsville Nine," *Variety*, posted 20 August 2007, 1:44 PT, http://www.variety.com/review/VE1117934459.html?categoryid=33&cs=1. Accessed 15 June 2009.

26. Philip Nobile, "The Priest Who Stayed Out in the Cold," 9.

27. Robert Cover, "Violence and the Word," 203.

28. Carol Martin, "Bodies of Evidence," 10.

29. Berrigan, *Catonsville Nine* (acting version; see note 8 above), 5. David Darst was killed in an automobile accident near Auburn, Nebraska, on 30 October 1969, after the trial but before he had served his sentence.

30. David C. Gill, "Review of *The Trial of the Catonsville Nine*, by Daniel Berrigan," 209

31. Martin, "Bodies of Evidence," 9.

32. Gordon Davidson, "Formative Moments in a Theatrical Life," A Rector's Forum presentation of Gordon Davidson. All Saints Church, Pasadena, CA. Electronic archives. 27 February 2005. http://www.allsaints-pas.org/archives/sermons /formative-moments-in-a-theatri.htm. Accessed 22 July 2010.

33. Ray Zeman, "Controversial Play Set at Music Center Prompts Criticism, D1.

34. Moylan was never caught by the FBI. In 1978, she turned herself in and served three years.

35. Clive Barnes, "Riveting Work by Berrigan," 40.

36. Barnes, "Catonsville 9 Makes the Broadway Scene," 38.

37. Simon, 291.

38. Dan Sullivan, "'Catonsville' Recites War Evils," *Los Angeles Times* 10 August 1970: E1, 17.

39. Sullivan, "Berrigan Play Given New Look," 11.

40. Sullivan, "'Catonsville'—Once a Sermon, Now a Play," E1.

41. Isaac, 124.

42. Paul Gewirtz, "Narrative and Rhetoric in the Law," 3.

43. Paget, 17.

44. Nussbaum, 240.

45. Jessica Silbey, "Patterns of Courtroom Justice," 97.

46. The *Los Angeles Times* reported at least two readings of the play done at Los Angeles churches during the years 1970–71. Both the Burbank Unitarian Fellowship and Saint Matthew's Episcopal Church in Pacific Palisades staged readings as part of their Sunday services; in the latter case, a discussion period followed. See, "Catonsville Reading," *Los Angeles Times* 22 November 1970: A2 and "'Catonsville' to Be Acted Out Sunday," *Los Angeles Times* 25 September 1971: 24. At the St. Matthew's reading, the rector Canon Cary read the part of the judge, and he was quoted as saying, "Officially as a parish we are advocating no particular position (but) it is this issue we wish to explore."

47. Gill, 209.

48. Simon, 292.

49. Richard K. Fenn, *Liturgies and Trials: The Secularization of Religious Language*, 11, 49.

50. Berrigan, 48.

51. Berrigan, 48.

52. Berrigan, 48–49.

53. Berrigan, 29.

54. Berrigan, 45.

55. James Boyd White, "The Judicial Opinion and the Poem," 132.

56. Fenn, 8.

57. Fenn, 51.

58. Berrigan (Fordham ed.), 73.

59. Berrigan, 33.

60. Berrigan, 49.

61. Berrigan, 50.

62. Berrigan, 48.

63. Berrigan, 48–49.

64. Berrigan, 46.

65. Berrigan, 48.

66. See Bela Kiralyfalvi, "The Catonsville 'Trilogy.'"

67. Fenn, 45.

68. Peter Babcox et al., Letter.

69. Babcox et al.

70. Ron Sossi and Frank Condon, *The Chicago Conspiracy Trial*.

71. The *New York Times* reported from London that a "verbatim documentary called 'Chicago/Conspiracy' played there for one night at the Open Space Theater, text by John Burgess." Also in 1970, the BBC aired a television documentary dramatization of the Chicago Conspiracy Trial. It used the actual trial transcripts in its creation and production, and the program ran for three hours during prime viewing time. It was acquired by Public station KCET in Los Angeles and broadcast there in 1975.

72. Julio Martinez, "Review of 'The Chicago Conspiracy Trial,'" *Variety* 16 October 2007 http://www.variety.com/review/VE1117935112.html?categoryid=33&cs=1. Accessed 8 August 2010. In the published script of the play, two jurors are listed as being played by women. However, there was no jury in the 2007 production, and, in fact, as is conventional in this form, the theater audience served as jury.

73. Frank Condon, "Director's Notes," in Sossi and Condon, *The Chicago Conspiracy Trial*, vi.

74. Steven Leigh Morris, "'The Chicago Conspiracy Trial': Boomer Town," *LA Weekly* 25 October 2007 http://www.laweekly.com/2007–10–25/stage/the-chicago-conspiracy-trial-boomer-town. Accessed 12 August 2010.

75. "Current Season," *Odyssey Theater Ensemble*, 15 December 2007. http://www.odysseytheater.com/current.htm. Accessed 15 February 2008.

76. Lahav, 23.

77. For a detailed account of the trial and its legal aftermath, see John Schultz, *The Chicago Conspiracy Trial*, new introduction by Carl Oglesby.

78. Condon, "Director's Notes," vi.

79. Sossi and Condon, 1–2-4, 1–2-5.

80. Sossi and Condon, 2–9-102.

81. Kahn, 116.

82. Kahn, 116.

83. Sossi and Condon, 2–1-58.

84. Sossi and Condon, 1–2-6.

85. Sossi and Condon, 1–3-11.

86. Sossi and Condon, 1–3-12.

87. Sossi and Condon, 1–4-18.

88. Sossi and Condon, 1–4-19.

89. Sossi and Condon, 1–4-19 and 1–4-20.

90. Sossi and Condon, 1–9-40.

91. Sossi and Condon, 1–9-41.

92. Sossi and Condon, 1–9-41.

93. Sossi and Condon, 1–9-40.

94. Lahav, 29.

95. Sossi and Condon, 1–9-41.

96. Lahav, 28.

97. Sossi and Condon, 1–10–42 and 1–10–43.

98. Sossi and Condon, 1–12–50.

99. Sossi and Condon, 1–12–53, 54.

100. Lahav, 29.

101. Sossi and Condon, 2–3-62.

102. Sossi and Condon, 2–2-60.

103. Kahn, 116.

104. Sossi and Condon, 2–9-102.

105. Paget, 30.

2. National Investigation: *Inquest* and *Are You Now or Have You Ever Been*

1. Freed, *Inquest* (Ecco Press ed.), 145.

2. Donald Freed, "The Case and the Myth: *The United States of America v. Julius and Ethel Rosenberg*," 200.

3. Freed, "The Case and the Myth," 201.

4. Freed, *Inquest*, (Ecco Press ed.), 147.

5. Walter Kerr, "'Inquest': Kerr Votes against It," 99.

6. Freed, *Inquest*, (Ecco Press ed.), 189. These words have not been altered by Freed and are taken verbatim from the trial transcript.

7. Ferguson, 238–39.

8. Ferguson, 245.

9. Freed, "The Case and the Myth," 199.

10. Freed, "The Case and the Myth," 200.

11. Donald Freed, *Inquest* (Samuel French ed.), 3.

12. Freed, *Inquest*, (Ecco Press ed.), 146.

13. Freed, *Inquest* (Ecco Press ed.), 146.

14. Freed, *Inquest* (French ed.), 5.

15. Freed, "The Case and the Myth," 201.

16. Freed, *Inquest* (French ed.), 8.

17. Freed, *Inquest* (French ed.), 9.

18. Freed, *Inquest* (French ed.), 9. The juror drum is still used in select districts or other voting areas; it is a barrel or drum that contained all the names of the possible jurors; a set number would be drawn from the drum.

19. Gad Guterman, "Reviewing the Rosenbergs: Donald Freed's Inquest and Its Jurors," 265–87; 273.

20. Kerr, 9.

21. Janelle Reinelt, "Notes for a Radical Democratic Theater: Productive Crises and the Challenge of Indeterminacy," 283–300; 286.

22. Ferguson, 245.

23. Martha Minow, "Stories in Law," 24–36; 26.

24. Minow, 26.

25. Freed, *Inquest* (French ed.), 55.

26. Freed, *Inquest* (Ecco ed.), 145.

27. Guterman, 277. Guterman ties Freed's playwrighting to his alleged resistance work supporting the Black Panther Party and to his efforts to provide grounds for overturning the Rosenberg-Sobell verdict.

28. Kerr, 99.

29. Guterman, 273.

30. Guterman, 266.

31. Martin, 9.

32. Kerr 99.

33. Freed, *Inquest* (Ecco ed.), 170.

34. See Ferguson, 246.

35. Clive Barnes, "Theater: 'Inquest' Opens," 37.

36. Freed, *Inquest* (Ecco ed.), 196.

37. Freed, *Inquest* (Ecco ed.), 197.

38. Freed, *Inquest* (Ecco ed.), 197.

39. Guterman theorizes that the harshest criticisms of the play came from those reviewers who were US born and already working for the press during the time of patriotic frenzy that led many Americans to assume the defendants' guilt (278).

40. Brenda Murphy, *Congressional Theater: Dramatizing McCarthyism on Stage, Film, and Television*, 3–4.

41. Eric Bentley, *Are You Now or Have You Ever Been, Rallying Cries: Three Plays*, 8–76, 167.

42. Stephen Farber, "A Play about HUAC Stirs Hollywood," 105.

43. Mel Gussow, "Bentley and the Committee," 77.

44. Farber, 105.

45. Farber, 105.

46. The other two plays are *The Recantation of Galileo Galilei* and *From the Memoirs of Pontius Pilate*.

47. Murphy, 103.

48. Bentley, 4.

49. Bentley, 4.

50. Bentley, 4.

51. Murphy, 96.

52. Murphy, 96.

53. Bentley, 3.

54. Bentley, 4–5.

55. Quoted in Bentley, 3.

56. Bentley, 3–4.

57. Bentley, 51.

58. Bentley, 51.

59. "The Motion Picture Production Code." http://productioncode.dhwritings. com/multipleframes_productioncode.php. Accessed 2 July 2011.

60. "Hollywood 'Red' Probe, HUAC Hearings Begin 1947/10/20," YTTM TV presents Video Time Machine, http://yttm.tv/v/5011. Accessed 15 August 2011.

61. Bentley, 11–12.

62. Bentley, 12–13.

63. Quoted in Bentley, ix.

64. Just days before Ethel and Julius Rosenberg were executed, Douglas granted a stay of execution on the grounds that Judge Irving Kaufman had sentenced them to death without the consent of the jury. Douglas's ruling might have provided the Rosenbergs up to six months additional time, since the Court was not in session at

that time. In his decision, Douglas wrote that it is "important that before we allow lives to be snuffed out we be sure—emphatically sure—that we act within the law. If we are not sure, there will be lingering doubts to plague the conscience after the event." See Walter and Miriam Schneir, *Invitation to an Inquest*, 243. Douglas himself was unsuccessfully targeted for impeachment because of his liberal views in 1970.

65. Bentley, 14.

66. Bentley's play provides a cross-section of the various attitudes that the witnesses adopted as they went before the committee.

67. Bentley, 29.

68. Bentley, 24–25.

69. Bentley, 31.

70. Bentley, 34.

71. Bentley, 21–22.

72. Bentley, 23.

73. Bentley, 29.

74. Bentley, 70.

75. Bentley, 70.

76. Bentley, 71.

77. Bentley, 71.

78. Bentley, 75.

79. Farber, 105

3. Ideological Confrontation: *Execution of Justice* and *Greensboro (A Requiem)*

1. Shoshana Felman, "Education and Crisis, or the Vicissitudes of Teaching," 17.

2. Felman, 17.

3. Ryan M. Claycomb, "(Ch)oral History: Documentary Theatre, the Communal Subject and Progressive Politics," 100. Claycomb's discussion of "staged oral histories," as he calls documentary theater, includes analysis of some plays included in this study, specifically Emily Mann's and Anna Deavere Smith's works. The naming difference nods once again to the fluctuation of this form of theater and to the difference in emphasis a discussion can take. Claycomb's interest in feminist forms seems to fit with his use of "staged oral histories" just as Mann's perspective favored "theater of testimony" and mine prefers "documentary theater."

4. Claycomb, 100.

5. In an article published by the *San Francisco Chronicle* on the twenty-fifth anniversary of the killings, chief defense attorney Douglas Schmidt is reported as saying, "I don't think Twinkies were ever mentioned in testimony," although he recalls "HoHos and Ding Dongs," but no Twinkies. In fact, the cream-filled confections were mentioned, but only in passing. Junk food was an insignificant part of the defense. The matter was raised briefly in testimony by Marin psychiatrist Martin Blinder, one of five defense therapists. Today, the entire episode is characterized by Schmidt as "a throwaway witness . . . with a throwaway line." See Carol Pogash, "Myth of the 'Twinkie Defense,'" D1.

6. Emily Mann, "Still Life," *Testimonies: Four Plays*, 34.

7. Naomi Siegel, "Daring to Disagree, and Sent to an Asylum," NJ12.

8. John Istel, "Emily Mann," 44.

9. Attilio Favorini, "The Documentary Plays of Emily Mann," 152–53.

10. After the play's debut in Louisville, the show was staged at various regional theaters before landing on Broadway, including the Empty Space Theatre in Seattle, Berkeley Rep, the Arena Stage in Washington, DC, and the Guthrie Theatre in Minneapolis. Like many of the plays examined in this book, *Execution of Justice* found its way to the screen in the form of an original television movie, this one airing on Showtime in 1999.

11. Favorini, xxxiii.

12. Emily Mann, Interview with Alexis Greene, 286–310, 294.

13. Mann, Interview, 299.

14. William Kleb, "You, the Jury: Emily Mann's *Execution of Justice,*" *Theater* 16 (1984): 55–61. Reprinted in Favorini, *Voicings,* 332–37; 332.

15. Mel Gussow, "Stage: Emily Mann's 'Execution of Justice,'" C3.

16. David Richards, "'Justice for All': At Arena, the Many-Sided Dan White Case," *Washington Post* 17 May 1985. Rpt. in Attilio Favorini, *Voicings: Ten Plays from the Documentary Theater,* 337–39.

17. Emily Mann, *Execution of Justice, Testimonies: Four Plays,* 149.

18. Mann, *Execution,* 151.

19. Mann, *Execution,* 151–52.

20. Mann, *Execution,* 152.

21. Mann, *Execution,* 153.

22. Mann, *Execution,* 152

23. Mann, *Execution,* 152.

24. Mann, *Execution,* 156.

25. Kleb, 333.

26. Kleb, 333.

27. Kleb, 333.

28. Mann, *Execution,* 155.

29. James Boyd White, "The Judicial Opinion and the Poem," 125.

30. Leslie Bennetts, "When Reality Takes to the Stage," H1.

31. Favorini, *Voicings,* xxxiv.

32. White, 121.

33. Mann, *Execution,* 159.

34. Mann, *Execution,* 179. Gwenn Craig and several other female characters are identified by their first names rather than their last throughout the script.

35. Mann, *Execution,* 178.

36. Bennetts, H1.

37. Felman, *Juridical Unconscious,* 165.

38. Mann, *Execution,* 182.

39. Elayne Rapping has argued that television and movies about crime have increasingly encouraged audiences to side with the police and district attorneys who prosecute criminals. See her book *Law and Justice as Seen on TV.*

40. Kleb, 334.

41. Susan Letzler Cole, "Emily Mann Directs Execution of Justice," 56–72, 61.

42. Mann, *Execution,* 245.

43. Mann, *Execution,* 244.

44. Richards, 337–38.

45. A full report on the events and their aftermath is available online at a website created to make public the work and the findings of the Greensboro Truth and Reconciliation Commission. In its own words, the commission was formed as an "independent, democratically selected body seeking truth and healing transformation for Greensboro, N.C., a city left divided and weakened by the events of Nov. 3, 1979. The seven commissioners were a respected group of individuals selected for their diverse perspectives, strengths and resolve to fulfill their Mandate." The panel began its work on June 12, 2004, and spent two years examining evidence, holding public hearings, and interviewing survivors before presenting its final report to the residents of Greensboro on May 25, 2006. See *Greensboro Truth and Reconciliation Commission Report*, 2 June 2008, http://www.greensborotrc.org/. Accessed 5 January 2010.

46. "Executive Summary," *Greensboro Truth and Reconciliation Commission Report*, 6 http://www.greensborotrc.org/exec_summary.pdf. Accessed 5 January 2010.

47. "Executive Summary," 11.

48. Emily Mann, *Greensboro (A Requiem), Testimonies: Four Plays*, 282.

49. "Transforming Tragedy into Triumph," web page, Mountain Area Information Network, 14 June 2008, http://www.main.nc.us/wncceib/GJFMARCH.htm. Accessed 5 January 2010.

50. "Injustice and the Justice System," *Greensboro Truth and Reconciliation Commission Report*, 311, http://www.greensborotrc.org/post1979_justice.pdf. Accessed 5 January 2010.

51. "Injustice and the Justice System," *Greensboro Truth and Reconciliation Commission Report*, 258, http://www.greensborotrc.org/post1979_justice.pdf. Accessed 5 January 2010.

52. Mann, *Greensboro*, 257.

53. Istel, 44.

54. *Greensboro Truth and Reconciliation Commission*, Welcome Page. http://www.greensborotrc.org. Accessed 5 January 2010.

55. Vincent Canby, "When Communists Clashed with Nazis and the Klan," C14.

56. Dudley Clendinen, "Theater; Of Old South Violence Only Yesterday," H5.

57. Istel, 44.

58. Claycomb, 110.

59. Mann, *Greensboro*, 330.

60. Mann, *Greensboro*, 330.

61. Alvin Klein, "Theater; Now, a Few Words with the Audience," NJ11.

62. Emily Mann, "In Conversation," 4.

63. Emily Mann, interview with Daniel Zwerdling, *All Things Considered*, Natl. Public Radio, 3 March 1996.

64. Mann, *Greensboro*, 265.

65. Mann, *Greensboro*, 267.

66. Mann, *Greensboro*, 267.

67. Mann, *Greensboro*, 267–68.

68. Mann, *Greensboro*, 270, 275.

69. Claycomb, 114 and n. 71.

70. Mann, *Greensboro*, 259.

71. Mann, *Greensboro*, 268.

72. Mann, *Greensboro*, 268–69.

73. Dawson, *Documentary Theatre in the United States: An Historical Survey and Analysis of Its Content, Form, and Stagecraft*, 41.

4. Individual Interrogation, Communal Resolution: *Unquestioned Integrity: The Hill/Thomas Hearings, Gross Indecency: The Three Trials of Oscar Wilde,* and *The Laramie Project*

1. At this writing, O. J. Simpson is behind bars for conspiracy, robbery, kidnapping, and assault in a 2008 case that involved sports memorabilia; on December 5, 2008, he was sentenced to fifteen years for his involvement.

2. Ruth Wilson Gilmore, "Terror Austerity Race Gender Excess Theater," 30.

3. Numerous studies of the 1992 riots have been published, and they reflect the concerns of sociologists, historians, artists, political scientists, media specialists. See Haki R. Madhubuti, ed., *Why L.A. Happened: Implications of the '92 Los Angeles Rebellion*; Mark Baldassare, *The Los Angeles Riots: Lessons for the Urban Future*; Nancy Abelman and John Lie, *Blue Dreams: Korean Americans and the Los Angeles Riots*; Robert Gooding-Williams, ed., *Reading Rodney King: Reading Urban Uprising*; Min Hyoung Song, *Strange Future: Pessimism and the 1992 Los Angeles Riots*.

4. Richard Stayton, "A Fire in a Crowded Theater: Anna Deavere Smith Relives the Los Angeles Riots," 22.

5. Stayton, 22.

6. As reported in the *Los Angeles Times* on May 18, 1993, the opening of *Twilight* at the Mark Taper Forum was postponed ten days while already in previews because Smith continued to gather interviews and add material to the script. See Don Shirley, "Artist Delays Opening of 'Twilight' Theater," *Los Angeles Times*, F1. Most significant was her interview, subsequently included, of Reginald O. Denny, the truck driver pulled from his cab and beaten in an incident during the first hours of violence.

7. These include *The O. J. Simpson Story* (1995), produced by Twentieth Century Fox Television; *The People vs. O. J. Simpson* (1996), a five-part series produced by CNN; and *O. J.: Monster or Myth* (2010), a documentary that stars Simpson talking about the trial, filmed before he was sent to prison in 2008.

8. Mamie Hunt's play, *Unquestioned Integrity: The Hill / Thomas Hearings*, is printed in Attilio Favorini, *Voicings: Ten Plays from the Documentary Theater*, 365.

9. Hunt, 356.

10. Quoted in Adolphson, 33.

11. Heather Mackey, "Review of *Unquestioned Integrity*," 10.

12. David Pellegrini, "*Unquestioned Integrity* Questioned," 373–76; 373.

13. Sue Adolphson, 33

14. Mackey, 10.

15. Hunt, 356.

16. See "The Decade of Woman: 1992–2002." *Women in Congress*. Web. 20 August 2010, http://history.house.gov/Exhibitions-and-Publications/WIC /Historical-Essays/Assembling-Amplifying-Ascending/Introduction./ Accessed 22 April 2011, and "Year of the Woman." *United States Senate*. Web. 20 August 2010, http://www.senate.gov/artandhistory/history/minute/year_of_the_woman.htm. Accessed 22 April 2011.

17. Hunt, 360.

18. Hunt, 356.

19. Hunt, 358.

20. Hunt, 365.

21. Hunt, 365.

22. Hunt, 366.

23. Hunt, 368.

24. Hunt, 365–66.

25. Robin West, *Caring for Justice*, 100.

26. Hunt, 364.

27. Adolphson, 33.

28. Steven Winn, "A Theatrical Rerun of Hill vs. Thomas, E1.

29. Mackey, 10.

30. Joe Adcock, "Drama Brings Back Frustrations of the Hill-Thomas Proceedings," 10.

31. Hunt, 371.

32. Hunt, 371.

33. Hunt, 356.

34. Hunt, 372.

35. Hunt, 371–72.

36. Hunt, 361–62.

37. Hunt, 362.

38. Peter Brooks, *Troubling Confessions: Speaking Guilt in Law and Literature*, 40.

39. Hunt, 365.

40. Hunt, 365.

41. Hunt, 367.

42. Hunt, 367.

43. Hunt, 372.

44. Hunt, 372.

45. West, 108.

46. Smith, Anna Deavere, *House Arrest: A Search for American Character In and Around the White House, Past and Present*, 102.

47. "The Story." *Tectonic Theater Project.* Web. 15 September 2010, http://www.tectonictheaterproject.org/Tectonic.html. Accessed 10 April 2011.

48. "The Story."

49. Moisés Kaufman, "Author's Introduction," *Gross Indecency: The Three Trials of Oscar Wilde*, xiii.

50. Moisés Kaufman, *Gross Indecency*, 1.

51. Indeed, a well-received bio-pic called *Wilde*, directed by Brian Gilbert and starring Stephen Fry, was in movie theaters in 1997, the same year that *Gross Indecency* was first staged.

52. Quoted in Robert Myers, "Nothing Mega about It Except the Applause," H28.

53. Myers, H1.

54. Ben Brantley, "Oscar Wilde, Stung by His Own Tongue," 18.

55. Brantley, "Oscar Wilde, Stung by His Own Tongue," C18.

56. Margo Jefferson, "Importance of Being Modern," C 11.

57. S. I. Salamensky, "Re-presenting Oscar Wilde: Wilde's Trials, *Gross Indecency*, and Documentary Spectacle," 577.

58. Kaufman, *Gross Indecency*, 21.

59. Salamensky, 578.

60. Myers, H28.

61. Brantley, "Oscar Wilde, Stung by His Own Tongue," C13.

62. Rich Brown, "Moisés Kaufman: The Copulation of Form and Content," 55.

63. Brown, 55.

64. Brown, 55.

65. Kaufman, *Gross Indecency*, 5.

66. Kaufman, *Gross Indecency*, 35.

67. Stephen Bottoms, "Putting the Document into Documentary," 62.

68. Bottoms, 57–58.

69. Bottoms, 61.

70. Bottoms, 63.

71. Salamensky, 576–77.

72. Kaufman, *Gross Indecency*, 31.

73. Kaufman, *Gross Indecency*, 51.

74. Kaufman, *Gross Indecency*, 65.

75. Kaufman, *Gross Indecency*, 65.

76. Kaufman, *Gross Indecency*, 76.

77. Kaufman, *Gross Indecency*, 75.

78. Brantley, "Oscar Wilde, Stung by His Own Tongue," C18.

79. Kaufman, *Gross Indecency*, 28.

80. Morris B. Kaplan, "Literature in the Dock: The Trials of Oscar Wilde," 118.

81. Jefferson, C13.

82. Kaufman, *Gross Indecency*, 56.

83. Kaufman, *Gross Indecency*, 56.

84. Kaufman, *Gross Indecency*, 57.

85. Kaufman, *Gross Indecency*, 58.

86. Kaufman, *Gross Indecency*, 114.

87. Kaufman, *Gross Indecency*, 127.

88. Kaufman, *Gross Indecency*, 130.

89. Kaplan, 130.

90. Moisés Kaufman and the Members of Tectonic Theater Project, *The Laramie Project*, 9.

91. Kaufman, *Laramie*, 10.

92. Ten years after Shepard's death and despite the introduction of bills that would allow for hate-crime legislation, no hate-crime law has been passed in Wyoming. Indeed, among all the states in the Intermountain West, only Wyoming has resisted passing any hate-crime legislation. Colorado is the only state in the region that has voted to include sexual orientation in its hate-crime categories. See the Anti-Defamation League's web site, http://www.adl.org/learn/hate_crimes_laws/map_frameset.html. Accessed 30 April 2011.

93. Michael Janofsky, "A Death in Laramie, Reimagined as Drama," AR10, 28.

94. Kaufman, *Laramie*, vi.

95. Don Shewey, "Town in a Mirror," 14.

96. Claycomb, 99.

97. Ben Brantley, "A Brutal Act Alters a Town," E4.

98. Brantley, "Brutal Act," E4.

99. Brantley, "Brutal Act," E4.

100. Quoted in Janofsky, AR28.

101. Judith Graham, "Erasing Stereotypes in 'Laramie,' A Small Town Faces Its Fears and Prejudices," 5.

102. Don Shewey, "A Play Has Second Life as a Stage for Discussion," A7.

103. Kaufman, *Laramie*, xiv.

104. Janofsky, AR28.

105. Shewey, 14

106. Kaufman, *Laramie*, xiv.

107. Kaufman, *Laramie*, xiv.

108. Bottoms, 64.

109. Brown, 58.

110. Kaufman, *Laramie*, 10, 14.

111. Kaufman, *Laramie*, 10.

112. Kaufman, *Laramie*, 29, 60.

113. Kaufman, *Laramie*, 27.

114. Kaufman, *Laramie*, 58–59.

115. Kaufman, *Laramie*, 44.

116. Kaufman, *Laramie*, 44.

117. Kaufman, *Laramie*, 45.

118. Kaufman, *Laramie*, 44.

119. Kaufman, *Laramie*, 45.

120. Kaufman, *Laramie*, 81.

121. Kaufman, *Laramie*, 83.

122. Kaufman, *Laramie*, 58.

123. Kaufman, *Laramie*, 33.

124. Kaufman, *Laramie*, 64.

125. Kaufman, *Laramie*, 64–65.

126. Kaufman, *Laramie*, 64.

127. Kaufman, *Laramie*, 79.

128. Kaufman, *Laramie*, 84.

129. Shewey, "Play Has Second Life," A7.

130. Ferguson, 2.

131. Charlie Savage, "Clarence Thomas's Wife Asks Anita Hill for Apology," A1.

Conclusion: Cultural Legislation

1. Alison Forsyth and Chris Megson, *Get Real: Documentary Theatre Past and Present*, 2.

2. Court TV went on to produce a film version of *The Exonerated*, widely available on DVD.

3. Bob Verini, "Review of 'The Trial of the Catonsville Nine,'" *Variety* 20 August 2007. http://www.variety.com/review/VE1117934459.html?categoryid=33&cs=1. Accessed 30 June 2011.

4. Vernini.

5. Berrigan (Fordham ed.), 122, 48.

6. Online archives document these cases and their investigations. The sources provide detailed information on the history of abuse: the Church's response to accusations; the journalistic coverage; victims' stories. Extensive details are available online at the *Boston Globe*'s Spotlight site, a complete archive of the scandal and of the prize-winning investigative reporting that placed the *Globe* in the center of the controversy. http://www.boston.com/globe/spotlight/abuse/. Accessed 15 July 2011.

7. The molestation scandals were back in the news during 2010, when Pope Benedict XVI was accused of not acting on abuse accusations during the 1990s, when as Cardinal Ratzinger he headed the Vatican office that dealt with child-abuse cases. An investigation that had been authorized by the then cardinal's deputy into allegations made against an American priest, Father Lawrence Murphy, was halted when Murphy wrote to the cardinal to explain that he was ill and to beg that he be allowed to live out his life "in the dignity of the priesthood." "Pope Accused of Failing to Act on Sex Abuse Case," BBC News, 25 March 2010, http://news.bbc.co.uk /2/hi/8587082.stm. Accessed 18 July 2011. Legal debates connected to the press investigation of the scandals also continue: the *New York Times* reported in October 2009 that the United States Supreme Court rejected a request from the Roman Catholic diocese of Bridgeport, Connecticut to delay the release of thousands of legal documents from lawsuits filed against priests. The diocese argues that the ruling threatens the First Amendment rights accorded to religious groups. See Paul Vitello, "Diocese Loses Bid to Keep Abuse Records Sealed," A28.

8. Kevin Cullen and Charles M. Sennott, "A Respite, Then Firestorm Ignites," A20.

9. Michael Murphy, *Sin (A Cardinal Deposed)*. *Sin* was initially produced in Chicago and a suburb of Boston before a new production opened at the Clurman Theatre in New York City in September 2004, where it received a 2005 Obie Award and two Drama Desk nominations.

10. See *BishopAccountability.Org*, an online source for updated and extensive information on the child abuse cases brought to light within the Catholic Church: http://www.bishop-accountability.org/. Accessed 20 April 2011. Among its documents are the "Charter for the Protection of Children and Young People," first composed in 2002 and then revised in 2005 (publication date 2006). It sets out norms that it described as "complementary to the universal law of the Church and [that] are to be interpreted in accordance with that law" (12). It proposes that privacy of victims will be foremost, as will be the work with them pastorally, necessary so that they may move past the pain. It promises that the Church will work with parents, civil authorities, and law enforcement to bring cases to justice. It pledges to evaluate personnel and take special care to see that anyone with access to children be vetted carefully. It requires each diocese to have a written policy for how it will proceed in child abuse cases.

11. "Who We Are," *BishopAccountability.Org*. 15 December 2010. http://www .bishop-accountability.org/Who_We_Are/. Accessed 20 April 2011.

12. David Cote, "Filtering Priests' Sins through Two Prisms," B9.

13. Tim Unsworth, "The Stage Trial of Cardinal Law," 21.

14. Charles Isherwood, "The Anguish Is Plausible, but His Eminence Forgets," E1.

15. Murphy, 163.

16. More information, including a timeline of Shanley's life, is available on *BishopAccountability.Org.* http://www.bishop-accountability.org/assign /Shanley-Paul-Richard.htm. Accessed 20 April 2011. At every turn the narrative provides links to primary documents, all available digitally in their original formatting by way of the Shanley page; this archival record of Shanley's career contributes a tragic but nonetheless important and detailed history of a man with unchecked power.

17. Murphy, 156.

18. Murphy, 168.

19. Cote, B14.

20. Murphy, 181.

21. Murphy, 181.

22. Peter Weiss, "Fourteen Propositions for a Documentary Theatre," 377.

23. Weiss, 383.

24. Martin, "Bodies of Evidence," 10.

25. Claycomb, 95.

26. See Nussbaum, 240, and Paget, 17.

27. Elayne Rapping, *Law and Justice as seen on TV*, 16, 17.

28. Rapping, 263.

29. James Boyd White, "The Judicial Opinion and the Poem," 123.

Select Bibliography

Primary Texts

Bentley, Eric. *Rallying Cries: Three Plays by Eric Bentley*. Washington, DC: New Republic Book 1977.

Berrigan, Daniel. *The Trial of the Catonsville Nine*. New York: Fordham University Press, 2004.

———. *The Trial of the Catonsville Nine*: A Play by Daniel Berrigan. Text prepared for the production by Saul Levitt. New York: Samuel French, 1971.

Freed, Donald. *Inquest*. New York: Samuel French, 1969.

———. *Inquest. Voicings: Ten Plays from the Documentary Theater*. Edited and with an introduction by Attilio Favorini. Hopewell, NJ: Ecco Press, 1995. 144–99.

Hunt, Mamie. *Unquestioned Integrity: The Hill/Thomas Hearings. Voicings: Ten Plays from the Documentary Theater*. Edited and with an introduction by Attilio Favorini. Hopewell, NJ: Ecco Press, 1995. 356–72.

Kaufman, Moisés. *Gross Indecency: The Three Trials of Oscar Wilde*. With an afterword by Tony Kushner. New York: Vintage Books, 1998.

Kaufman, Moisés, and members of the Tectonic Theater Project. *The Laramie Project*. New York: Vintage Books, 2001.

Mann, Emily. *Execution of Justice. Testimonies: Four Plays*. With an introduction by Athol Fugard. New York: Theatre Communications Group, 1997. 133–246.

———. *Greensboro (A Requiem). Testimonies: Four Plays*. With an introduction by Athol Fugard. New York: Theatre Communications Group, 1997. 247–330.

Murphy, Michael. *Sin. TDR: The Drama Review* 50.3 (2006): 155–81.

Sossi, Ron, and Frank Condon. *The Chicago Conspiracy Trial.* New York: Theatre Communications Group, 1979.

Secondary Texts

Abelman, Nancy, and John Lie. *Blue Dreams: Korean Americans and the Los Angeles Riots.* Cambridge, MA: Harvard University Press, 1995.

Adcock, Joe. "Drama Brings Back Frustrations of the Hill-Thomas Proceedings." *Seattle Post* 5 November 1993: 10.

Adolphnson, Sue. "Hill-Thomas: A Reconfirmation Hearing." *San Francisco Chronicle* 21 February 1993: 33.

Babcox, Peter, et al. Letter, *New York Review of Books* 19 July 1969. Web. Accessed 29 August 2011.

Baldassare, Mark. *The Los Angeles Riots: Lessons for the Urban Future.* Boulder, CO: Westview Press, 1994.

Bandes, Susan A, ed. *The Passions of Law.* New York: New York University Press, 2001.

Barnes, Clive. "Catonsville 9 Makes the Broadway Scene." *New York Times* 16 June 1971: 38.

———. "Riveting Work by Berrigan." *New York Times* 8 February 1971: 40.

Bennetts, Leslie. "When Reality Takes to the Stage," *New York Times* 9 March 1986: 2.1.

Bottoms, Stephen. "Putting the Document into Documentary." In "Documentary Theatre," edited by Carol Martin, special issue, *Drama Review* 50.3 (2006): 56–68.

Brantley, Ben. "A Brutal Act Alters a Town," *New York Times* 19 May 2000: E4.

———. "Don't Send In the Clowns," *New York Times* 27 March 2000: E1, 8.

———. "Oscar Wilde, Stung by His Own Tongue," *New York Times* 19 March 1997: C 13, 18.

Brooks, Peter. "The Law as Narrative and Rhetoric." *Law's Stories.* Edited by Brooks and Paul Gewirtz. New Haven, CT: Yale University Press, 1996. 14–22.

———. *Troubling Confessions: Speaking Guilt in Law and Literature.* Chicago: University of Chicago Press, 2000.

Brown, Rich. "Moisés Kaufman: The Copulation of Form and Content." *Theatre Topics* 15.1 (2005): 51–67.

Burnett, D. Graham. *A Trial by Jury.* New York: Knopf, 2001.

Canby, Vincent. "When Communists Clashed with Nazis and the Klan." *New York Times* 12 February 1996: C14.

Claycomb, Ryan M. "(Ch)oral History: Documentary Theatre, the Communal Subject and Progressive Politics." *Journal of Dramatic Theory and Criticism* 17.2 (2003): 95–122.

Clendinen, Dudley. "Theater; Of Old South Violence Only Yesterday." *New York Times* 4 February 1996: 3.

Cole, Susan Letzler. "Emily Mann Directs Execution of Justice." *Directors in Rehearsal: A Hidden World.* New York: Routledge, 1992. 56–72.

Cote, David. "Filtering Priests' Sins through Two Prisms." *New York Times* 20 November 2004: B9.

Cover, Robert. "Violence and the Word." In *Narrative, Violence, and the Law: The Essays of Robert Cover.* Edited by Martha Minow, Michael Ryan, and Austin Sarat. Ann Arbor: University of Michigan Press, 1993.

Crotty, Kevin M. *Law's Interior: Legal and Literary Constructions of the Self.* Ithaca, NY: Cornell University Press, 2001.

Cullen, Kevin, and Charles M. Sennott. "A Respite, Then Firestorm Ignites." *Boston Globe* 14 December 2002: A20.

Davidson, Gordon. "Formative Moments in a Theatrical Life." A Rector's Forum presentation of Gordon Davidson. All Saints Church, Pasadena, CA. Electronic archives. 27 February 2005. http://www.allsaints-pas.org/archives/sermons/formative-moments-in-a-theatri.htm. Accessed 22 July 2010.

Dawson, Gary Fisher. *Documentary Theatre in the United States: An Historical Survey and Analysis of Its Content, Form, and Stagecraft.* Westport, CT: Greenwood Press, 1999.

Doyle, Michael William. "Staging the Revolution: Guerilla Theater as a Countercultural Practice, 1965–68." *Imagine Nation: The American Counterculture of the 1960s and '70s.* Edited by Peter Braunstein and Michael William Doyle. New York: Routledge, 2002. 71–98.

Farber, Stephen. "A Play about HUAC Stirs Hollywood." *New York Times* 7 September 1975: 105.

Favorini, Attilio. "The Documentary Plays of Emily Mann." *Get Real: Documentary Theatre Past and Present.* Eds. Alison Forsyth and Chris Megson. New York: Palgrave Macmillan, 2009. 151–66.

———, ed. *Voicings: Ten Plays from the Documentary Theater.* Hopewell, NJ: Ecco Press, 1995.

Felman, Shoshana. "Education and Crisis, or the Vicissitudes of Teaching." In *Trauma: Explorations in Memory,* edited and with introductions by Cathy Caruth. Baltimore, MD: Johns Hopkins University Press, 1995. 13–60.

———. *The Juridical Unconscious: Trials and Traumas in the Twentieth Century.* Cambridge, MA: Harvard University Press, 2002.

Felman, Shoshana , and Dori Laub, MD. *Testimony: Crisis of Witnessing in Literature, Psychoanalysis, and History.* New York: Routledge, 1992.

Fenn, Richard K. *Liturgies and Trials: The Secularization of Religious Language.* Oxford: Basil Blackwell, 1982.

Ferguson, Robert. *The Trial in American Life.* Chicago: University of Chicago Press, 2007.

Filewood, Alan. *Collective Encounters: Documentary Theatre in English Canada.* Toronto: University of Toronto Press, 1987.

Forsyth, Alison, and Chris Megson. *Get Real: Documentary Theatre Past and Present.* New York: Palgrave Macmillan, 2009.

Freed, Donald. "The Case and the Myth: *The United States of America v. Julius and Ethel Rosenberg.*" In *Voicings: Ten Plays from the Documentary Theater,* edited by Attilio Favorini. Hopewell, NJ: Ecco Press, 1995. 199–203.

Gewirtz, Paul. "Narrative and Rhetoric in the Law." *Law's Stories: Narrative and Rhetoric in the Law.* New Haven, CT: Yale UP, 1996. 2–13.

Gill, David C. "Review of *The Trial of the Catonsville Nine,* by Daniel Berrigan." *Educational Theatre Journal* 23.2 (1971): 209–10.

Gilmore, Ruth Wilson. "Terror Austerity Race Gender Excess Theater." In *Reading Rodney King: Reading Urban Uprising*, edited by Robert Gooding-Williams. New York: Routledge, 1993. 23–37.

Gleb, Hal. "Theater." *Nation* 6 April 1992: 462–64.

Gooding-Williams, Robert, ed. *Reading Rodney King: Reading Urban Uprising*. New York: Routledge, 1993.

Graham, Judith. "Erasing Stereotypes in 'Laramie,' A Small Town Faces Its Fears and Prejudices." *Chicago Tribune* 19 May 2000: 5.

Gussow, Mel. "Bentley and the Committee." *New York Times* 12 November 1972: 77.

———. "Stage: Emily Mann's 'Execution of Justice.'" *New York Times* 14 March 1986: C3.

Guterman, Gad. "Reviewing the Rosenbergs: Donald Freed's Inquest and Its Jurors." *Theatre Survey* 48.2 (2007): 265–87.

Haithman, Diane. "Present-Tense Playwright; Anna Deavere Smith's Take on the Presidency, Media Keeps Evolving." *Los Angeles Times* 8 February 1999: 1.

Hammond, Will, and Dan Steward, eds. *Verbatim Verbatim: Contemporary Documentary Theatre*. London: Oberon Books, 2008.

Hariman, Robert, ed. *Popular Trials: Rhetoric, Mass Media, and the Law*. Tuscaloosa: University of Alabama Press, 1990.

Hulbert, Dan. "Theater Review 'House Arrest: First Edition.'" *Atlanta Constitution* 20 November 1997: D9.

Hyoung Song, Min. *Strange Future: Pessimism and the 1992 Los Angeles Riots*. Durham, NC: Duke University Press, 2005.

Irmer, Thomas. "A Search for New Realities: Documentary Theatre in Germany." In "Documentary Theatre," edited by Carol Martin, special issue, *Drama Review* 50.3 (2006): 16–28.

Isaac, Dan. "Theatre of Fact." *Drama Review* 15.3 (1971): 109–35.

Isherwood, Charles. "The Anguish Is Plausible, but His Eminence Forgets." *New York Times* 27 October 2004: E1.

Istel, John. "Emily Mann." *American Theatre* 13.2 (1996): 44.

Janofsky, Michael. "A Death in Laramie, Reimagined as Drama." *New York Times* 27 February 2000: AR10.

Jefferson, Margo. "Importance of Being Modern." *New York Times* 12 May 1997: C11, 13.

Kahn, Paul. *The Reign of Law: Marbury v. Madison and the Construction of America*. New Haven: Yale University Press, 1997.

Kaplan, Morris B. "Literature in the Dock: The Trials of Oscar Wilde." *Journal of Law and Society* 31.1 (2004): 113–30.

Kerr, Walter. "'Inquest': Kerr Votes Against It." *New York Times* 3 May 1970: 99.

Kiralyfalvi, Bela. "The Catonsville 'Trilogy': History, Testimony and Art. *Theatre History Studies* 6 (1986): 132–41.

Klein, Alvin. "Theater; Now, a Few Words with the Audience. *New York Times* 18 February 1996: NJ11.

Lahav, Pnina. "Theater in the Courtroom: The Chicago Conspiracy Trial." September 30, 2002. Boston Univ. School of Law Research Paper No. 02–16. Available at SSRN: http://ssrn.com/abstract=335921 or http://dx.doi.org /10.2139/ssrn.335921. Accessed 20 April 2008.

Lewis, Barbara. "The Circle of Confusion: A Conversation with Anna Deavere Smith." *Kenyon Review* 15.4 (1993): 56.

Mackey, Heather. "Review of Unquestioned Integrity." *American Theatre* 10.3 (1993): 10.

Mandell, Jonathan. "In Depicting History, Just How Far Can the Facts Be Bent?" *New York Times* 3 March 2002: A7.

Mann, Emily. "In Conversation." *Theatre Topics* 10.1 (2000): 1–16.

———. Interview with Alexis Greene. In *Women Who Write Plays: Interviews with American Dramatists*, edited by Alexis Greene. Hanover, NH: Smith and Kraus, 2001. 286–310.

Martin, Carol. "Anna Deavere Smith: The Word Becomes You." *Drama Review* 37.4 (1993): 45–62.

———. "Bodies of Evidence." In "Documentary Theatre," edited by Carol Martin, special issue, *Drama Review* 50.3 (2006): 9–15.

Mason, Gregory. "Documentary Drama from the Revue to the Tribunal." *Modern Drama* 20.3 (1968): 263–77.

Madhubuti, Haki R. *Why L.A. Happened: Implications of the '92 Los Angeles Rebellion*. Chicago: Third World Press, 1993.

McLellan, Dennis. "Manuel Reyes, 1925–2008; Defendant in Notorious '42 Sleepy Lagoon Murder Case Was Unjustly Convicted." *Los Angeles Times* 7 March 2008: B8.

Minow, Martha. "Stories in Law." In *Law's Stories: Narrative and Rhetoric in the Law*, edited by Peter Brooks and Paul Gewirtz. New Haven, CT: Yale University Press, 1996. 24–36.

Murphy, Brenda. *Congressional Theater: Dramatizing McCarthyism on Stage, Film, and Television*. Cambridge, UK: Cambridge University Press, 1999.

Myers, Robert. "Nothing Mega about It Except the Applause." *New York Times* 25 May 1997: H1, 28.

Nobile, Philip. "The Priest Who Stayed Out in the Cold." *New York Times* 28 June 1970: 9.

Nussbaum, Laureen. "The German Documentary Theatre of the Sixties: A Stereopsis of Contemporary History." *German Studies Review* 4.2 (1981): 237–55.

Paget, Derek. *True Stories? Documentary Drama on Radio, Screen and Stage*. Manchester, UK: Manchester University Press, 1990.

Pellegrini, David. "*Unquestioned Integrity* Questioned." In *Voicings: Ten Plays from the Documentary Theater*, edited with an introduction by Attilio Favorini. Hopewell, NJ: Ecco Press, 1995. 373–76.

Phillips, Michael. "Building an Arresting House." *Los Angeles Times* 19 April 1999: 3.

Pillsbury, Samuel H. "Harlan, Holmes, and the Passions of Justice." In *The Passions of Law*, edited by Susan A. Bandes. New York: New York University Press, 1999. 330–62.

Pogash, Carol. "Myth of the 'Twinkie Defense.'" *San Francisco Chronicle* 23 November 2003: D1.

Pogrebin, Robin. "Ms. Smith, Alone Again, Is Going to Washington." *New York Times* 27 February 2000: 2.11.

Posner, Richard A. *Law and Literature*. Rev. and enl. ed. Cambridge, MA: Harvard University Press, 1998.

Rapping, Elayne. *Law and Justice as Seen on TV*. New York: New York University Press, 2003.

Reinelt, Janelle. "Notes for a Radical Democratic Theater: Productive Crises and the Challenge of Indeterminacy." In *Staging Resistance: Essays on Political Theater*, edited by Jeanne Colleran and Jenny S. Spencer. Ann Arbor: University of Michigan Press, 1998. 283–300.

Richards, David. "'Justice for All': At Arena, the Many-Sided Dan White Case." *Washington Post* 17 May 1985. Rpt. in *Voicings: Ten Plays from the Documentary Theater*, edited by Attilio Favorini. Hopewell, NJ: Ecco Press, 1995. 337–39.

Rokem, Freddie. *Performing History: Theatrical Representations of the Past in Contemporary Theatre*. Iowa City: University of Iowa Press, 2000.

Rose, Lloyd. "'House Arrest': Too-Early Release." *Washington Post* 21 November 1997: C1.

Salamensky, S. I. "Re-presenting Oscar Wilde: Wilde's Trials, *Gross Indecency*, and Documentary Spectacle." *Theatre Journal* 54.4 (2002): 575–88.

Savage, Charlie, "Clarence Thomas's Wife Asks Anita Hill for Apology." *New York Times* 20 October 2010: A1.

Schechner, Richard. "Guerilla Theater: May, 1970." *TDR* 14.3 (1970): 163–68.

Schultz, John. *The Chicago Conspiracy Trial*. With a new introduction by Carl Oglesby. Rev. ed. of *Motion Will Be Denied*, 1972. Cambridge, MA: De Capo, 1993.

Shewey, Don. "A Play Has Second Life as a Stage for Discussion." *New York Times* 1 December 2002: A7.

———. "Town in a Mirror," *American Theatre* 17.5 (2000): 14.

Shirley, Don. "Taper to Redo Show Due to 'Arrest'-ing Developments." *Los Angeles Times* 29 January 1999: 2.

Siegel, Naomi. "Daring to Disagree, and Sent to an Asylum." *New York Times* 27 May 2007.

Silbey, Jessica. "Patterns of Courtroom Justice." *Journal of Law and Society* 28.1 (2001): 97–116.

Simon, John. "Theatre Chronicle." *Hudson Review* 24.2 (1971): 291–300.

Smith, Anna Deavere. *House Arrest: A Search for American Character In and Around the White House, Past and Present*. New York: Dramatists Play Service, 2003.

Stayton, Richard. "A Fire in a Crowded Theater: Anna Deavere Smith Relives the Los Angeles Riots." *American Theater* 10.7–8 (1993): 20–22, 72–75.

Sullivan, Dan. "Berrigan Play Given New Look." *Los Angeles Times* 26 February 1971: 11.

———. "'Catonsville'—Once a Sermon, Now a Play." *Los Angeles Times* 18 June 1971: E1.

———. "'Catonsville' Recites War Evils." *Los Angeles Times* 10 August 1970: E1, 17.

United States of America v. Mary Moylan, Appellant, et al., United States Court of Appeals for the Fourth Circuit, nos. 12988–96, 417 F.2d 1002, 1969.

United States of America v. Philip Berrigan et al., United States District Court for the District of Maryland, Criminal Trial #28111, 225.

Unsworth, Tim. "The Stage Trial of Cardinal Law." *National Catholic Reporter* 16 April 2000: 21.

Vitello, Paul. "Diocese Loses Bid to Keep Abuse Records Sealed." *New York Times* 5 October 2009, A28.

Weber, Bruce. "On Stage and Off." *New York Times* 22 April 1994: C2.

Weiss, Peter. "Fourteen Propositions for a Documentary Theatre." *World Theatre* 17 (1968): 375–89.

West, Robin. *Caring for Justice.* New York: New York University Press, 1997.

White, James Boyd. *Acts of Hope: Creating Authority in Literature, Law, and Politics.* Chicago: University of Illinois Press, 1994.

———. "The Judicial Opinion and the Poem." *Heracles' Bow: Essays on the Rhetoric and Poetics of the Law.* Madison: University of Wisconsin Press, 1989. 107–38.

Winn, Steven. "A Theatrical Rerun of Hill vs. Thomas." *San Francisco Chronicle* 25 February 1993: E1.

Winner, Lucy. "Democratic Acts: Theatre of Public Trials." *Theatre Topics* 15.2 (2005): 149–69.

Zeman, Ray. "Controversial Play Set at Music Center Prompts Criticism." *Los Angeles Times* 26 May 1971: D1.

Zilliacus, Clas. "Documentary Drama: Form and Content." *Comparative Drama* 6.3 (1972): 223–53.

Index

Actors' Gang, 192n25; *Catonsville* revival by, 172

Adcock, Joe, 137

Adolphson, Sue, 137

affirmative action: erosion of, 128; executive order for, 97; Thomas and, 130

agitator figure, 100–101, 107, 115, 121, 123

Alice Tully Hall, production of *Laramie Project: Ten Years Later* at, 167

Allen, Jessie, 18

American Communist Party, attraction of. *See also* communist threat

American Nazi Party, 115

Angels in America (Kushner), 144

antiriot legislation, 47–49

antiwar protests. See *Chicago Conspiracy Trial, The* (Sossi and Condon); protests; *Trial of the Catonsville Nine, The* (Berrigan)

Arena Stage, production of *Execution* at, 198n10

Are You Now or Have You Ever Been (Bentley), 5, 65, 80–96; historical context for witnesses in, 85; language modes in, 92–95; sources for, 65–66, 84; witnesses in, 84–85

art, legislation of, 152, 154

audience: *Are You Now* and, 82; deliberate upset of, 16; documentary theater's challenges to, 170; *Execution* and, 112–14; *Greensboro* and, 122; *Gross Indecency* and, 147; as jury, 8, 71–72, 194n71; *Laramie* and, 159–60; role of, 11–12, 15, 105

Auschwitz trials, 190n28

Bandes, Susan A., 19

Bank of America, student protestors and, 24

Barnes, Clive, 35–36, 77

Bentley, Eric, 4–5, 65, 80, 81–83, 90

Berkeley Rep, *Execution* production of, 198n10

Berle, Milton, 70

Berrigan, Daniel, 24, 30–31, 40, 49, 83, 158, 172–73; arrest of, 34; Catholicism of, 38–39; closing statement of, 44; intent of, 31

Berrigan, Philip, 30, 40, 43, 172; Catholicism of, 38–39

BishopAccountability.org, 176

blacklisting, 73, 79, 81–82, 88, 96

Black Panther Party, 47, 50; Freed and, 195n27

Blank, Jessica, 172

Blinder, Martin, 197n5

Bloch, Emanuel, 70, 78

Bottoms, Stephen, 148–49

Brantley, Ben, 145, 147, 152, 158

Brecht, Bertolt, 3, 42, 189n3; Kaufman and, 160

Brittain, Victoria, 170

Brooks, Peter, 18, 139

Brown, Rich, 147–48, 160

Burbank Unitarian Fellowship, 193n46

Burgess, John, 194n71

Burnett, Graham, 25

Burrows, Abe, 85–86, 89, 93

Bush, George H. W., 130

Byrd, James, 155–56

Cambodia, invasion of, 22

Canby, Vincent, 119

Carson, Edward, 148, 153

Cary, Canon, 193n46

"Case and the Myth: *The United States of America v. Julius and Ethel Rosenberg*" (Freed), 66

Castro neighborhood, 98, 102–3

Catholic Church, in *Catonsville Nine*, 45–46

Catholic church sexual abuse scandal, 173–80; investigative journalism and, 174; priests involved in, 173–75, 178. See also *Sin (A Cardinal Deposed)* (Murphy)

Catholicism: Catonsville Nine and, 27, 32, 38–39, 172–73; separation of church and state and, 175

Catonsville Nine: conviction of, 28; defense arguments of, 80. See also

Trial of the Catonsville Nine, The (Berrigan)

Cauce, Floris, 117

Center Theatre Group, Smith's commission by, 128–29

"Chicago/Conspiracy" (Burgess), 194n71

Chicago Conspiracy Trial, 73; BBC dramatization of, 194n71; constitutional issues in, 48; cultural importance of, 48; defendants in, 26

Chicago Conspiracy Trial, The (Sossi and Condon), 1, 46–62; versus *Catonsville*, 49; and conscience versus government, 51; current relevance of, 52–53; democratic process and, 18; Hoffman (Abbie) in, 47, 51–52, 60–61; Hoffman (Judge) in, 24–25, 55–57, 181; ideological issues in, 45, 53–54; Lahav's exploration of, 17–18; Rubin in, 47, 51, 52; Seale and, 57–61; stagings and filming of, 50–52; structure of, 55; symbolic significance of, 53; transcript sources of, 53–54; US government and, 49–59; verdict in, 62

Chicago Eight, 46; defense arguments of, 80; Seale's removal from, 57–61

child abuse, church reporting requirements for, 175. *See also* Catholic Church sexual abuse scandal

Chomsky, Noam, 48

Chorus: in *Inquest,* 78; of Uncalled Witnesses, 107–9

Churchill, Winston, 64

Citizens Legal Defense Alliance, 34–35

civil disobedience, philosophy of, 24

civil disputes, 169

Civil Rights Act of 1964, 115

Civil Rights Act of 1968, 47; "conspiracy" provisions of, 51

civil trials, as source material, 17

Clarke, Edward, 151

class issues: in *Greensboro*, 115–16; Hill/Thomas hearings and, 138

Claycomb, Ryan M., 101, 123, 157, 182, 197n3

Clendinen, Dudley, 120

Clinton, Bill, 1

Cohn, Roy, 74–75

Cold War, origins of, 64. See also *Are You Now or Have You Ever Been* (Bentley); HUAC hearings; *Inquest, The* (Freed)

Cole, Susan Letzler, 113

Committee to Defend the Conspiracy, 48

Communism: attraction of, 85–86; Klan attitude toward, 124

Communist threat: documentary trial plays and, 64–65; HUAC hearings and, 65, 76–96; public's reaction to, 75; Rosenbergs and, 70–76. *See also Are You Now or Have You Ever Been* (Bentley); *Inquest, The* (Freed)

Communist Workers Party (CWP), 115, 124–25

community: in documentary theater, 100–101, 182; Laramie, 168

community trauma, 14, 125, 199n45; *Execution* and, 110–12, 115; *Greensboro* and, 119–20, 123; Hill/Thomas hearings and, 131–32. See also *Greensboro (A Requiem)*; Greensboro Truth and Reconciliation Commission; *Laramie Project, The* (Kaufman)

Condon, Frank, 24, 50, 51, 61. See also *Chicago Conspiracy Trial, The* (Sossi and Condon)

congressional hearings, 1; similarities to civil/criminal cases, 2–3

Connelly, Catherine, 161–62

constitutional issues, *Chicago Conspiracy* and, 48–49

continuum of publication, Ferguson's concept of, 9

Cooper, Murdock, 163

Corrie, Rachel, 170–71

Cote, David, 176

courtroom, 4; versus community context, 100; ritual of, 13; stage as, 39; theater ritual and, 36

Cover, Robert, 16, 33

Cowlings, Al, 127

Craig, Gwenn, 110–11, 198n34

criminal trials, as source material, 17

Crito, 16

Cromwell, John, 89

cultural factors, 5–8, 16, 19–20, 24, 36, 39, 46; American rule of law and, 5; *Are You Now* and, 82, 85–88; in *Chicago Conspiracy*, 48, 51; HUAC and, 79–80; in *Inquest*, 72; race and gender issues and, 110, 113, 118–21, 132, 137, 142; revelations about, 13; Wilde's trials and, 145, 149, 152–53

cultural product, 37, 40

cultural trauma, 9, 12

Culture Project, *Exonerated* production of, 172

culture wars, 97

Daley, Richard J., 53, 61

Darst, David, 27, 33, 43, 192n29

Davidson, Gordon, 34, 128, 172, 190n28, 192n25

Davis, Rennie, 47, 61

Dawson, Edward, 116, 122–23

Dawson, Gary Fisher, 125

Debree, Rob, 163

Dellinger, David, 56

democracy: Chicago Conspiracy Trial and, 18–19; documentary theater and, 9, 72

Democratic Convention of 1968, 48–49

Denman, Jim, 107

Denver Center Theatre, *Laramie* production of, 156

Deputy, The (Hochhuth), 190n28

Dmytryk, Edward, 89–90

docudramas, 3–4

documentary film, 4

documentary theater: achievements of, 11–12; character fashioning in, 75–76; as democracy forum, 72; development and origins of, 3; evolution of, 181–82; German, 190n28; high-profile cases represented in, 170; issues implicated in, 21;

documentary theater (*continued*)
political and emotional roles of,
180–81; ritual of, 13; rule of law
and, 181; and search for truth and
justice, 184–85; shift from individual to wider community in, 182;
terminologies of, 3–4
Douglas, Alfred, 146
Douglas, William O., 90–91, 196n64
Douglass, Frederick, 95
draft records, destruction of, 26–28,
32, 44, 173. *See also Trial of the
Catonsville Nine, The* (Berrigan)
Drake, Kerry, 164
Drama Critics Circle Award, 104
Duke, David, 122

Eichmann Trial, 59
Eilenberg, Larry, 131
Emerson, Michael, 152
emotional component: exposure of, 13;
of law, 19
Empty Space Theatre, *Execution* performance at, 198n10
ethical issues, 10; interrogating, 15
Ethiopia, 89
Eureka Theatre, *Execution* and, 104
Execution of Justice (Mann), 98–115;
audience responses to, 112–14;
critics' response to, 105; departures
from legal testimony in, 110–11;
diverse perspectives in, 106–11; jury
selection in, 108–9; representative
characters in, 106–7; sources for,
104–6; stagings of, 198n10; transcript versus play script in, 108; TV
movie of, 198n10; Twinkie defense
and, 1, 102, 106, 197n5; uncalled witnesses in, 107–9; verdict in, 110–11
Exonerated, The (Blank and Jensen), 172
extralegal narratives, 17, 108, 110, 116

facts, challenging faith in, 37–38
Falzon, Frank, 112
Farber, Stephen, 81–82
Favorini, Attilio, 103–4, 108, 189n3
FBI, in *Inquest*, 74–75

Federal Theatre Project, 27, 88–89
Feinstein, Dianne, 105
Felman, Shoshana, 13–15, 17, 101
Fenn, Richard K., 39, 42, 45–46
Ferguson, Robert, 2, 9, 26, 68, 152, 166
Fifth Amendment, 95
film, documentary, 4
film industry, Hays Code and, 86–88
*Fires in the Mirror: Crown Heights,
Brooklyn and Other Identities*
(Smith), 10, 128
Flanagan, Hallie, 88–89
Forsyth, Alison, 171
Frankfurter, Felix, 66
Freed, Donald, 64, 68, 70, 73, 76,
195n27. See also *Inquest, The* (Freed)
Freedom of Information Act, 73
Freitas, Joseph, Jr., 107–8
French, Samuel, 191n9
Frost/Nixon (Morgan), 171
Fry, Stephen, 201n51

Gauvreau, Jackie, 178
gay activists, 102
gender politics, 97–99; plays focusing
on, 130; in *Unquestioned Integrity*,
140–42. *See also* identity politics
Geoghan, John, 178
*Get Real: Documentary Theatre Past
and Present* (Forsyth and Megson),
171
Gewirtz, Paul, 37
Gild, David C., 33–34, 39
Gilmore, Wilson, 128
Ginsberg, Allen, 51, 61
global terrorism, 171
Goldman, Ronald, 127
Good Shepherd–Faith Church, and
staging of *Catonsville Nine*, 39,
192n25
government. *See* US government
Great Depression, HUAC witnesses
and, 85, 88–89
Greensboro (A Requiem) (Mann), 98–
99, 115–25; community trauma and,
119–20; Interviewer in, 122–24, 159;
sources for, 118–19

Greensboro Massacre, 115–16; trials following, 117–18

Greensboro Truth and Reconciliation Commission: findings of, 116, 118, 199n45; support of, 119

Grizzard, George, 75

Gross Indecency: The Three Trials of Oscar Wilde (Kaufman), 130, 143–54; and legislation of art and morality, 152; sources for, 144–45, 147–48; structure of, 148; and transformation of plaintiff into defendant, 149; trial verdicts in, 150–52

Guantanamo: Honour Bound to Defend Freedom (Brittain and Slovo), 170

Gussow, Mel, 81, 105, 109

Guterman, Gad, 71, 73, 75, 78, 196n39

Guthrie Theatre, *Execution* production of, 198n10

Halliday, George, 126

Hammond, Will, 10

Harlan, John Marshall, 191n3

Harris, Frank, 152

hate-crime legislation: absence of, 155, 157; argument against, 163; federal, 168; in Intermountain West, 202n92; Matthew Shepard Foundation and, 168

Hayden, Tom, 51, 52

hearings: government, 169; as source material, 17. *See also* Hill/Thomas hearings; HUAC hearings

Henderson, Russell, 155, 161–63; excommunication of, 165

high-profile trials, 166; documentary theater representations of, 170

Hill, Anita, 130–42; as accused, 149–50; background of, 136–38; interrogation of, 138–39; Virginia Thomas and, 167. *See also* Hill/Thomas hearings; *Unquestioned Integrity: The Hill/Thomas Hearings* (Hunt)

Hilliker, Rebecca, 159

Hill/Thomas hearings, 130–42; accuser as accused in, 149–50; similarity to rape trials, 136–37

historical record, cultural product and, 37

Hochhuth, Rolf, 190n28

Hoffman, Abbie, 47, 51, 52, 60–61

Hoffman, Julius J., 1, 51, 55–57, 181

Hollywood Ten, 79, 81, 85, 93

Holmes, Oliver Wendell, 191n3

Holocaust: documentary plays about, 190n28; law and art in processing of, 14; trial-trauma connection and, 19

homosexuality: English law in Wilde's time and, 144; religion and, 164. *See also Execution of Justice* (Mann); *Gross Indecency: The Three Trials of Oscar Wilde* (Kaufman); *Laramie Project, The* (Kaufman)

House Arrest (Smith), 142

House Un-American Activities Committee: "American values" and, 87–88; establishment of, 79; Federal Theatre Project and, 89. *See also* HUAC hearings

HUAC hearings, 3, 5; political context and, 80–81, 85–89; Rosenbergs and, 65; source and authority in, 79–80; traumatic effects of, 90–91; witnesses in, 81–86, 88–89, 91–95. *See also Are You Now or Have You Ever Been* (Bentley)

Humana Festival of New American Plays, 104

Hunt, Mamie, 131

Hyde, H. Montgomery, 148

identity politics, 97; in *Gross Indecency*, 145–47, 149, 150, 152; Tectonic Theater and, 143; in *Unquestioned Integrity*, 135, 138–39, 142–43. *See also* gender politics

Innocence Project, 172

Inquest, The (Freed), 83, 92; critics' responses to, 67–68, 76; political context of, 69, 73 (*see also* Cold War); as political protest, 74; productions of, 66–67; sources for, 65–67, 70, 76, 195n6; staging of, 69–73

In Spite of Everything (Piscator), 3
Interviewer, in *Greensboro*, 122–24, 159
interviewers, in *Laramie Project*, 157, 159–60, 164
Investigation, The (Weiss), 42, 190n28
"Investigation of a Flame," 192n12
Investigator, in *Are You Now*, 83–84
Iranian hostage crisis, 99
Isaac, Dan, 26–27, 36, 98, 191n8
Isaacs, Ken, 70
Isherwood, Christopher, 177
Istel, John, 103

Jackson, Anne, 75
Janofsky, Michael, 160
Jefferson, Margo, 145, 152
Jefferson, Thomas, 58
Jensen, Erik, 172
Johnson, Eric, 87–88
Johnson, Lyndon B., 97, 115
Johnson, Nelson, 116, 122–24
Johnson, Sherry, 163, 164
Johnson, Stephen Mead, 164
judge: in *Catonsville Nine*, 56–57, 74, 181; in *Chicago Conspiracy*, 49, 55–57, 181; and imposition of violence, 33; in *Inquest*, 67–68, 74; as quintessential figure of justice, 25; representations in *Catonsville* and *Chicago Conspiracy*, 24–25; violence of, 16
judiciary, impacts of documentary theater and, 5–8
juror drum, 71, 195n18
jury, audience as, 8, 71–72, 194n71
jury selection, in *Execution*, 108–9
justice, documentary theater and search for, 184–85
justice system: art and enhanced understanding of, 16; critique of, 27; skepticism about, 2. *See also* law(s); legal system

Kahn, Paul, 25, 55–56, 61
Kaplan, Morris B., 152, 154
Kaufman, Irving R., 67–68, 159–60, 195n6, 196n64

Kaufman, Moisés, 142–43, 159–60; in *Gross Indecency*, 151–52; and *Laramie Project: Ten Years Later*, 167–68; moment work of, 160
Kazan, Elia, 85, 89
Kennedy, John, 97
Kennedy, Robert, assassination of, 46
Kent State University shootings, 23–24
Kerr, Walter, 67, 71, 76
King, Martin Luther, Jr., assassination of, 46, 47
King, Rodney Glen, 126–30, 156, 166, 200n3
Kiralyfalvi, Bela, 45
Kleb, William, 105–7, 112
Klein, Alvin, 121
Krieger, Orson, 178–79
Ku Klux Klan: *Greensboro* and, 101, 115–18; judgment against, 121; Reverend Nelson and, 121; self-defense argument of, 124
Kunstler, William, 28, 54, 55, 60, 62

Lahav, Pnina, 16, 17–18, 53, 59–61
LaHoste, Jeffrey, 142
Laramie Project, The (Kaufman), 130, 145; audience and, 159–60; *Catonsville Nine* and, 157–58; dissemination of, 158–59; HBO movie of, 156; impacts of, 165–66; interviewers in, 157, 159–60, 164; postscripts to, 167–68; sources for, 158
Laramie Project, The: Ten Years Later (Kaufman), 167–68
Lardner, Ring, 91
Laub, Dori, 19–20
law(s): accomplishments and limitations of, 14–15; *Catonsville Nine* perspectives on, 45; documentary theater challenges to, 183; emotion of, 19; links with other ideological issues, 20; religious challenge to, 39–40 (see also *Trial of the Catonsville Nine, The* [Berrigan]); shift from judge/government to community, 166–67; social function of, 18; unjust, 28; in Wilde's

England, 144, 151. *See also* justice system; rule of law
Law, Bernard, 174–80
legal narrative, notion of, 8
legal studies, psychoanalysis's intersection with, 17
legal system: versus community, in *Laramie*, 162; documentary theater and, 172; examination of, 11–12; limitations of, 2
Leopold and Loeb murder case, 2
Let Me Down Easy (Smith), 170
Levitt, Saul, 36, 42–43, 192n25
Lewis, Thomas, 40–41
Living Newspaper, 27, 88–89, 98
London Charter, Nuremberg court and, 64
Los Angeles, and rioting after King beating, 126, 128–30, 200n3
Lu, Joanna, 108–9
Lyceum Theater, 192n25

Mackey, Heather, 131–32, 137
Magic Theatre, *Unquestioned Integrity* and, 131
Mailer, Norman, 48
Maltz, Albert, 81
Mandel, Louis, 93
Mann, Emily, 98–100, 118–19, 189n3, 197n3; Dawson and, 122–23; as provocateur, 121–22. See also *Execution of Justice* (Mann); *Greensboro (A Requiem)* (Mann)
Manson, Charles, 1
Mark Taper Forum, 35, 36, 192n25
Marshall, Thurgood, 130
Martin, Carol, 5, 8, 11, 33, 75
Martinez, Julio, 51
master narrative, in Rosenberg trial, 68, 77
Matthew Shepard Act, 168
Matthew Shepard Foundation, 168
Matthews, David, 123
McCarter Theatre, 115
McCarthy, Joseph R., 48, 70
McKinney, Aaron, 155, 161–63
McSorley, Patrick, 177–79

Megson, Chris, 171
memory, trauma and, 19
Middle East, US involvement in, 170–71
Milk, Harvey, 1, 3, 101–2, 109–10, 113–14; election of, 102; murder of, 102–3
Milwaukee Fourteen, 32
Minow, Martha, 72–73
Mische, George, 40, 42, 45
moment work, Kaufman's, 160
morality, legislation of, 157, 164. See also *Gross Indecency: The Three Trials of Oscar Wilde* (Kaufman); *Laramie Project, The* (Kaufman)
Morris, Steven Leigh, 52
Moscone, George, 1, 101–2, 109, 110, 113–14
Motion Picture Alliance for the Preservation of American Ideals, 89
Motion Picture Production Code (Hays Code), 86–88
Moynihan, Mary, 35
Mrs. Packard (Mann), 103
Murdock, George, 50–51, 56
Murphy, Brenda, 79–80, 82–83
Murphy, Michael, 178. See also *Sin (A Cardinal Deposed)* (Murphy)
Music Box Theater, 66, 67
Myers, Robert, 147
My Lai Massacre, 22
My Name Is Rachel Corrie (Rickman and Viner), 170–71

napalm: *Catonsville Nine* and, 27, 44; protests using, 32
narratives: contributions of, 18–19; extralegal, 17, 108, 110, 116
Nathan, Marty, 117
national crises, replaying of, 9
National Mobilization to End the War in Vietnam (MOBE), 47
national security issues: global terrorism and, 170; HUAC and, 65–66
Nelson, Reverend, 121
Neruda, Pablo, 42
New Theater for Now, 191n9, 192n25

New York Theater Workshop, *Gross Indecency* production of, 144
Nicola, James, 144
Nixon, Richard M., 22, 96
Nobile, Philip, 32
Norman, Tom, 109
not-guilty plea, unjust laws and, 28
nullification doctrine, 28
Nuremberg trials, 13, 63–64
Nussbaum, Laureen, 11, 12, 15, 38

Obama, Barack, 168
Odyssey Theater Ensemble, *Conspiracy Trial* production of, 26, 50, 52–53
Oklahoma City bombing, 119
oral history, staged, 101, 120, 157, 197n3
Overlie, Mary, 160

Pabich, Richard, 110
Paget, Derek, 3–4, 37–38, 62, 70
Paris, Andy, 160
Parks, Garrett, 82
Parks, Larry, 82, 85–86, 91–95
Passions of Law, The (Bandes), 19
Patterson, Romaine, 164
Peck, Gregory, 192n25
performance art, 98
performers, impacts of, 75–76
Peterson, Donald, 61
Phelps, Fred, 164
Phoenix Theater Company, *Catonsville Nine* production of, 39, 192n25
Pillsbury, Samuel H., 25, 191n3
Piscator, Erwin, 3, 189n3, 190n8, 190n28
Pitts, Lewis, 117, 124
political contexts, 12; HUAC hearings and, 80–81, 85–89; *Inquest* and, 69, 73; race and gender in, 97–99; Rosenbergs and, 63–64, 67–70, 73–74, 78–79. *See also* US government
political dissent, *Chicago Conspiracy* and, 48–49
Porter, James R., 173–75
postwar period, presumed cultural values of, 86–87

priests: antiwar activism of, 24–46; sexual abuse by, 173–80. *See also Sin (A Cardinal Deposed)* (Murphy); *Trial of the Catonsville Nine, The* (Berrigan)
protests: against Bank of America, 24; in HUAC hearings, 81; against Vietnam War, 22–25, 26. *See also Chicago Conspiracy Trial, The* (Sossi and Condon); *Trial of the Catonsville Nine, The* (Berrigan)
psychic release, testimony and, 13
psychoanalysis, and intersection with legal studies, 17
public perceptions, of rule of law, 30
public records, script use of, 189n8
Public Theater, *Let Me Down Easy* production and, 170
Pulitzer Prize committee, theatrical legitimacy and, 10

Queensbury, Marquess of, 146, 149–50

race, as political focus, 97–99
racism: Chicago Eight and, 59; in *Greensboro*, 115–16; Greensboro massacre and, 124; in Hill/Thomas hearings, 132–33, 138; King beating and, 126–27; in urban conflicts, 128–29
Rallying Cries (Bentley), 90
Rapping, Elayne, 183, 198n39
Reinelt, Janelle, 72
religion: *Catonsville Nine* and, 38–46, 173; and morality of homosexuality, 164; sexual abuse by priests and, 173–80. *See also* Catholicism; *Sin (A Cardinal Deposed)* (Murphy); *Trial of the Catonsville Nine, The* (Berrigan)
Rent, 144
Reserve Officers' Training Corps (ROTC), decreased enrollments in, 23–24
Richards, David, 105, 114
Rickman, Alan, 170
riots, after King beating, 126, 128–30, 200n3

ritual: of theater and courtroom, 13, 36; trials as, 38–39

Robbins, Tim, 172, 192n25

Robeson, Paul, 94–96, 99

Roosevelt, Franklin, 64

Rosenberg, Ethel, 65

Rosenberg, Julius, 65, 73

Rosenberg trial: charges and verdict in, 66; defense arguments in, 80–81; disproven charges in, 67–68; Douglas and, 90; political context and, 63–64, 67–70, 73–74, 78–79. See also *Inquest, The* (Freed)

Rosenbergs: execution of, 68, 71, 74, 77–78, 196n64; privilege renounced by, 99–100

Rubin, Jerry, 47, 51, 52

rule of law: *Catonsville's* challenge to, 173; and impact of documentary theater, 181; public perception of, 30–31, 33. *See also* law(s); legal system

Ryan, George, 172

Sacco-Vanzetti trial, 2

Saint Matthew's Episcopal Church, 193n46

Salamensky, S. I., 146, 149

Salmon, Zackie, 161

San Francisco: changing demographics in, 97–98; 1970s political struggle in, 102

Satrom, Leroy, 23

Savage, Charlie, 167

Saypol, Irving, 65–66, 74

Scales of Justice award, 172

Schmidt, Douglas, 197n5

Schultz, John, 54, 57

Scopes trial, 2

Screen Directors Guild, 89

Screen Writers Guild, HUAC and, 79

Seale, Bobby, 46, 47, 51, 52, 99, 117, 182; removal and isolation of, 57–61

September 11, 2001, 170

sexual abuse, by Catholic priests, 173–80. See also *Sin (A Cardinal Deposed)* (Murphy)

sexual harassment: Hill/Thomas hearings and, 133–43; as public concern, 135–36; Thomas candidacy and, 131

sexual orientation, criminalization of, 157. *See also* homosexuality

Shanley, Paul, 178

Sheen, Martin, 172

Shepard, Daniel, 163

Shepard, Dennis, 162, 165

Shepard, Judy, 168

Shepard, Matthew, 166, 168; interviewer testimonies and, 161; murder of, 154, 156, 157. See also *Laramie Project, The* (Kaufman)

Sherman, Cindy, 98

Shewey, Don, 159, 165

Siegel, Naomi, 103

Silbey, Jessica, 38

Simon, John, 29, 36

Simpson, Nicole Brown, 127, 129–30

Simpson, O. J., 127, 129–30, 166, 200n1; documentaries/dramatizations of, 129–30, 200n7

Sin (A Cardinal Deposed) (Murphy), 175–80; sources for, 175

Slonaker, Jonas, 161

Slovo, Gillian, 170

Smith, Anna Deavere, 10, 128, 142, 158–59, 170, 197n3

Snipes, Wesley, 106

social justice, documentary theater and, 172

Sondergaard, Gale, 96

Sontag, Susan, 48

Soon Ja Du, 129

Sossi, Ron, 24, 50, 61. See also *Chicago Conspiracy Trial, The* (Sossi and Condon)

source material, 17, 189n8; selection process for, 11

Spencer, John, 113

Stalh, David E., 57–58

Stalin, Joseph, 64

state, power of, 25. *See also* US government

State of Tennessee v. John T. Scopes, 2

Stayton, Richard, 129

Steger, Trish, 162–63

stereopsis, 12, 15, 38, 182

Steward, Dan, 10

Still Life (Mann), 103–4

storytelling, contributions of, 18–19

Stuff Happens, 170

Sullivan, Dan, 36

Taylor, Marvin, 151–52

Tectonic Theater Project, 142–43, 154–58, 167–68. See also *Gross Indecency: The Three Trials of Oscar Wilde* (Kaufman); *Laramie Project, The* (Kaufman)

television docudramas, 3–4

terrorism, global, 171

testimony: psychic release and, 13; theater of, 103–4, 107

Theater of Fact, 26–27, 76, 98, 189n3, 191n8

theater of testimony, 98–99, 103–4, 107

theater performance, trials and, 12–13

Theaters of Justice, 14

Thirty Years of Treason (Bentley), 82

Thomas, Clarence, 1, 130–42; background of, 136–38; opposition to candidacy of, 130; sexual harassment accusations against, 130–31. *See also* Hill/Thomas hearings; *Unquestioned Integrity: The Hill/Thomas Hearings* (Hunt)

Thomas, Virginia, 167

Thurmond, Strom, 132

trauma: of Holocaust, 19; public's response to, 104–5; release from, 13–14, 20. *See also* community trauma

Trial of the Catonsville Nine, The (Berrigan), 22, 24–46, 92; versus actual trial, 32–33; Catholicism in, 38; and challenge to rule of law, 173; versus *Chicago Conspiracy*, 49; conflicting narratives in, 42; defendant arguments in, 40–43; defense position in, 29; Fordham script of, 42; initial run of, 192n25; judge in, 24–25, 56–57, 181; *Laramie Project* and,

157–58; prosecution statement in, 28–29; protest against, 34–35; readings of, 193n46; reviews of, 35–36; revised version of, 36; revival of, 172; *Sin* and, 179; trial records used in, 30; versions of, 191n9; views of law in, 45

trials: artistic recountings of, 3; choice of, 8; high-profile, 166; post–World War II paradigm of, 13; public events and, 2; as ritual, 38–39; theater performance and, 12–13

trials of the century, concept and influence of, 2

Tricycle Theater, *Guantanamo* production of, 170

True Stories: Documentary Drama on Radio, Screen, and Stage (Paget), 3–4

truth: crisis of, 101; facts versus, 37, 62

Tubman, Harriet, 95

Twilight: Los Angeles, 1992 (Smith), 10, 129, 200n6

"Twinkie defense," 1, 102, 106, 197n5

Union Square Theatre, *Laramie* and, 156

US government: in *Are You Now*, 83–84; *Catonsville Nine* and, 38, 40, 43–44, 47; *Chicago Conspiracy* and, 49–59; citizen clashes with, 27; Cold War and, 64–65; destruction of property of, 26, 29; distrust of, 29; in *Inquest*, 74–77; and silencing of protests, 24

US government hearings, as source material, 17

United States of America v. Julius and Ethel Rosenberg, 65. See also *Inquest, The* (Freed)

Unquestioned Integrity: The Hill/Thomas Hearings (Hunt), 130–42, 149; critics' response to, 137; gender imbalance in, 134; Hill's interrogation in, 138–40; identity issues in, 135, 138–39, 142–43; lynching metaphor in, 139–40; postscripts to, 167;

sources for, 131–33, 138; televising of, 131–32; Thomas's character in, 139–40
Unsworth, Tim, 176
Untitled Film Stills, 98

verbatim theater, 189n3
Vernini, Bob, 172, 192n25
Vietnam War: opposition to, 22–25, 26, 169. See also *Chicago Conspiracy Trial* (Sossi and Condon); *Trial of the Catonsville Nine, The* (Berrigan)
Viner, Katharine, 170
violence, judicial, 16, 33

Waiting for Lefty (Odets), 88
war crimes trials, Nuremberg, 63–64
Washington, George, 58
Watergate hearings, 51, 96
Weiss, Peter, 10–11, 12–13, 180, 190n28
West, Robin, 136, 142
White, Dan, 1, 100–101, 105, 109, 110, 113; confession of, 112–13; resignation of, 102; suicide of, 114; trial, imprisonment, and suicide of, 102–3
White, James Boyd, 16–17, 41, 107–8, 183–84

White, Mary Ann, 106, 113
white men/women, privilege renounced by, 99–100
Wilde, Oscar, 143–54, 155, 166; bio-pic of, 201n51; charges against, 146–47; and criminalization of sexual preference, 157; imprisonment of, 153–54; as public example of homosexual subject, 145. See also *Gross Indecency: The Three Trials of Oscar Wilde* (Kaufman)
Winn, Steven, 137
Winner, Lucy, 18
witnesses: versus actual persons, 5; HUAC, 81–86, 88–89, 91–96; of trauma, 19–20; uncalled, 107–11
witnessing: role of, 103–4; of sexual abuse survivors, 176
women's movement, Hill/Thomas hearings and, 132
Wood, Sam G., 89–90, 91
Wyoming, hate-crime legislation and, 163, 168, 202n92

Yalta Conference, 64
Year of the Woman, 133
Youth International Party (Yippies), 1, 47, 54

Jacqueline O'Connor is a professor of English at Boise State University and the author of *Dramatizing Dementia: Madness in the Plays of Tennessee Williams.*

Theater in the Americas

The goal of the series is to publish a wide range of scholarship on theater and performance, defining theater in its broadest terms and including subjects that encompass all of the Americas.

The series focuses on the performance and production of theater and theater artists and practitioners but welcomes studies of dramatic literature as well. Meant to be inclusive, the series invites studies of traditional, experimental, and ethnic forms of theater; celebrations, festivals, and rituals that perform culture; and acts of civil disobedience that are performative in nature. We publish studies of theater and performance activities of all cultural groups within the Americas, including biographies of individuals, histories of theater companies, studies of cultural traditions, and collections of plays.

Other Books in the Theater in the Americas Series

*Shadowed Cocktails: The Plays of
Philip Barry from "Paris Bound" to
"The Philadelphia Story"*
Donald R. Anderson

*A Gambler's Instinct: The Story of
Broadway Producer Cheryl Crawford*
Milly S. Barranger

*Unfriendly Witnesses: Gender, Theater,
and Film in the McCarthy Era*
Milly S. Barranger

*The Theatre of Sabina Berman: "The
Agony of Ecstasy" and Other Plays*
Translated by Adam Versényi
With an Essay by Jacqueline E. Bixler

*Staging Social Justice: Collaborating to
Create Activist Theatre*
Edited by Norma Bowles and
Daniel-Raymond Nadon

*Messiah of the New Technique: John
Howard Lawson, Communism, and
American Theatre, 1923–1937*
Jonathan L. Chambers

*Composing Ourselves:
The Little Theatre Movement and
the American Audience*
Dorothy Chansky

*Ghost Light: An Introductory
Handbook for Dramaturgy*
Michael Mark Chemers

*The Hanlon Brothers: From Daredevil
Acrobatics to Spectacle Pantomime,
1833–1931*
Mark Cosdon

*Richard Barr: The Playwright's
Producer*
David A. Crespy

*Women in Turmoil: Six Plays by
Mercedes de Acosta*
Edited and with an Introduction by
Robert A. Schanke

*Rediscovering Mordecai Gorelik: Scene
Design and the American Theatre*
Anne Fletcher

*A Spectacle of Suffering: Clara Morris
on the American Stage*
Barbara Wallace Grossman

American Political Plays after 9/11
Edited by Allan Havis

*Performing Loss: Rebuilding
Community through Theater
and Writing*
Jodi Kanter

*Unfinished Show Business: Broadway
Musicals as Works-in-Process*
Bruce Kirle

Staging America: Cornerstone and
Community-Based Theater
Sonja Kuftinec

Words at Play: Creative Writing
and Dramaturgy
Felicia Hardison Londré

Entertaining the Nation: American
Drama in the Eighteenth and
Nineteenth Centuries
Tice L. Miller

Stage, Page, Scandals, and Vandals:
William E. Burton and Nineteenth-
Century American Theatre
David L. Rinear

Contemporary Latina/o Theater:
Wrighting Ethnicity
Jon D. Rossini

Angels in the American Theater:
Patrons, Patronage, and Philanthropy
Edited and with an Introduction by
Robert A. Schanke

"That Furious Lesbian":
The Story of Mercedes de Acosta
Robert A. Schanke

Caffe Cino: The Birthplace
of Off-Off-Broadway
Wendell C. Stone

Teaching Performance Studies
Edited by Nathan Stucky and
Cynthia Wimmer
With a Foreword by
Richard Schechner

Broadway's Bravest Woman: Selected
Writings of Sophie Treadwell
Edited and with Introductions by
Jerry Dickey and
Miriam López-Rodríguez

The Humana Festival:
The History of New Plays at
Actors Theatre of Louisville
Jeffrey Ullom

Our Land Is Made of Courage and
Glory: Nationalist Performance of
Nicaragua and Guatemala
E. J. Westlake